THE VILLAGE ON THE HILL

Aspects of Colerne History

Volume 2

THE VILLAGE ON THE HILL

Aspects of Colerne History

Volume 2

Edited by
Joyce and John Utting

Colerne History Group
1995

First published in 1995 by
Colerne History Group
c/o Colerne Parish Council
Council Offices, Market Place, Colerne
Chippenham, Wiltshire SN14 8DF

Cover design by William Knight and Marian Pollard

Filmset in Monotype Plantin by
Bath Typesetting Limited
London Road, Bath, Avon BA1 5NL

Printed in Great Britain by
Antony Rowe Limited
Bumpers Farm, Chippenham, Wiltshire SN14 6QA

ISBN 0 9515728 3 0

Contents

Some Colerne Buildings

Introduction
Adrian Wood 1

Colerne Manor House
James Norton 3

Vale Court
Lavinia Wilson 7

The Rectory
Roger Clifton 22
Charcoal House 28
The Gazebo 28

Lucknam House 32

Trunnells Farm 42

Ragge Farm 50

Trimnells Farm and Doncombe Farm 57

Chapps Mill and Farm 63

No 8 Market Place 75

Thickwood and Euridge 82

The Village Centre 92

Artefacts and Extras 112

Conclusion 118

The Walmesleys of Lucknam
Simon Garrett 121

The Colerne Drewetts
Adrian Wood 147

RAF Colerne: The Early Years 1940–46
David and Annette Hitch 158

The Junior Leaders Regiment at Colerne:
A Personal Memoir
David Coates 246

A Naval Connection
Barrie Austin 252

J. Mullins and Sons: Water Finders
Lesley Yeo and Joyce Utting 260

Berwyn Engineering
Beryl Winter 264

Memories of the Vineyard Restaurant
Iris Fuller 266

The Village Constable
Ron Read 273

Medical Care in Colerne
Jocelyn Berry, Donald Taylor and Joyce Utting 282

Colerne Parish Council
Chris Phillips 293

Preface

Like the first volume of *The Village on the Hill*, this book covers a wide variety of topics. The principal criterion for the choice of these subjects has been the interest in them and the willingness to write about them of our various authors, all of whom either live in the village or have some direct connection with their subjects, often both. This has made for a diversity of both subject matter and its treatment which will be immediately apparent to the reader. As editors, we have thought it important that our contributors should speak with their own voices, and we have not sought to impose uniformity except in such matters as layout, spellings and other publisher's conventions.

Nevertheless, the book does have a central theme, which is to show how history is shaped by a living community as it reacts with regional, national and international events and legislation. Occupations change, dwellings are adapted to new circumstances and the pace of life changes with the coming of rapid communications systems. There is no doubt that the rate of change in the twentieth century is unprecedented. In Colerne it was greatly accelerated by the coming of the RAF. Yet the bedrock of this ancient settlement is still beneath us, solid and constant. And so we present the second volume of *The Village on the Hill*.

Acknowledgements

Our thanks are due first to our authors; among them, special mention must be made of Adrian Wood who besides coordinating the whole of the first part of the book, on Colerne buildings, wrote much of it himself and took most of the photographs which illustrate it.

Secondly, we thank Donald Thompson who has again handled all our typesetting arrangements and contributed his typographic expertise to the production of a book which we hope is good to look at, as well as interesting to read. We are also grateful to Barbara and David Hoskins, Frank Trumper and Lesley Yeo who have assisted with the task of proof-reading.

Our authors have provided their own lists of acknowledgements; among them are recurring mentions of the Wiltshire Record Office, the Wiltshire Buildings Record and the Local Studies Library at Trowbridge. We thank them and their staffs for their continuing and unfailing help.

We are again indebted to members of Colerne History Group and other village residents who, although not themselves authors, have contributed their old documents, photographs and memories to add to what is available from formal records.

Colerne Parish Council continues to allow us the use of a room in the council offices. It now houses the History Group's growing collection of archival material, as well as providing valuable office space.

Finally, we thank all those who have helped to finance the production of this book by ordering their copies in advance of publication.

Illustrations

We are grateful to all those who have allowed us to reproduce copyright photographs and documents to illustrate our text. We have provided individual acknowledgements in parentheses following the captions, using abbreviations for the most frequent contributors. These are Adrian Wood (AAW), the Wiltshire Buildings Record (WBR), Simon Garrett (SG) whose photos are all taken from a Walmesley family album, Frank Champion (FC) and the Imperial War Museum (IWM followed by reference); other names are given in full. We emphasize that our use of these illustrations in no way authorises their reproduction in any other publication.

Besides providing a number of cross-references between different pages of this volume, we have sometimes referred to the first volume of *The Village on the Hill*. We have usually abbreviated this to *V on H*.

J. and J. U. *September 1995*

Some Colerne Buildings

This part of our book (pp 120) has been collected, collated and, in most cases, written by Adrian Wood. The sections on the Manor House, Vale Court, and Colerne Rectory have been written by the named authors; but in all other cases the primary author is Adrian Wood, often with the help of present occupiers, and always with the assistance of the sources named in his list of acknowledgements. Most of the photographs illustrating this section are also his.

As is said in the Introduction below, a good deal of attention has been paid to the occupancy of the buildings described. The principal sources for this information are the map and schedule accompanying the 1787 Inclosure Award, the similar map and schedule for the 1875 Tithe Award, and the six publicly available census returns covering the period 1841–1891 at ten-yearly intervals. These dates, therefore, recur frequently in the accounts which follow, but there is little certainty about the dates in between. It should also be noted that, in those days before house numbers, the census returns do not always identify buildings unambiguously.

A glossary of architectural terms used in this section is appended (p 120).

Introduction

Adrian Wood

"They lived sluttishly in poor houses where they ate a great deale of beefe and mutton and drank good Ale in a brown Mazard: and their very kings were but a sort of Farmers." So wrote John Aubrey of the Saxons in Wiltshire. Whether his comments were entirely true is not our concern. We can be certain that the poor houses were rudely constructed and no remains exist in this area. Indeed the only artefacts in the parish which have been identified as of Saxon origin are fragments of decorated stonework now built into the interior of the north wall of the church. The church architecture is described in Pevsner's *Wiltshire*. Parts of it date from the very end of the twelfth century and there are no other buildings in Colerne which can be said to have parts of the fabric which are as old, with the possible exception of Euridge Manor House in which a Norman arch is still preserved. Daubeneys has a claim to be the oldest surviving secular building in the village, although it has been much altered over the centuries. The house is comprehensively described in *Longhouse on the Hill* by Arthur and Joan Platt.

The accounts which follow concentrate on older buildings in the parish and the treatment of the subjects varies considerably. Details of construction have usually received brief attention but the history of occupancy has been given much more, and thanks are due to those who have made available old documents relating to their houses. Hopefully, others will be prompted to make information available which would be useful in extending our knowledge of the history of our village on the hill.

Fig 1 The heart of the Village (AAW)

Colerne Manor House

James Norton

A short account of the early history of the Manor of Colerne will be found in *V on H* pp 8–10. Eventually, in 1388, the reversion was sold to William of Wykeham who conveyed it to his own foundation of New College Oxford the next year. New College did not sell it until 1877.

The present Manor house dates from an Elizabethan building erected in 1570 by the tenant of New College at that time, Robert ffreeland. This date can be determined accurately from the Estate records in the archives of New College. Two years earlier, in 1568, an entry in the records denotes that the same Robert ffreeland spent "ffortey markes in repayring of that theire [New College] Manor place at Colerne". This entry suggests that there was a building on the site prior to the erection of the 1570 House. Further documentation at New College refers to a "dove house" built in 1596.

Fig 2 The Manor House, showing all thirteen chimneys

Of some interest is an entry in 1662 from the Progress Notes of Warden Woodward. "Mr. Harris our tenant will talke with his workmen about a staire cast, and if the charge be not above £10 he will spend soe much about it, this hee promised at Marshfield. His wife is much for it." This indicates that the staircase, which survives, was almost a hundred years later than the Elizabethan house. This date is consistent with the construction of the staircase which is typical of the period [see *Editors' note*, p 6].

The next firm date of interest is 1689 which is referred to on a datestone now above the front door of the Manor. The inscription reads:

> This stone was set by
> Elizabeth
> Anne
> & Frances
> April XI., MDCLXXXIX
> The day of Coronation
> W. & M., King & Queen

The stone is known not to have been above the front door of the Elizabethan house but above the door of a wing to the left which joined the house to the farm buildings. This means that the house must have been extended after the 1570 date presumably by the New College tenant of that time, the Misses Hunt.

Although the 1570 house does not survive, much is known about it from a paper read by the Rev Wynter E. Blathwayt to the Bath natural History and Antiquarian Field Club in 1901. This paper included a sketch of the house, reproduced in *V on H* (p 10).

This indicated rather a square structure and the author describes four sloping roofs dropping down to a well at centre. The house contained attractive panelled rooms and was configured around a courtyard on the west side.

The 1570 house would have had cellar space, and building works in 1990 revealed the existence of previously unrecorded cellar windows beneath the windows to the current reception rooms on the east side of the house. Excavations did not reveal a void beneath these rooms, which suggests that the cellar space was filled in when the house was rebuilt in 1901.

An important feature of the 1570 house was the wood panelling in the main reception room on the south side, although this may have been added at a later date.

Modern history

The Elizabethan house fell into disrepair in Victorian times and it is likely that when it was sold by New College in 1877 it was fairly dilapidated. The Manor was sold to Richard Walmesley and formed part of his Lucknam Park estate. Colerne Manor was used as a farmhouse residence but the Elizabethan house was pulled down at the turn of the century except for the southernmost block which remains. This was incorporated into a new house by appending a northern section to the house. In the 1930s a flat-roof service extension was added still further to the north.

The southernmost block of the existing house is thus of the Elizabethan structure and contains the 1662 staircase. The foundations for this part of the building may relate to an even earlier structure prior to Robert ffreeland's tenancy. In the cellar under the hall of the existing house there is clear evidence of a door to another cellar below the Elizabethan building, which has subsequently been filled in. There is also evidence of stairs going downwards parallel to the existing staircase, but to a lower level. Nothing of any earlier construction remains, however.

Architectural details

Wall thicknesses, one surviving moulded beam and the cellar mullioned window with reversed chamfer mouldings suggest the stone house of today originated in about 1570.

The ovolo (quarter round) moulded mullion windows and the twisted balusters of the staircase suggest a late seventeenth century date for alterations. These might well be contemporary with the 1689 datestone.

The bolection moulded fireplace in the south-east room and the windows in the stable block are probably early eighteenth century.

The stone tanks in the stable block, one of which has been removed at some time but is still outlined on the floor, may be storage cisterns for the water supply mentioned in the plaque outside in the street commemorating the owner's sharing of the overflow of his supply with the villagers (see *V on H* p 149). There is a pump to supply the yard or house at the east end of the stable block.

The present roof of the house is a kingpost structure likely to date from the repairs and renovation of *c.* 1900.

Editors' note: The "staire cast" mentioned above has also been taken to refer to the enclosure of the former outside staircase at Daubeneys; see *Longhouse on the Hill* pp 12 and 13.

Vale Court

Lavinia Wilson

Situated as it was on the southern edge of the village of Colerne, overlooking the beautiful By Brook valley, it is perhaps hardly surprising that a small farmstead grew and multiplied over the centuries to become the substantial dwelling known today as Vale Court.

Fig 3 The original T-shaped building (note blocked upper windows) (AAW)

Sixteenth century

There is no documentation in existence with which to plot the precise origins of the house. However, we can speculate on two possibilities. The first is that the original T-shaped stone building dating from the latter half of the sixteenth century consisted of two cottages, one running east–west and facing south, following the ground plan of the present day hall, and the other running north–south and facing west, where the kitchen is now. The second possibility is that the house originated as a single dwelling which would have been one of the better farmsteads of the village, already well built for the sixteenth century. This would have consisted of a stone wing running north–south attached to an older hall to the east which was the main reception area of the house, as with the great hall of a manor house.

Fig 4 Seventeenth century mullioned window (AAW)

In either case, later improvements suggest that both wings may have been open to the roof inside, with no upper chambers. The kitchen walls dating back to this period are 36 inches thick, and at the north end there are still visible signs of a large kitchen stack with a cornice and roll moulding remaining.

Seventeenth century

It is possible to speculate that members of the Drewett (or Druett) family lived at the house during the seventeenth century. An account of the Colerne Drewetts is given elsewhere (pp 147–57); here we will refer only to their links with the house.

The house was undoubtedly 'modernised' during the seventeenth century, and it would by now have become a single dwelling, if this was not already the case. Upper chambers were added over both wings, and a gable dormer window with ovolo-moulded mullions and a hood mould was inserted to light the chamber over the kitchen on the west side. The window remains today, and the quoins which were at the sides of the dormer are still visible in the outside wall at the first floor level. A first floor fireplace was also put into the kitchen stack; the stone surround and another small sixteenth century fireplace are both still in use elsewhere in the house.

The hall wing was probably rebuilt in the seventeenth century – the walls are not exactly at right angles. The chimney stack to the hall fireplace has the orange-coloured mortar and rounded side typically found in seventeenth century chimney stacks.

Eighteenth century

By the eighteenth century the Drewett family was definitely in residence at Colerne House, or Belle Vue House as it was increasingly becoming known, and they progressively improved the house to suit their needs.

Early in the century both wings were raised in height to three storeys – the present roof dates from that time. The top floor of the west wing consisted of one large room, well lit with windows on three sides, which would have been ideal for weaving. The room exists largely

Fig 5 The various stages of development on the west side (AAW)

unchanged today, except for the south window which was partly blocked towards the end of the century by the addition of a further two-storey extension to the south. It may be assumed that by then weaving was no longer taking place in the house but in outside workshops, so the room would no longer have needed such excellent light. The extension is clearly visible on the 1785 Inclosure map of Colerne, but is not easy to find on the less clear 1767 map, so was probably built between those dates. There was a further small extension when a panelled room in the Queen Anne style was added to the west side of the new south wing. This room still contains a fireplace of the late eighteenth century.

Nineteenth century

There is no evidence to indicate any structural alterations during the nineteenth century. Indeed the house seems to have been sub-let to different tenants for much of the latter half of the century, and to have fallen into somewhat of a state of disrepair. At the very end of the century we find the Warden and Scholars of New College, Oxford, chastising the copyholders – descendants of Peter and Frances Drewett – " . . . and reciting that owing to the state of want of repair of the said messuage called Belle Vue House . . . the said Warden and Scholars as Lords of the said Manor had then lately threatened to seize the said tenements and heredits . . ." Much of the interest during the nineteenth century lies in following the fortunes of Peter Drewett and his descendants through detailed Abstracts of Title amongst the Deeds of the house.

Although he retained the copyhold, Peter and his family do not appear to have lived at Belle Vue House for long. There is no record of a Peter Drewett being buried at Colerne in 1817 or 1818, confirming the impression that he was not living in the village at the time of his death, although his Will is dated 13th December 1817 and was proved 8th October 1818. In this Will he leaves his property at Colerne valued at £1284 to his unmarried daughter Mary Ann subject to her taking up residence there within two years.

Mary Ann

Mary Ann certainly seems to have followed her father's wishes and lived at Colerne House (as she called it), though it is puzzling that in 1828 we find her nephew Frederick William Brown approaching the Court of New College and being granted first reversion on the property (see below).

Mary Ann married Morgan James Morgan in 1829 but was subsequently widowed, and then on 30th July 1845, at Colerne Parish Church, she married Thomas Arnold Loxley, who was only 27, or thereabouts, at the time. Mary Ann must have been quite a 'catch' for all her 53 years, her father having bequeathed her £1331 as well as Colerne House, and she may even have received an annuity from her first husband. She died the following year on 11th November 1846, and is buried at Corsham.

Mary Ann left a Will dated 29th October 1846 in which she "devised and bequeathed her copyhold house with land attaching at Colerne Wiltshire called Colerne House as well as the furniture in the same namely books pictures and all generally understood as furniture to my two sisters Susanna Brown and Fanny Harding to be enjoyed by them for their natural lives only on condition that they live . . ." At her sisters' deaths she willed the same to her two nephews, Thomas Drewett Brown and Frederick William Brown, and their heirs forever. She appointed as executors her husband Thomas Arnold Loxley and the two nephews.

Frederick William

Among the Title Deeds of the house there is a note dated 9th April 1828 referring to ". . . a General Court Baron and Customary Court of the Revd Philip Nicholas Shuttleworth DD the Warden and the Scholars of New College in Oxford held in and for the Manor of Colerne in the County of Wilts . . ." at which the Lords by their Steward "did grant unto Frederick William Brown aged 10 years or thereabouts"

> The first reversion of and in one messuage or tenement one close and one yard Land called Gregorys
>
> And also to a Cotsettle of land called Williams with their appurts situate and being within the Manor aforesaid late in the tenure of Peter Drewett deceased . . .
>
> To have the premises aforesaid with the appurts unto him the said F.W. Brown immediately when by death surrender or forfeiture of Mary Ann Drewett then in possession or by any other means the same should happen to come into the hands of the Lords of the said Manor . . .
>
> In Trust nevertheless for said M.A. Drewett
>
> Paying therefor to the Lords by the year for the premises in the first Copy 5s 5d and 2 Bushels of Wheat at Michaelmas and for Lords silver 9d and for those in the 2nd Copy 7s 0d and a heriot for each when it should happen
>
> And doing and performing all other burthens customs and services therefor due and of right accustomed . . .

The "messuage or tenement . . . called Gregorys" and the "Cotsettle of land called Williams" seem to refer to the whole estate as described in a Schedule dated 21st November 1859, when Frederick's brother Thomas and his wife Isabella were granted by the Court first reversion on the premises and land. This comprised some 67 acres and included "Bellevue House Lawns Garden & Bldgs." There is no other record of the names 'Gregorys' or 'Williams.'

The estate included the cottage (now part of the garage and log/tool store) adjoining the main gate which would have been Nos 2 and 4 Watergates. No 4 belonged to Frederick William until his death on 29th September 1909, at the advanced age of 91, when it was sold by his executor, Mr George Lee, to the owner of Vale Court for £15. The small yard behind the cottage had been sold in 1907 when the main house changed hands, but it was let back to Frederick William for his lifetime at 6d a year.

Following the death of his aunt Mary Ann, Frederick went back to the Court on 7th April 1847 and was admitted tenant of the premises, though it is not clear whether he actually lived in the house for any length of time. Certainly at this time his mother Susanna was living in London, where she died on 2nd December 1854, and Frederick spent his last years in Putney. He never seems to have married.

Thomas Loxley

As noted above, at a General Court held on 7th April 1847 Frederick William was admitted as tenant of the premises. However, at the end of the following year on 23rd December 1848 we find Mary Ann's husband, Thomas Arnold Loxley, being granted "first reversion of all the said premises to hold the premises . . . for the term of his natural life . . . paying and performing the said several rents heriots and services." At that time Thomas Loxley was a merchant living at Tower Hill in the City of London, and he died some ten years later on 2nd April 1858 at Northchurch, Herts, so it is not certain that he ever lived at Colerne House following his wife's death. In the census of 1851 (the house here called Vale View) only two servants are listed – Harriot Bush, married aged 52, and Sarah Bush, aged 12.

Thomas Drewett

Thomas Drewett Brown, Mary Ann's other nephew, and his wife Isabella are discovered again in 1847, in which year he makes a Will in favour of Isabella and appoints her as the sole executrix.

On 21st November 1859 we find them living in Jarrow Gateshead in the County of Durham and being granted first reversion of the premises, for the first time fully described in a Schedule. This by now comprises a large estate of some 67 acres including Green Lane Tining, Fall Tining, Ruckle, Little Fall Tining, Rag Farm Coppice and Old Orchard, Rag Farm Field 1 and 2, Dry Leaze near Drewetts Mill, Bellevue House Lawns Garden & Bldgs, The Close and Orchard, the Lower Close.

In September 1867 Thomas Drewett Brown changed his surname to Drewett by Royal Licence (*London Gazette* 17th September 1867) thus becoming Thomas Drewett Drewett. Was this perhaps because he and his brother were the last remaining members of the Drewett family of Colerne and Thomas had a son, Drewett Ormonde, to carry on the name, whereas Frederick seems never to have married or had children?

Thomas died in September 1870. In January 1887 Isabella, then living at East Hall, Middleton Tyas, York, made a Will in favour of their son Drewett Ormonde Drewett, leaving him her estate of Jarrow, County of Durham, and all her estate and effects. She died in December 1894, and the Will was proved in February 1895 by Drewett Ormonde Drewett.

Therefore, as previously noted, it seems likely that the estate was tenanted for much of the nineteenth century following Mary Ann's death. Frederick William seems to have lived in Putney much of his life and Thomas Drewett and his family have various addresses in the north of England.

Tenants

Among other names that appear regularly on the census returns for the latter half of the nineteenth century are those of the Dowding family, papermakers, who were working Chapps Mill at Slaughterford at that time (see pp 66–70). In 1881 and in *Kelly's Directory* of 1885 Samuel Dowding was living at Vale View with his widowed mother Eleanor, his wife Emily, and three small children – Eleanor, Samuel and Marguerite – who were all born in Slaughterford. Also in the house were a ladies' help and a domestic servant, and in Vale View Cottage lived Ann Pinchin aged 90 and her nieces Mercy and Mary Brokenbrow, all listed as annuitants.

In *Kelly's Directory of Wiltshire, Hampshire & Dorsetshire* of 1889 Samuel Dowding is listed at Elmsleigh. His name does not appear at all in the 1891 census, though his mother Eleanor is still at Vale View with three small children – Mary and Charles (children of Samuel?) and Florence, a niece – a governess and two servants. William Dowding (Samuel's brother?) paper manufacturer, was at Elmsleigh in that year, and George Dowding (another brother?) was at Chapps Mill. The ages would fit with the three being brothers, though George was born in America.

The only other names mentioned at Vale View are those of a Mr Glassbrook (no name or initial) in *Harrod's Directory* of 1865, and a Major Garrard in *Owen's Directory of Wiltshire and Somerset* in 1878 and 1879.

Twentieth century

The present century has seen many changes of ownership of the property, and major structural work during the 1930s when the house was thoroughly renovated to a very high standard, and almost doubled in size. We, the present owners, are the longest inhabitants this century, having lived here now for nearly 24 years. Strangely, the previous record goes to another Wilson family (no relation) though it is odd that such an ideal family house has never remained in the same ownership for so long before. It has been easy to piece together the history of Vale Court during the twentieth century thanks to the long memories of many Colerne people. In January 1904 Frederick William Brown and his nephew Drewett Ormonde Drewett surrendered to the Lords of the Manor, the Warden and Scholars of New College, all rights to the property "and each of them did grant & release unto the said Warden & Scholars all the estate & interest whatsoever to which they or either of them was or might be entitled in the said tenements & heredits described in the said schedule thereto under or by virtue of the Will of the said M. A. Loxley . . . to the intent that the same heredits might thenceforth be held . . . freed and discharged from any claim whatsoever in law or in equity on the part of the said F. W. Brown & D.O. Drewett . . . " The estate at this time comprised some 5 acres, 2 roods and 9 perches.

In December 1904 Joseph Mullins of Colerne bought "the freehold messuage known as Belle Vue otherwise Vale View situate at Colerne together with outbuildings gardens and two paddocks . . . for the sum of £610 . . ." The two paddocks are named on the Tithe map accompanying the conveyance as Mr Drewitt's Orchard and Druids Close. The small strip of land at the bottom of Druids Close running east–west along Ark Lane belonged to John Walmesley of Lucknam Park until it was sold to the owners of Vale Court in 1913.

Joseph Mullins was perhaps living at Elmsleigh at the time he bought Vale View. He was certainly living there in January 1907 when he sold the house, and older people in Colerne can remember him living at Elmsleigh until probably about 1920. He was a water diviner and water engineer (see pp 258–63).

In January 1907 the house "known as Vale Court previously known as Vale View" was bought by Mr John Wilson of Dorchester-on-Thames for £1100. One must assume that during Mr Mullins' three years' ownership of the property he had worked to renovate and refurbish the house, as we know it had fallen into disrepair at the end of the previous century. This would account for the sale price almost doubling in three years, and the first appearance of the grander name still used today. Mr and Mrs Wilson lived at Vale Court for some twenty years until their deaths within a short time of each other at the end of the 1920s. They are well remembered by older Colerne people, many of whom worked in the house at that time. Mrs Wilson seems to have been somewhat fey and claimed to have seen several ghosts in and around the house, including that of a dog in the drive.

Mrs Gray was housekeeper/caretaker at the house after Mr Wilson's death, and her daughter, Katie Trumper, well remembers living and playing there as a child.

Fig 6 Southern extension to the old core. Twentieth century bay windows (AAW)

In 1931 John Wilson's executors sold the entire property to Mrs M A Forester of Bristol for £1650, though it is not certain how much she actually lived in the house. Mr Roy Russell who called recently and introduced himself as having worked on the house as a fourteen-year-old apprentice joiner in 1936–7 remembers an atmosphere of unused musty deterioration about it when he first arrived, as if it had been empty for quite a long time, and the gardens also quite overgrown in parts (see Appendix for some of his memories).

Captain R D Wills

In 1936 Capt Ronald Dewhurst Wills bought the property from Mrs Forester for £2050. He was a member of the wealthy W.D. & H.O. Wills tobacco family of Bristol – he was a philanthropist and supporter of boys clubs and destitute children, and of the poor and needy of Bristol. He had set up a poultry farm at West Littleton for a young man named Fry, who may have been his adopted son, but for some reason this venture failed to work out so Capt Wills purchased and renovated Vale Court for him. However, Mr Fry was killed in an accident before he could live there and Capt Wills himself died in 1937 aged only about 50. This was apparently not very surprising as he was a very large man, tall and overweight, and was always chauffeured around in a black Daimler. Captain Wills himself lived at Hill House, Corston, on the other side of Bath. In the summer of 1936 he started a major programme of additions and renovations to the house, with the main contractors being Geo. Mannings & Sons of Claverton Down. The work involved building a new east wing with one long room downstairs and rooms above on the first floor. This large downstairs room was designed as a billiards room – the game was very popular during the 1920s and 30s but largely faded out because of the size of room required to accommodate the large tables, and the cumbersomeness of the tubular containers in which players carried their cues around to matches. The much more convenient size of present day tables and cues became popular after the war.

At the same time a further extension was built for staff quarters, all older roofs were strengthened, a new heating system was introduced, and electrical wiring and plumbing were renovated. Various old doorways, fireplaces and other features were introduced into the house, including a very fine Adam entrance porch. The present hall fireplace – probably Tudor with a fine design of birds and gryphons – was inserted into the old stack at this date. The back wall has been brought forward and the area above the fireplace opening has been rebuilt. A window in the dining room looking eastwards up the drive was blocked up, and there is now a small niche by the front door where this window used to be. A somewhat indistinct photograph exists showing this window and the house before alterations started.

Fig 7 Part of the Tudor fireplace frieze (AAW)

The garden and grounds were also extensively altered at this time. The entrance drive had always followed the wall of the Bank footpath, indeed this can be seen on the 1787 Inclosure map of Colerne. Captain Wills had it relaid through the walled fruit garden, the north and east walls of which still remain, along with several fruit trees – a fig tree, a pear tree, and espalier pears on the north wall.

During 1936 also, Captain Wills purchased Tutton Hill House from Mr E J Jenkins for use as a butler's cottage. It remained part of the Vale Court estate until 1945 when the then owners, the Bowes-Lyon family, sold it to Dame Muriel Albina Powell for £3800, a big increase on the £400 that Captain Wills had paid in 1936.

After Captain Wills' death, his executor, Wilfred Dewhurst Wills, sold the house at auction on 18th March 1938 at Fortts Restaurant, Milsom Street, Bath. The estate at that time comprised about six and a half acres, including Tutton Hill House. It was sold for £6000 to Captain G F Bowes-Lyon who lived there with his family through the war. The house changed hands again in 1946 when it was bought by Mr and Mrs H B Tate of the Tate & Lyle sugar family, and they were followed in 1958 by the Hagenbach family and in 1968 by Mr and Mrs John Pile. We bought the house from Mr Pile in 1971 and moved in during March 1972, having completed various alterations to make it more of a family home. For instance, the rear (servants) wing could only be reached by a back staircase from the kitchen, so we were able to bring it more into the rest of the house by making ways through on upper floors.

We were very restricted about making any changes to the outward appearance of the house as the building is listed Grade 2. Without intending to be critical, it might well be claimed that the planning authorities of today would never have allowed the original sixteenth century buildings to develop into the large house that it is now, enriched by the variety of architectural styles which have been incorporated over the intervening centuries.

Appendix

The following is extracted from a memoir by Roy F Russell, sub-titled "A milestone in the history of a lovely old country house and the life of a young apprentice lad." He gives a fascinating account of his experiences in his first job, and of the building methods in use, sixty years ago. Regrettably, we only have space here for some amusing anecdotes.

> Mr Charlie Mannings usually arrived on site just after 11.30am and would give me half a crown (12½p). I would then run up to the Fox and Hounds public house to fetch a flagon of 'India Pale Ale' brewed, I think, by Ushers of Trowbridge and priced about one shilling and three or six pence (7 or 7½ pence). I had to run to get the beer in hope to get back inside Vale Court gateway before Colerne School came out at 12 o'clock, because some half dozen of the oldest lads and us three lads [the apprentices] were not on good terms at all, and if caught out on the road it was not too good when the odds were three or four to one. It all started when Charlie Jukes, a carpenter from Marshfield, told us to shout "Go and polish the donkey's hoofs." This really annoyed them. After the trouble had started, Charlie

told us some tale about a village donkey being buried in Colerne churchyard with its hooves sticking up out of the turf because they had not dug the grave deep enough! I recall that I never dared to make any clever suggestions to the Colerne workmen on the site over this matter.

During lunchtime one Monday before Christmas 1936, Mr Mannings was sat in his 'reserved place' on the right nearest the fire. He finished his sandwiches, looked around and said "Cyril Beazer (a mason who was off sick) has now got pneumonia and is on his 'uppers' (in need of money); I think we should have a 'nobbin' (collection)." He took off his old trilby hat and passed it around, the men giving such coins as they could afford. All I had was my sixpence ($2\frac{1}{2}$p) pocket money from the Saturday before. I felt I must put in something, so in it went. Altogether the firm raised about £5. Some weeks later, again at lunchtime, Mr Mannings arrived late and somewhat annoyed. He sat down, looked at us saying "Beazer won't be coming back, he is better and he has used your money to buy trucks (handcart) and ladder, and has started up on his own and one day he will have your jobs." How true this turned out to be in the following years as the huge Beazer construction empire flourished beyond belief. I have wondered many times over the years what my sixpence would have been worth as a share in the business when at its peak!

Christmas eve 1936 arrived, and I remember Mr Ronald Wills came with Mr Arnold (Jolly's land and property contracts agent) into the entrance hall and wished everyone goodwill and a merry Christmas, together with a bottle of whisky for Mr Mannings, 100 box cigarettes for Harold Player, two 200 boxes cigarettes between the workmen, but the three apprentices (a mason, a plumber and myself) nil!

The Rectory

Roger Clifton

For centuries the Church of England built parsonage houses which suited the social status, and often generous income, of the incumbent. In the twentieth century, rapid changes in society, and the rising cost of maintaining large old buildings, have led the church to replace most of its rectories with modern properties. This has not always been a good thing, and there is often a good case to be made for retaining the traditional house. In Colerne, thanks to the slightly unusual nature of the building, this proved possible, and (at least at the time of writing) the Victorian rectory is still in use. It is not the original parsonage, as will be seen, though many questions remain. Researching local history is a continuing process, and no doubt others will in turn find things to fill out what I have written here.

The old vicarage

It seems likely that the parish priest has always lived somewhere near the church, but there are no early records of this. Before the present rectory was built, the parsonage house and garden were on the land where the old school now stands, in Vicarage Lane. The Inclosure Award map of 1785 shows a large, irregularly shaped building at the top of the site, near the gate into the churchyard. A print of the church seen from the east – undated, but later than 1819 as it shows a tombstone of that date – gives a tantalising glimpse of a corner of the old vicarage, and beyond it, on the site of the present rectory, a large building with dormer windows. (The view also shows the church tower without its staircase pinnacle which must have been added later, perhaps in the restoration of 1877.)

It seems likely that the vicarage had been on that site for a considerable period, as the lane was named after it. The present house is of course called a rectory, and it is worth explaining how the change of title came about. The ancient parish of Colerne was formed in the seventh century. For several centuries it was a double benefice; the rectors (who were entitled to the income of the benefice) were appointed by the Lords of the Manor, and the vicars (who actually lived in the village and did the work) were appointed by the rector. From 1740 to 1903, the rectorate was held in plurality with the wardenship of New College, Oxford. Presumably the incumbent would have spent most of his time in Oxford, and left the vicar to care for the parish. One hopes that he also gave him a suitable share of the income.

During the tenure of Dr Sewell (1860–1903) the wardenship became open to a layman. Obviously a lay person could not also be a parish priest, so an Act was specially passed in the latter part of the nineteenth century to separate the wardenship and restore the rectorate to Colerne. The clergyman with the benefice once more came to live here, and the title of 'Rector' was restored in 1903. The title remains, though clergy are now paid centrally (and equally) through the Church Commissioners. The link with New College also remains, as they are patrons of the living.

The new rectory – Gilbert Heathcote

With the arrival of the Reverend Gilbert Heathcote, the days of the old house were numbered. He obviously did not like the vicarage. An indenture dated 23rd March 1848 (still in the possession of the church) states: "the parsonage house belonging to the said vicarage of Colerne is inconvenient and too small and is not fit for the habitation of the Minister." The deed goes on to convey "a newly built messuage house or tenement ... lying within a distance of fifty yards from the church", the property of Gilbert Heathcote, to be "for ever hereafter deemed and taken to be the Parsonage or Glebe house, outbuildings, gardens and appurtenances of the said vicarage of Colerne." The consideration was the nominal sum of ten shillings. In other words, it would appear that Mr Heathcote had built and given the new rectory.

With its dignified proportions and its prominent position in the Market Place, he must have been well pleased with it.

One of the parties to the deed is "The Right Reverend James Henry, Lord Bishop of the diocese of Gloucester and Bristol (within which diocese the said vicarage of Colerne is situate)." This is odd, because *The English Dioceses* by Geoffrey Hill states that Colerne was in Salisbury diocese until 1875. At that date there was a reorganisation under which North Wiltshire, including Colerne, was transferred to the combined diocese of Gloucester and Bristol. These two were divided in 1884, and the separate diocese of Bristol revived. Hill states that Colerne was then assigned to Bristol, where it has remained ever since. Clearly more research is needed on this point.

We are now faced with another oddity. The table of incumbents in the church shows that Gilbert Heathcote came to be vicar in 1796, when Dr Gauntlett was warden of New College, and that he resigned in 1799. One wonders why he resigned so quickly. Another Gilbert Heathcote was then appointed in 1846, and stayed as vicar until 1868. We know it must have been another of the same name because the 1851 census shows him as aged 36, living in the vicarage with a wife, servants and three infant children. This man was not even born in 1796. (As an aside on the problems facing us when using old records, the census of 1861, ten years later, gives his age as 44, only eight years older. His wife had died in childbirth in 1854, at the age of 34, and he ceased to be vicar in 1868.) Presumably the two men were father and son. It was the second Heathcote who owned the new house, because the indenture states that Gilbert Heathcote is the owner and is "the vicar for the time being of the said vicarage" and gives the Vicarage as his address. He had clearly wasted no time in building, because this was only two years after he came to the parish.

It seems unlikely that Heathcote senior had stayed on in the village after his resignation, as the 1841 census, the first for which records are available, does not record any Heathcotes as being resident – but then it does not record the name of any incumbent either!

Building the new house

The plans attached to the deed show the rectory and garden largely as

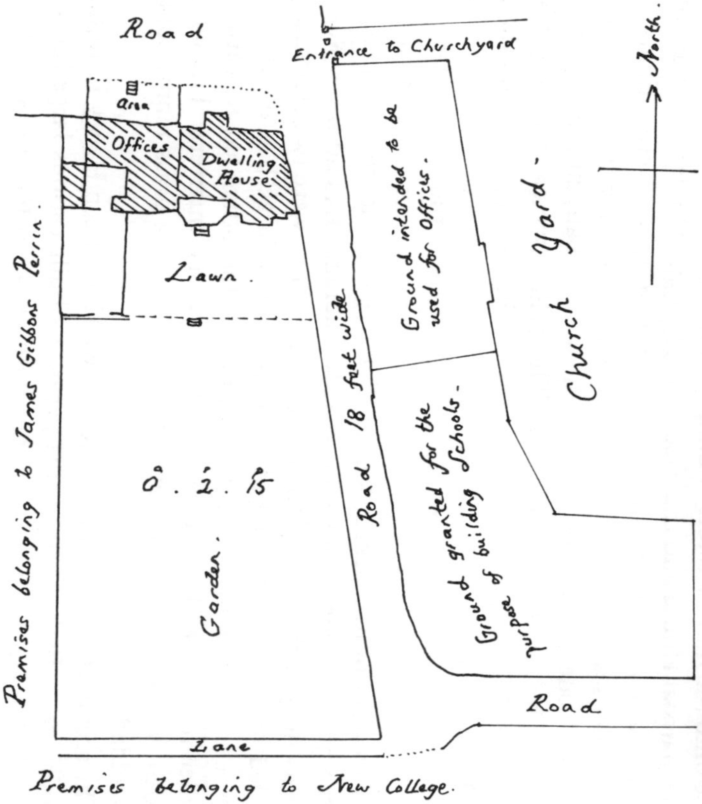

Fig 8 Copy of plan attached to original deed

Fig 9 East end of Rectory from the garden (AAW)

they are now, though the gazebo is not indicated. This is something of a mystery, as the gazebo, at the bottom of the garden beside The Bank footpath, appears to be older than the house and is shown on earlier plans. The new house must have been on the site of an earlier one. The map of 1785 shows two separate plots. On the eastern half (numbered 6014 and corresponding with the present-day rectory) there is a large house in the shape of a hollow square at the front of the plot, and an L-shaped house below that, about half way down what is now the garden. The property is shown as one, and is described as "Miss Drewett, Lewis's and Jones. House and Homestead." Adjoining it is a house the same size as the present day Charcoal House, with a long narrow plot (numbered 6015 but with no names) extending behind it the same width as the house, and including the gazebo. This charming building is described in a note which follows.

It seems most likely that Mr Heathcote bought both plots, demolished the properties on the eastern one, and built the new house onto the more westerly building. Certainly the styles differ, and both Charcoal House and the gazebo would appear to date from about the late seventeenth century. The fact that there were originally separate houses on the site would also account for the rectory having two wells – one in the front room of the western half, and the other in the cellar below the eastern half. The cellar (which was possibly incorporated from the previous house) also had a supply of rainwater piped down from a catch tank at the rear of the main roof.

The 1842 plan includes an outline of the house – the eastern (larger) end is described as "Dwelling House" and the western end, with the 'area' in front of it, marked "Offices." There was a large rear opening on the ground floor at this end, used for storage etc, and there was a conservatory at the back of the main house. There were two staircases: one led up to a bathroom and then on to three large bedrooms (one with a small dressing room attached), and the other led to various smaller rooms which were presumably servants' quarters. The large garden was laid out with gravel paths, and later a grass tennis court was added.

The architect is not known, but may well have been Henry Edmund Goodridge of Bath. During this period he built various large houses with Italianate features in the Bath area, often in situations commanding a good view, and Colerene Rectory fits his style.

The rectory stables were most probably built at the same time, although no contemporary record has yet been found. They were erected on the site of the old vicarage, and what had been the vicarage garden was later used for the new school, which was built in 1885. The ground floor of the stables still has relics of the days when it was used for horses, while the upper storey was used by staff and still contains the old fireplaces and other fittings.

Later developments

For many years the house was unchanged. During the Second World War the children from the school opposite used to come and cultivate their own allotments in the bottom part of the garden and 'dig for victory.' Part of the garden continued to be let as allotments for some years after the war. With the passage of time the house became too large and expensive for its purpose, and, as in so many villages, it might easily have become 'The Old Rectory.' Various schemes were mooted, such as building a new rectory in the garden or even demolishing the smaller (western) section and building garages in its place. However, a plan was devised after the retirement of the Revd Lewis Ramell to divide the house into two, and this was very successfully done in 1977 by the firm of A J Neal of Sherston. The original 'offices' were extended slightly by covering in the open area at the back and, together with a part of the garden, were sold as a private house. The larger part was kept as the parsonage. This left the rector without a kitchen, which had been in the other half, so a new kitchen was constructed in place of the (now derelict) conservatory. Regrettably, the large projecting eaves of the house were removed during this work.

The stables remained as garaging and storage, as they had been for many years. For some years after the war the upstairs rooms were used as a meeting place for the village scouts, but became increasingly decrepit. At the time of writing (1994) plans have been approved to renew the roof, convert the upper storey into a flat, and restore the whole building to something like its original appearance.

Charcoal House

It appears that this building dates from the middle of the eighteenth century or earlier. Its present appearance suggests that when it was reconstructed as a service wing to the new vicarage there was a clear intention that the two buildings should complement each other, without there being any doubt as to which one was the more important. The chimney stacks on both buildings are virtually identical and presumably that on Charcoal House is a replacement of an older chimney. The exterior walls are of rubble-stone, stuccoed to match those of the vicarage. The low pitched, concrete tiled roof must have replaced an earlier one. The windows, in raised, moulded surrounds are in the style of the eighteenth century. The front door is set in a plain stone surround with a heavy, ridged hood on brackets.

The Gazebo

The building is evidently older than the rectory and obviously dates from the period when the vicarage occupied the site on which part of the old National School now stands. It appears to be shown on the map of New College properties dated 1767. It is a building which reflects the status and wealth of those who caused it to be erected. The obvious candidates are the Drewetts who at one time occupied Elmsleigh and Vale Court, as well as a large house on the rectory site.

A remarkable feature of the building is the ornamental bulls-eye window at ground floor level on the western side (fig 10). Why would such a decorative feature have been placed where it is out of view of anybody casually walking in the garden? Perhaps the explanation lies in a timber lintel on the inside of the garden wall of Vale Court, almost opposite the gazebo, which indicates that there was probably a door through the wall at that point many years ago. If there was a similar opening on the opposite side of the footpath at that time, then the

Fig 10 The ornamental bulls-eye window (AAW)

occupiers of Vale Court would have entered what is now the rectory garden and would have observed the bulls-eye window immediately on their right. This would explain its positioning.

Since the gazebo was in existence long before the Wills' extension to Vale Court, the south window would have afforded a marvellous unimpeded view across the By Brook valley towards Rudloe and Pickwick.

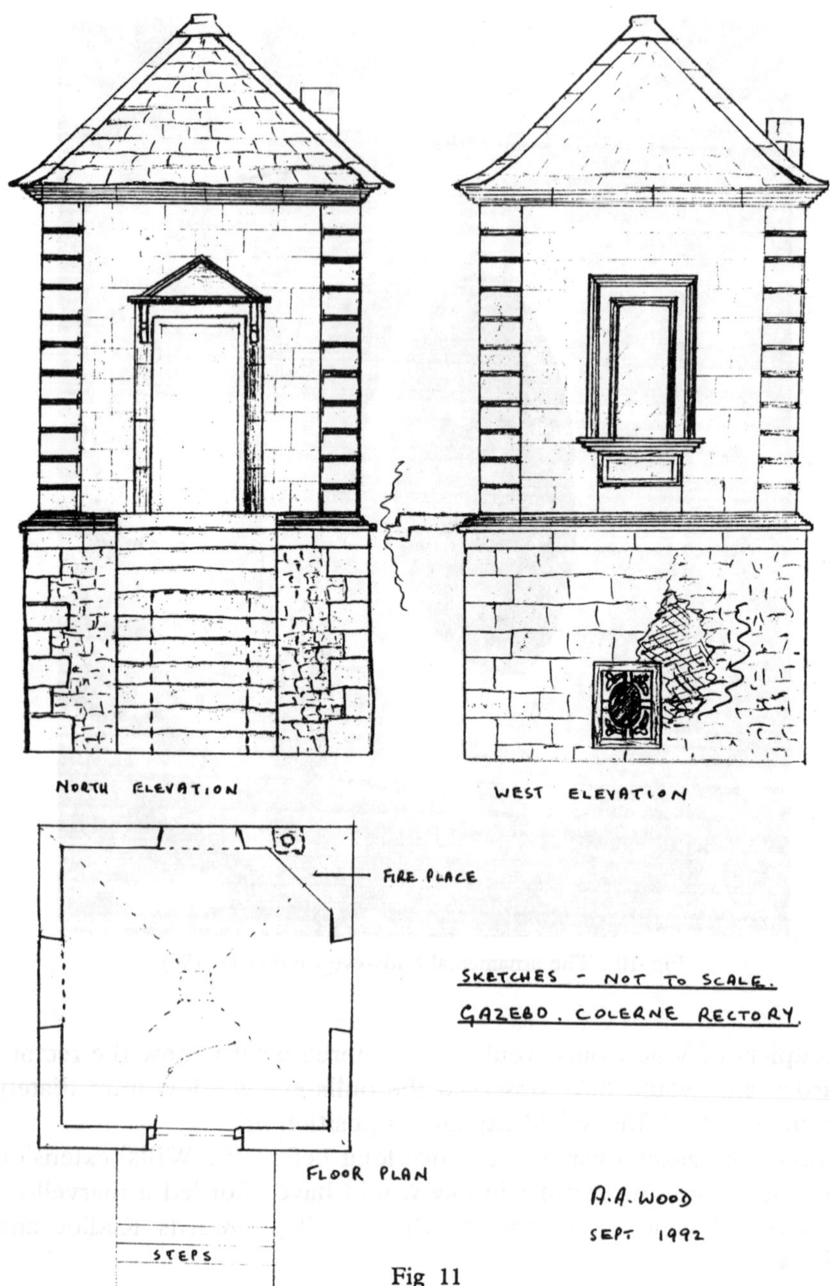
NORTH ELEVATION
WEST ELEVATION
FIRE PLACE
SKETCHES - NOT TO SCALE.
GAZEBO. COLERNE RECTORY.
FLOOR PLAN
STEPS
A.A. WOOD
SEPT 1992

Fig 11

Architectural details

The gazebo is a two storey building of local limestone under a Welsh slate roof. The upper storey is finished externally with ashlar whereas the exterior of the ground floor room is of rubble stone on three sides with ashlar facings on the westerly side. The quoins are of ashlar on both levels. The lower room has a doorway which is positioned under the stone built stairway which gives access to the upper room. The west side of the ground floor room is pierced by the decorated stone bulls-eye window. The frame of this window is monolithic and the embrasure is splayed into the room.

The stone staircase leading to the upper room has ten treads and has an iron balustrade on each side. The door has a moulded stone frame in the Renaissance style (triangular pediment). Tall windows, now blocked up, gave light from the other three sides. Externally, these windows have moulded stone frames. Internally, those on the east and south walls have green painted wooden window seats, the tops of which are hinged to give access to storage below. There may at one time have been a window seat on the west wall. There is a plain fireplace in the southwest corner of the room. The floor is plain board about $\frac{3}{4}$-inch thick. This is in a state of decay. Much of the lath and plaster ceiling has fallen in.

The slate roof may not be original. One might have expected a roof of Cotswold stone on a building of this size and age. The roof is centrally capped with a flat stone which once supported a stone ball. The latter was removed some years ago on safety grounds. The chimney is of square section and is of local stone. There is an ashlar string course on the exterior walls below floor level of the upper storey. Above this, a moulded stone joint is made between the two storeys.

Internally the gazebo is about ten feet square.

Lucknam House

The history of the house and the estate has been researched by R and B Harvey and the following account owes much to them and the Wiltshire Buildings Record; their contribution is gratefully acknowledged.

Early history

The oldest known spelling of the name is Luckenham and, the Saxon name for a settlement being 'ham', it seems more than likely that the Saxons farmed here, continuing a tradition which had started with the Romans. Somewhat surprisingly, Lucknam is not mentioned in the Domesday survey, but the fact is that the estate of modern times was divided between the Manors of Colerne and Euridge. It was cut off to the south by the Manor of Thickwood.

In 1199, when King John was on the throne, 'Lukeham' was divided between William FitzOsbert and Roger de Limoges. Robert de Luckenham appeared on the scene a century later when he granted land to Beatrice de Limoges and her daughters. Robert had died when in 1333 a deed of gift mentions Thomas and Richard, his son and grandson respectively. It appears that Robert's family owned Lucknam Park but not the farm.

Lucknam Park was sold in 1513 by Richard Clements, a farmer, to John Horsington, another farmer. A house was included in the sale. The price of the farm was £26 13s 4d. Thomas Holbrooke of Norton Malreward was the next owner. He made the purchase in 1559. The Holbrookes were a prosperous family with land in Somerset as well as at Lucknam. In 1612 Samuel Holbrooke was at Lucknam and the farm at that time extended to 100 acres. When Samuel died at his other farm in Keynsham in 1615, his goods and chattels were valued at £379, about three times the average for a yeoman farmer of that time. The last Holbrooke to live at Lucknam was Anne, the unmarried grand-daughter of Samuel. She died in 1671 and left the farm to be divided between her nine cousins. It was eventually sold to a wealthy

Bristol merchant, James Wallis, and from this time on it became part of a landed estate.

The Wallis occupation

James Wallis bought the property in 1688 and when he died it passed to his surviving son Ezekiel who died on the last day of 1735, leaving a widow but no issue.

The Wallis family were prosperous clothiers of Trowbridge and James's grandfather, Ezekiel, a second son, had left his home town to seek his fortune in Bristol, also as a clothier. He was so successful that he was elected Lord Mayor in 1638. John, the father of James, was also a clothier who married Elizabeth Hulbert of Slaughterford, the daughter of another clothier. They lived at Manor Farm there and it is possible that John used the fulling mill there, which is now referred to as Rag Mill from its most recent usage. John and his family were Quakers and John was buried at the Quaker meeting house opposite Chapps Mill when he died in 1661. His son, James, was one of ten children. It is thought that he went to Bristol shortly after the death of his father and paid for his religious beliefs by being imprisoned there. His elder brother, also named Ezekiel, remained at Slaughterford until his death in 1699, when James inherited his property. The minute book of the Bristol Quaker Meeting records that on 23rd November 1678, "James Wallis and Mary Gouldney signified their intention of marriage and desire to accomplish the same in the way of friends." In 1682 James embarked on a programme of acquiring land in the area around his birthplace, his first purchase being the Manor of North Wraxall. He subsequently bought the Manor of Biddestone before taking over Lucknam which cost him £500.

The initials of James and Mary with the date 1689 appear on a stone built into the stables at Lucknam but it is unlikely that this is its original position. No doubt the stone recorded some early rebuilding of the mansion, including the centre portion, but not the two bow-windowed rooms, pillared portico, or much of the rear wings. The house was not quite symmetrical and some of the internal walls are thicker than would be expected for the period. It could be that there was already a sizeable farmhouse there and that James considered it worthwhile to incorporate parts of it into his new house. It appears that James and Mary did not take up residence at Lucknam, for they were both buried in Bristol in 1708 and 1719 respectively.

Their son, another Ezekiel, was the only survivor of several children when his father died. He was then aged fourteen. No doubt he was able to play the country gentleman because of his wealth. It was recorded by Thomas Smith, the uncle of Lucas Selfe, Ezekiel's kinsman and lifelong friend, that he had gone to Beanacre to welcome home his nephew and Ezekiel after their *fourteen-month* journey through Holland, southern Germany, and Italy.

Ezekiel was obviously much respected for he was appointed High Sheriff. For this to happen he must have forsaken his Quaker tenets. He had married Cecilia Selfe, the youngest sister of his friend Lucas, the previous September, at Ditteridge. Her marriage portion was £2500, and Ezekiel settled upon her the Manors of North Wraxall and Biddestone as well as the mansion (Lucknam) he was living in and 40 acres of land adjoining.

On his death at the age of 41, everything he owned went to his widow with the exception of money bequests to Lucas Selfe and others. To each of his servants he left a suit of mourning. After two years of widowhood, Cecilia married Dr John Coxed, Warden of New College, Oxford, in the church at Colerne. Cecilia lived long enough to be a widow for a second time and died in 1760 at the age of 60.

The succession of Paul Methuen

Cecilia left no will. On her death all of her property, which included Lucknam, went to her nephew, Paul Methuen, the son of her sister Ann and her husband Thomas Methuen, a clothier of Bradford-on-Avon. Paul had been orphaned at the age of fourteen when his widowed father died. In 1747, at the age of 24, he moved into Corsham Court which he had recently purchased. He married Christian Cobb in 1749 and they had three children, the eldest being Paul Cobb Methuen who was later to be associated with other property in Colerne. Having inherited Lucknam in 1760, Paul Methuen had no interest in taking up residence there and so James Clutterbuck became tenant. In about 1786 Paul Methuen added to his property by purchasing Thickwood Farm, lately the property of John Oseland who had inherited it from the Fisher family of Worcestershire. Paul Methuen died in 1795 and, like his wife, he was buried in North Wraxall. Their tomb in the church there is highly decorated and is a splendid memorial.

In 1776 Paul Cobb Methuen married Matilda Gooch from Suffolk and his father made an agreement allowing his son to occupy Lucknam Park rent free. There is no record of substantial alterations or additions being made to the house during his occupancy, although some of the fireplaces date back to this period. Like Ezekiel Wallis before him, Paul Cobb Methuen became High Sheriff of Wiltshire and he was also Member of Parliament for Great Bedwyn, 1781–84. When his father died in 1795 he moved to Corsham Court and sold Lucknam and Thickwood.

1796 to 1806

John Clements was the next owner of Lucknam and Thickwood farm. Lucknam Grove was the name given to the house at that time and when he bought the property in 1796 it cost him £7750. As well as the house, there were 191 acres of land in addition to Thickwood Farm which had a further 70 acres. The sale included much of the contents of the mansion, and there was a gallery in Colerne church for the family as well as a pew for the servants. John Clements died in 1806 and was buried at Colerne. Lucknam Grove was sold by his widow the following year to William Tonge.

Another Bristol link

William Norris Tonge's family had once been prosperous merchants in Bristol. His father was Henry Tonge and his mother Anne Eliza was the daughter of Vice-Admiral Henry Norris. When William married Mary-Ann, the daughter of the Revd John Bryan of West Charlton, in 1804, he already had estates at Alveston, Glos., Charlton Mackrell, and Highway, near Calne. Three years after his marriage he purchased Lucknam Park and several of his children were born there. The Tonges did not remain long at Lucknam and it was let for a time to

George Sawyer. When the property was advertised for sale or to let, 112 acres of land were included and the outbuildings included laundry, dairy, brewhouse, coachhouse and stabling. A large conservatory was mentioned, but it is clear from the details given that the portico and the rooms with the bow windows had not yet been added.

The Boode family

Andreas Christian Boode was the next owner. He was the son of a wealthy owner of five coffee plantations in Demarara. He was one of six children and he went to the University of Halle near Leipzig, with his brother Jacobus, to read law. They both finished with doctoral theses. Andreas came to England where he met Phebe Dannet, a daughter of the Rector of Liverpool, and married her in 1800. They lived in Amsterdam for a time, where their two children, Phebe and John Christian, were born. Andreas bought Lucknam Park in about 1827, two years after his wife Phebe died. His son John Christian had attended Oriel College, Oxford, and it may be assumed that the older Boode bought the property to pass on to his son. Andreas enlarged the mansion and in 1831 he also acquired Lucknam Farm, which had 368 acres, at a cost of £10 591. He subsequently added the Manor of Euridge, Thickwood, Eastrop (now Eastrip), and Sewell Farms.

His son, John, married Clementina Elizabeth Mary Bayntun, daughter of Admiral Sir Henry Bayntun, in 1834; she was then nineteen years old. A few days after the wedding a great party was held at Lucknam to celebrate the event. According to a contemporary report, about 800 people attended, including most of the population of Colerne who entered the field preceded by music at just before one o'clock. A cannon was fired to signal the start of the feast. Mr Boode and his friends were accommodated in a tent where they had a commanding view of the tables. A larger tent was provided for the benefit of the tenants and tradesmen. The festivities went on until midnight.

The marriage was also marked by the placing of a dated tablet, with the initials J.C.B., on the stables. John and his bride spent their lengthy honeymoon travelling in Europe and continued their tours there in later years. They had a son, born in Naples, but he and two daughters died in infancy. Their youngest daughter, Constance, was born at Lucknam in 1845. The family wealth enabled John to entertain in the most lavish fashion at Lucknam and he accumulated 500 distinguished calling cards in an album. He was also able to keep the number of staff necessary to support his lifestyle. These included a housekeeper, lady's maid, upper housemaid, under housemaid, servant for the schoolroom, butler, under butler, kitchen maid, scullery maid, valet, livery servant, coachman, groom, two helpers in the stables, gas man, bailiff, gardener, under gardener, woodman, carter, stable boy, gamekeeper and an individual called Jerry whose function is not described, a total of 24 servants to make life easy. The wages bill amounted to £614 4s a year. At that time Lucknam Mansion shared a certain distinction with The Rocks, in that they both had their own gas making plant and a gasholder. The marriage, despite its auspicious start, lasted only twelve years. Clementina abandoned John, leaving their two surviving daughters with him, and a divorce followed, a rarity in those days. She remarried, her second husband being the Comte de Villefranche, and died in France in 1888.

John, a bitter man, did not remarry, but continued to live at Lucknam and saw both his daughters married in Colerne church. After he died in 1870, his younger daughter, Constance, lived there for a further three years with her husband, Benjamin Winthrop.

Some of the Boode family wealth was used to make improvements to the mansion. It is thought that Andreas made most of the additions, including the portico and the two end rooms with the bow windows. At second floor level, above the portico, was an open space with false pedimented windows having balustrades between, providing a belvedere from which the view could be taken down the avenue and to either side of it. After Andreas had died, in 1844, architectural fashion changed and the gothic style became fashionable at the expense of the classical tradition. The gothic alterations date from John's time as owner.

Photographs of the exterior and interior of the house were included with the later sale particulars of 1918. The hall was panelled with oak, with an oak screen in the gothic style, leading to the staircase. The hall ceiling had carved beams, and carried the coats of arms of the Boode and Bayntun families. The library was at the west end of the main range and it was fitted with pedimented mahogany bookcases and had a handsome plaster cornice, which still remains. Upstairs in the west wing was the boudoir, a very heavily furnished room with Jacobean arcaded panelling and stained glass windows. The bow-windowed room at the east end of the house was a conservatory with a billiard room behind.

The Boodes had installed a bathroom and there was, of course, the ultimate in modernity, the gas making equipment. Water was pumped to the top of the house by hydraulic ram near Sewell Springs. The tower, to which water is still pumped, was not then built. The mansion had two lodges to its main approaches. Bath Lodge, opposite the airfield, was demolished when the airfield was built (see p 170) but Chippenham Lodge still exists, in separate ownership. The latter building was erected in 1854, but there is no date for the construction of Bath Lodge. The dovecote, which was originally at Euridge and dates from the late eighteenth century, is mentioned in the sales brochure of 1873, prepared when the Boodes sold Lucknam. It was used as a fruit store in more recent times and the pigeon holes can only be seen from its interior. There was also an icehouse, a brewhouse, an orchard house, and vineries.

The Walmesleys

When the estate came up for sale in 1873 it was bought by Richard Walmesley. It then amounted to 1100 acres. An account of the Walmesley family is given elsewhere in this volume (pp 121–46). Their major addition to Lucknam Mansion was the water tower, which is not as tall today as it was when first built. Then it had an embattled top from which a flag would be flown.

After the Walmesleys

Sir Alfred Read bought Lucknam in 1918. He also became High Sheriff of the County, in 1925. During his residence, he made many alterations to the interior of the mansion. The oak interiors installed by the Boodes were removed and rooms were refurbished in the

Fig 12 Lucknam House (note the embattled water tower) and the library *c* 1900 (SG)

Fig 13 Chippenham Lodge, 1995 (AAW)

Fig 14 Lucknam Park Hotel, 1995 (AAW)

Georgian style. In 1925 the house was described as having been practically reconstructed internally, and by that time electric light, radiators and the telephone had been installed. The number of bedrooms had been increased to seven. Sir Alfred moved in 1928 and he was succeeded by Colonel Merry. It was he who had the top of the water tower removed and commissioned the architect, Oswald Brakspear, to produce a design which was more sympathetic to the mansion as a whole. Middle Lodge was also built by Merry.

Mr Stevens was the next owner after Col Merry and after him came Mr Beck. In 1987 the property was sold and became Lucknam Park Hotel.

Building resources

From the earliest times there was no shortage of timber and it is likely that the first buildings at Lucknam would have been largely constructed of wood cut from woodland around. The topsoil is of no great depth locally in the areas which had been clear of trees from perhaps Roman, or even earlier times. As a consequence the original builders need not have dug far before reaching stone which would have been suitable for infilling a timber framed house and necessary outbuildings. Later on, the owners of the estate obviously wanted to erect something rather more substantial, in keeping with their positions in the community and reflecting their wealth. Near Sewell Springs there are two quarries with faces of considerable height. The quality of the limestone varies throughout the depth of the faces, with the better, building stone in the lowest ten feet or so. It can be assumed that the quarry faces would have been cut back progressively, with stone from the upper levels being used for walling and buildings of lesser importance, whilst the better quality stone was used for the house, and probably the lodges in later times. One of the quarries was eventually worked on the cave and pillar system which is common under Box Hill, Monkton Farleigh and Combe Down. The Sewell quarry has two parallel adits (or tunnels) entering the face at a low level, these being cross-linked a little way in from the entrances. It has been said that the last time that these quarries were worked was when Middle Lodge was built. The possibility exists that other adits may have been driven and since lost through rock and earth falls.

Trunnells Farm

It is clear from the map and schedule of the Inclosure Award of 1787 that the farm was then known as Trimnells Farm, the name being transferred to its more recent location during Victorian times.

The original farm was probably one of those around which the medieval village grew and there are elements of the farmhouse which support this.

The farmhouse

The house has obviously been subject to many alterations over the centuries. It is probable that the oldest parts of the structure date back to 1480–1520. The style and quality of the original features which still remain indicate that the house was built for a prosperous yeoman.

Fig 15 Trunnells Farmhouse (AAW)

Occupancy

Wentworth Parsons was the owner of the property in 1787 but it is unlikely that he lived there since he then held the Manor of Euridge and other properties in the parish amounting to about 920 acres in all.

During the nineteenth century, as recorded in the census returns from 1841 onwards, it is apparent that the farm changed hands frequently. It is not possible to identify the occupier in 1841 but the 1851 census names George Smith, a farmer of 30 acres, and a Somerset man, as resident at "Trimlins Farm." Also resident were his wife and four children, William, Henry, Charles and Mary Jane.

They had departed by 1861 and had been replaced by Isaac Webb and Elizabeth, his wife, and their five children. Also in the house was an eighteen-year-old boarder, James Bright, an agricultural labourer. Isaac was described as a farmer, butcher and carrier. Like George Smith, he was an incomer, having been born at Tormarton.

By 1871, George Cook was in residence, described as a farmer of 28 acres. He hailed from Bath and his wife Elizabeth came from Batheaston. They had two sons, John and William. At the time of the Tithe Award of 1875 the property was recorded as being in the hands of the trustees of the Revd John Allen but George Cook was the occupier. The property was described as "house, shop, stable, yards, etc."

In 1881 James Butler was resident in the property (still described as Trimnells House, although Trimnells Farm was also recorded beyond the other side of the street). He was an Atworth man and his wife Emily came from Chippenham. They had been resident in Colerne for some time and in 1871 they had lived in the Market Place. James was a carpenter and there were five children recorded in 1871 only three of whom, Henry, Ellen and Emily, were still present in 1881. It is likely that the eldest children, Julie and George, would have been married by then and have moved away, but there was a new, youngest daughter, nine-year-old Annie.

It is interesting to note that James Butler was referred to in the Tithe Award, as being the occupier of the ruins of a brewery, and also a shop. He and his wife were still resident in 1891 but none of their children was with them at that time, and the property was no longer given a name in the census return.

The farmhouse – structural details

This was probably originally a timber-framed house with a three room and cross passage plan. The cross passage still exists with access by the front door. The end of the house furthest from the Post Office would have been the service end; it has been considerably altered over the years.

Some of the old timber-framed partitions have survived as have the remains of a very old timber mullioned window on the side of the main chimney stack.

The ground floor room nearest to the Post Office has a partition in which there are mortices and pegholes for a doorway which probably gave access to another part of the house, long since demolished. The existing room at the north end of the house appears to have been the hall of the original building and this would have extended upwards to the rafters (see fig 16). When the house was first built there would not have been a fireplace in the modern sense. Instead there would have been an open hearth in the middle of the hall floor, and smoke would have risen and been dispersed in the rafters.

One of the more interesting features which still remains is an internal jetty projecting into the upper part of the hall, which allowed the construction of a larger first floor chamber than would otherwise have been possible, by using some of the upper part of the hall (figs 16 and 17).

From the cross passage there is a step up to the hall. This was a common feature which facilitated cleansing of the floor of the hall, since it could be swilled out and rubbish and water could be swept into the lower level of the passage floor and thence into the yard.

The doorway to the hall is a fine example of the period. Unfortunately, the original, arched head has been largely lost in order to accommodate a flat topped door. Some of the features of this door are similar to those of the old mullioned window, suggesting that they were constructed at about the same time. The large stone fireplace was probably installed about 1560–70, with the consequent blocking up of the old window. This has also suffered with the passage of time. All that remains of a moulded cornice is a side section. Since the installation of the fireplace and its associated chimney made the open

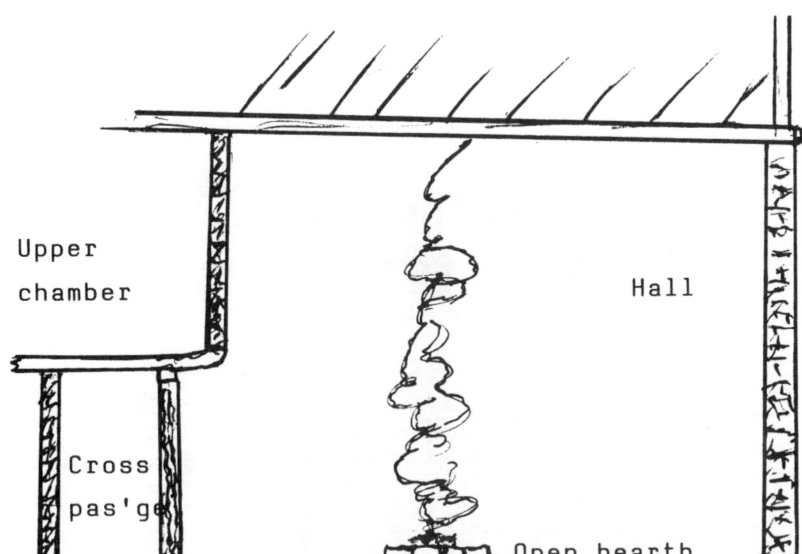

Fig 16 Sketch of medieval hall at Trimnells (now Trunnells) farmhouse

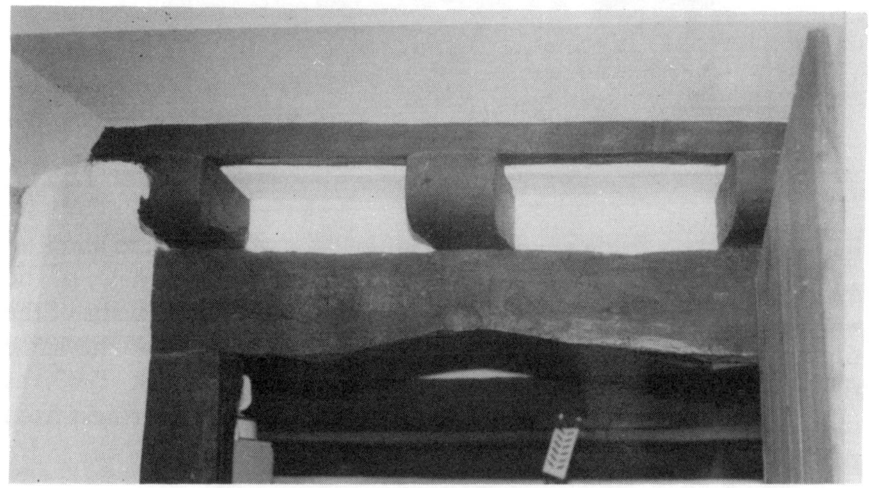

Fig 17 Jetty over hall doorway (WBR)

Fig 18 Doorway from passage to hall (note the step up) (WBR)

hall redundant, a ceiling and upper-storey floor were built, to allow an additional upper chamber to be added. A mullioned window, of the same period, on this upper floor suggests that the exterior walls of the timber-framed house were rebuilt or cased with stone at the same time. Further work was probably undertaken in about 1700, as indicated by the age of the roof on the end of the house furthest from the Post Office.

Fig 19 Sixteenth century fireplace (WBR)

The threshing barn

The barn has also been altered considerably over the centuries. It is a substantial building, constructed for the most part in coursed rubble stone with a gabled roof, now covered with pantiles though it may well have been thatched when first built. Unlike other local barns there are no covered porches but merely waggon entries, reaching to the eaves, at the centres of the longest walls. The exterior corners of the barn have rough-dressed quoin stones, but the exterior and interior corners of the entries have ashlar (smooth faced) quoins. Inside the main entry in the northernmost wall, a dirt threshing floor remains. In the same wall, adjacent to the end wall at the westerly end, a small door with a timber lintel and red brick quoins was added at some time. In the western end wall there is a square pitching door which has been blocked up. This would have given access to a hay loft. There is no lintel over the blocked door and the stone work blocking the aperture extends upwards beyond the original confines of the door. It seems likely that a partial collapse of this wall occurred, maybe because the lintel rotted. It was certainly found necessary to install two tie rods with X-shaped anchors above the door. Between the ends of the tie rods there is a narrow lancet vent. The top of the west end wall is covered with stone copings as are the end walls of the house, but the wall at the other end of the barn does not have coping stones.

The wagon entrance on the south side has been closed up with a breeze-block curtain wall. On either side of this old entrance two outbuildings have been attached, both of them have catslide roofs, that is to say the line of the main roof is continued over these additions. The building to the east was obviously a stable, since it has a cobbled floor with a drainage channel running out into the back yard. There are the remains of harness hooks in this stable and it appears that a partition may once have divided it into two stalls.

Stable extension to farmhouse

At the southerly end of the farmhouse there is a two-storey extension which appears to have been much altered. The walls are of rubble stone, some of which is random and some in courses. The corners, doors and windows have ashlar quoin stones and the gable has stone coping with stepped ashlar quoins under. At the time of a survey carried out in 1988 it was noted that this part of the building had probably been raised at some time, because an owl hole (filled in) was not at the apex, as is usual, but was five or six feet below it. However, this may have been in sympathy with the owl hole or vent in the adjacent barn which is in a similar position relative to the apex.

The farmhouse roof is clad with stone but the stable extension had triple roman tiles until they were replaced by pantiles matching those on the barn. In 1988 there was a typical two-part stable door on the east side and a pitching hole to a hay loft, a double door being provided. There was also a smaller pitching hole low down on the southern wall.

This extension has recently been converted to a residential unit and a separate staircase has been provided to give access to a relaid first floor.

Acknowledgement

The threshing barn and the stable were surveyed in 1988 by members of the Manpower Services Commission Community Programme, whose report was lodged with the Wiltshire Buildings Record. The farmhouse itself was the subject of a separate survey carried out in 1990 by WBR and grateful thanks are due to them for making the results of both surveys available. Special thanks are also due to the WBR for allowing the photographs of internal features to be reproduced.

Ragge Farm

This farm was previously called Jacques Farm and like many other properties in the parish, it was originally owned by New College, Oxford.

The farmhouse

At a casual glance this building presents itself as an ordinary village house, probably not more than two hundred years old. In 1849 the house was described as containing a cellar and bakehouse underground, a room and shop on the ground floor and two attics. The house was stone-built and slated. But a survey during 1988–9 by Mrs Pamela Slocombe for the Wiltshire Buildings Record revealed features dating from about 1500–1700.

The house which is parallel to the road and right against the pavement has two cellar windows of which only the upper parts now project above the footpath. Two horizontal lights have been inserted into the pavement to provide some of the light which has been lost due to the gradual rise in the height of the road surface over the years. These cellar windows would, presumably, at one time have been above ground level. A lean-to at the west end of the rear of the house, known to have been in existence in 1919, was removed sometime before 1987.

Moving inside the house, a major feature is the cellar which extends the full length of the building. The walls are built of stone throughout. Stone access stairs descend into the middle of the space creating a central area and there is a room at each end, to the east and west. There are two north facing windows which have already been mentioned. Both the east and west walls have fireplaces. The dressing of the stone of the west end surround indicates sixteenth century construction, but, more importantly, the stone surround in the east wall has traces of stone work prevalent around 1500.

The ceiling is a mixture of original and re-used timbers. For

Fig 20 Ragge Farm (note parapet and the almost obscured cellar window) (AAW)

Fig 21 The cellar window at the western end (AAW)

instance, one joist has a groove for a wattle and daub panel. Some timbers are heavily encrusted with soot, and it would be reasonable to deduce that they could have come from the roof of an earlier medieval structure which had an open fire in a room open to the rafters. Over the years, these beams would have become encrusted with the black resinous soot produced by wood smoke.

The upper storeys of the house have been much altered, particularly during the last hundred years or so, but some unusual and fascinating features still remain. The main staircase is stone, thought to be granite, which is not fully shaped on the underside. On the ground floor the large chimneys have been adapted to accommodate smaller and modern grates. The east room on the first floor has iron bound holes in the floor boards. They run across the room, north to south, about four inches inside the wall. They could well have anchored weaving looms or other machinery.

Above eaves level almost all the roof has been replaced in this century. A few old joists remain in the central area and east end, and there are also the remains of a lead rain channel running across the roof to carry water between the front and back parapets. The fact that there is an unused stair head still in existence indicates that the attic rooms were once used. There is no evidence of windows in the gable ends, but it is possible that there were once dormer windows which would have been removed when the house was re-roofed.

Architectural details

Exterior

The exterior walls of the house are of coursed rubble stone and the front and rear original walls are about twenty inches thick. The front doorway has an unchamfered ashlar stone surround. The facade has a high string course continuously forming the sills of the first floor windows. There is a coved cornice under the parapet at the top of the facade. The quoins are of ashlar stone and the chimney stacks are of stone with moulded tops. The sash windows of 4 panes are probably of nineteenth century origin. A separately roofed extension parallel to the original house in matching stone work has been added in recent years. The building formerly had a parapet at the rear as well as at the front.

Interior

The north-facing west cellar window has a two-light ovolo moulded mullion. The fireplace in the west wall has a three-inch chamfered surround and the remains of stops on the jambs, possibly 'urnstops'. Its flat arch points to a sixteenth century date. Also in this room there are trimmers for the ground floor fireplace above, and that on the north side has narrow mouldings of mid–late seventeenth century work. There is one original beam which runs east–west at the rear. It is set into the eastern end of the cellar partition wall, and has a three-and-a-half inch chamfer and step and concave stops. There is an old iron hook in the east end of the beam. The joist behind this original beam has a timber ovolo moulding along one edge and is probably a re-used seventeenth century door jamb.

The east cellar room fireplace has moulded lower jambs, but the lintel has been renewed. Its flue leads up to the south and has a hook on a short chain in the back wall. In 1849 the house was described as having a cellar and bakehouse underground. No strong evidence now exists of an oven, but there is a possibility that it might have been in the north-east corner of the east room next to the chimney stack. The stack of neither fireplace extends more than four inches into the cellar. The north facing window also has a two-light ovolo moulded mullioned window, but in a splayed opening. This window is now blocked with air bricks.

Ground floor

The stone staircase leading to the first floor has a heavy turned newel post of mid-nineteenth century type. There is a toadback handrail which may have had wooden balusters below, replaced by iron rods.

The east room has a modern (1970s) axial beam. The fireplace surround has been replaced in the nineteenth or more probably twentieth century. The inside of the chimney narrows sharply above the surround and the chimney itself appears to have been designed for a nineteenth century hob grate or an early small fireplace. The west room fireplace has a modern timber lintel and rebuilt jambs. Like the

Fig 22 Fireplace at west end of cellar (WBR)

Fig 23 Fireplace at east end of cellar (WBR)

one in the east room, the inside of the chimney narrows sharply. The stack protrudes about 6 inches into the room.

First floor

The west room has been divided into two during this century. The holes in the floorboards in the east room have already been mentioned. The windows have two panes per sash, elongated ovolo moulded glazing bars and horns on the sashes. Doorway openings in the house have timber lintels.

Roof

The former stairhead, which is no longer in use, is situated in the centre rear of the roof vertically above the three feet wide west section of the centre part of the cellar. It is surrounded by lath and plaster partitioning.

The outbuildings

The copyhold of 1849 refers to a four-bay barn and midsty (threshing floor), stone-built and tiled, a two-stall stable and loft over and a cart hovel, stone-built, thatched. The barn and attached stable have been substantially rebuilt within the last few years. They were surveyed by the Community Programme Industrial Archaeology project in 1988 and at that time it was noted that the barn and stable were of random rubble stone construction, built to courses with rough faced quoins around doors and windows. The barn was a one-and-a half storey building, the roof of which was about nine inches higher than that of the stable. The barn roof was partly covered with the original stone tiles but about three quarters of the roof was now covered with double roman tiles. The ridge tiles were of stone. The roof of the stable had been covered entirely with double roman tiles. The barn had had an upper floor put in probably after the 1939–45 war, and it had been used as a clothing store. Wide, wooden steps had been inserted in order to give access to the upper floor. Two windows on the north east side were probably pitching doors as was an opening in the gable end facing into the street. The gable there had stepped quoins with stone coping and there was a saddlestone at the apex. In the gable end of the stable there was a rectangular owl hole just below the apex and a similar, but larger, embrasure lower down in the same wall. Both of these were monolithic constructions (carved from a single block of stone). Although the outside walls of the barn and the stable are twenty inches thick, as is the case with the house, it is often the case that the walls of farm buildings were less massive than a dwelling erected at the same time. This together with the large quoins, the monolithic windows and the splayed front window of the stable suggest that it was built in the seventeenth century and is older than the barn and the house. The front walls of the barn and stable are not in the same straight line. It is more than possible that an earlier barn once stood on the site and that the plinth at the rear of the present barn is all that remains of the original back wall. The barn has been converted into a dwelling house during the last decade.

Occupancy

The earliest information available about occupants is that Ferdinand Aust held the copyhold plus thirty two acres of farmland in 1849. The ownership changed in 1893 when it was bought by Giles Tanner of Westonbirt but from 1851 until at least 1891 John Knight was the tenant. During this century the May family lived in the house and in more recent years the occupants, a Mr and Mrs Neeve ran a small agricultural and sporting clothing business, using the barn for storage and selling goods at agricultural shows, point-to-point meetings etc. The property has changed hands twice during the last decade.

Trimnells Farm and Doncombe Farm

We have grouped these two properties together, although neither of them now exists as a farm, because they were sold by auction at the Castle Hotel, Bath, on 6th July 1867, and the sale document gives a detailed account of the buildings at that time. In the case of Trimnells Farm, many of the buildings still exist, having been converted into modern dwellings and garages; but the Doncombe Farm buildings were demolished to make way for the airfield (see p 169).

Prior to the 1867 sale, the farms had been owned by Thomas Harding, lately deceased; and Frederick Perren, the owner of No 8 Market Place (see p 78), was the tenant of both. The Six Bells public house and two adjacent cottages were also included in the sale (see p 95).

Earlier still, according to the 1787 Inclosure Award, both properties were owned by Wentworth Parsons of Euridge Manor. Up to this time most of the land in the parish (with the exception of some older enclosures) was in common field and the farmer had strips or parcels of land scattered all over. It may well have been that the buildings on Doncombe Farm were erected following the 1787 awards.

Trimnells Farm

The original Trimnells Farm was that which is now called Trunnells. The name was transferred some time after 1787 but its derivation is uncertain.

The 1867 sale particulars describe the farm in some detail. It extended to just over 183 acres and had "A convenient Stone-built and Slated Farm House, with garden in front, enclosed from the road by a stone fence". The farmhouse contained, on the upper floor four attics, on the first floor six good bedrooms, and on the ground floor a parlour, drawing room, entrance hall, dairy, pantry, kitchen with oven, wash-house, yard, water closet, coal and wood house etc. In the basement there was good cellarage. There was a kitchen garden with summer-house etc. The farm buildings were stone built, partly tiled and thatched. They included a barn with two bays, twelve-horse cart stable, chaff-house, loft, cattle sheds, cow and calf pens, piggeries, nag stable, detached waggon-house, granary, three farm yards and good rick yard. Many of these buildings still exist having been converted to modern dwellings and garages. The farmhouse appears to have been demolished at about the time of construction of the Victorian farmhouse which is now a nursing home.

By the time of the 1861 census Frederick Perren was in residence with his wife Margaret and five children. He employed a governess, Henrietta Brokenbrow, and a domestic servant Esther Alford from Atworth. Esther had been with his family for at least ten years, appearing in the census of 1851, when Frederick was at No 8 Market Place and his father was the tenant of Trimnells Farm. In 1861, Frederick employed seven men and four boys on the two farms of which he was the tenant. Ten years before, his father had employed fifteen labourers, and the reduction in the workforce continued, perhaps reflecting a continual decline in the fortunes of Frederick. By 1871 there were no longer any servants at the farmhouse but there were then nine children. The eldest, Augustus, was 22 years old and probably worked for his father on the farm. Daughters Elizabeth, Emily and Alice, aged 20, 18, and 16 respectively, were no doubt kept busy with housework or looking after the younger children, the youngest of whom was Herbert, three years old. Frederick was then employing only five men and one boy. It is clear that he had lost the tenancy of Doncombe Farm, as his 1871 acreage was given as 200, compared with 425 ten years before.

Noah's Ark

Included in the same lot as Trimnells in 1867 was a cottage and close called "Petty's", as well as "A small plot of land on which are the ruins of a cottage known as Noah's Ark", in the occupation of William Hicks, as a yearly tenant. The annual rent was £4 with the landlord paying all rates and taxes. Noah's Ark Piece covered an area of 20 perches (one-eighth of an acre). The earliest identifiable resident of

Fig 24 The barn in 1995 (AAW)

Fig 25 The converted granary (before conversion, stone steps led up to a pitching door) (AAW)

The Ark appeared in 1851 when Henry Mullings (or Mullins) lived there with his 26-year-old son William. Henry was then 73 years old and was described as being a pauper agricultural labourer. William was a farm labourer.

William Hicks was living at The Ark by 1861 and, although it must surely have been in a dilapidated condition even then, it afforded shelter to him, his wife, Edith, and four young children.

Isaac Weeks, shepherd, and his wife Jemima, with two young children, George and Sarah, were living at The Ark in 1871. By 1881 the cottage had been demolished.

Doncombe Farm

When Doncombe Farm was put up for sale by the Trustees of Thomas Harding, it was referred to as Duncombe's Farm and said to be "Bounded on the North West side by the celebrated Fosse Road, and on the East by the road leading from Colerne to Marshfield." The farm covered 243 acres of "very productive arable, sheep and pasture land." The farm buildings were described as commodious, comprising, a large double-bay barn, stone-built and tiled, a range of cattle sheds, a detached waggon-house, cow sheds, cart stable for six horses, chaff-house, with hay and straw loft over, two enclosed farm yards and rick yard. Also on the farm was a substantial stone-built and slate roof cottage divided into two tenements, each containing four rooms and wash house, with good gardens attached. Slate roofs were then a modern form of roof covering and it seems that the cottage had been re-roofed or had been built much later than the barn and other farm buildings.

It is quite difficult to identify particular buildings in the early census returns, but it seems probable that in 1841 the cottage at Doncombe Farm was occupied by James Gaby and his wife, Elizabeth, with their son, Jacob, and daughters, Sarah and Lucy. Father and son were both described as yeomen. Elizabeth Billett was also resident with her sons, five-year-old Daniel and one-year-old James. Elizabeth Billett was James Gaby's daughter but the relationship to two other young children, Robert Bryan, one, and Elizabeth Povey, five, also in the cottage at the time, is unknown. Ten years later the Gabys were still at

Doncombe but only five people were resident when the census was taken, Jacob and Sarah having departed. Daughter Lucy, then 25 years old, was still there and Daniel and James Billett, recorded as nephews of James Gaby, were both at work on the farm, Daniel as a labourer and James as a ploughboy at the tender age of eleven.

In 1861 both Gabys were still there, and Elizabeth Billett was on record again, described as a domestic servant. Daniel Billett and John Brown, both nephews of James Gaby were the fourth and fifth members of the household; they were both agricultural labourers. Whereas the rest of the family were all born locally, John Brown's birthplace is given as Liverpool.

It is clear from the census returns that James Gaby farmed only a small area of land, 50 acres in 1851, 59 in 1861. He does not appear to have employed more than three men, though he may well have used casual labour at harvest time.

The enumerator for the 1851 and 1861 censuses, walking from the village towards Marshfield, came to 'Field Cottage' before he reached the Gabys. Shepherds lived there on both occasions, the Gale family in 1851 and the Shells (or Snells) in 1861.

The last appearance of the Gabys was in 1871. James was then farming 26 acres at Starvall Farm, Doncombe, employing a man and a boy. He was 86 years old, a widower, and his widowed daughter Elizabeth Billett aged 58 was still with him, as was his grandson Daniel. Arthur Sumsion, a Colerne boy aged sixteen, completed the household; he was a "general servant, domestic."

We have already seen that Frederick Perren had lost the tenancy of Doncombe Farm after it had been bought by Poynder. The 1871 census records that Charles Bevan had taken over and employed four men and three boys. Charles was 35 years old, unmarried and shared the cottage with his brother Albert and sister Catherine, both in their twenties and unmarried. Henry Bright, a Colerne man, aged about 50, slept in a hayloft on the farm.

By 1881 Charles Bevan and his brother Albert had Doncombe Farm between them. Charles, 46, had 120 acres and employed four labourers, and lived at Colerne Field with his wife Sarah, 30, and daughter, Tilley, seven. Albert, 39, also had 120 acres and employed four men, living at Brownings, the next property to his brother's, with his wife Matilda, 30, and their three children, Marian, six, George, three, and one-year-old Arthur. The occupiers of 'Field Cottage' were William Whatley, 48, a farm carter, his wife Betty, 43, and their six children, the eldest of whom, Albert, was a thirteen-year-old plough-boy. In 1891 Albert Bevan was still at Doncombe Farm. By that time his wife Matilda had had three more children, Kate, Elizabeth and Ada. The adjacent house was uninhabited and Starvall Farm had become Northwood Farm with William Tanner in occupation with his family.

Chapps Mill and Farm

The first volume of *The Village on the Hill* (pp 81–8) included some notes on Chapps (later, Dowding) Mill. The history of the mill is lost in the mists of time but it is possible that a water mill with an undershot wheel stood on the site in medieval times. Such a mill would have been used to grind the corn produced on the arable fields of Euridge. Later on with the blossoming of the woollen industry the present leat (in this case, a complete diversion of the By Brook, see *V on H* p 82) was excavated and either a new mill was erected as a fulling mill, or the existing mill was adapted and a more powerful water wheel was installed. The adjoining farm points to the likelihood of a corn (or grist) mill, being operated within the same piece of land, a practice which was quite common in the area.

Fig 26 The back of the farmhouse (AAW)

The Chapps family

Unlike Drewetts Mill, we know nothing definite about the man or family after whom the mill was named. Nor do we know of any earlier name for it. What we do know is that the Chapp family was in Colerne in the seventeenth century. Jeremiah, son of Edward, was baptised in 1629, and Samuel, son of Robert, was baptised in 1630. In 1662 Joseph, son of John and Sarah, was baptised, and five years later Elizabeth was born, daughter of Anthony. Yet another member of the family appears in the Colerne records, for Thomas Chap [sic] was named in a list of those attending a manorial court on 10th April 1648, which was also attended by Anthony Drewett junior. In 1701 an entry in the minutes of the Society of Friends, Chippenham Monthly Meetings, reads, "Stephen Shewring of Bradford, Taylor [sic] and Sarah Allen daughter of Robert Allen of Slaughterford proposed their intention of taking each other in marriage. Philip Bryant and Thomas Parradice are chosen to inspect into the said Sarah's clearness from all others on the account of marriage and make report to our next monthly meeting." Sarah is also referred to as 'Chapp alias Allen.' It is known that several aliases appear in Wiltshire minute books and it seems that the children of a widow who remarried would adopt the surname of their stepfather, but for legal purposes their former name had to be retained. To complete the story of Sarah we have to look at the minutes of the Monthly Meeting held on 17th November 1701. Francis Broom, a Colerne man, was there and so was the couple to be married. "Philip Bryant and Thomas Parradice report that they find nothing to obstruct their intentions wherefore this meeting leave the consummating it to the ffriends of Slaughterford meeting as they in the wisdom of God shall direct." Now the Friends at Slaughterford had a meeting house in the wood on the opposite side of the By Brook, from Chapps Mill. Unhappily the building has been allowed to decay and very little of it remains. Of course one can only speculate that the mill was named after the family of which Sarah was a member.

It does seem likely that the Chapps ran the mill sometime in the seventeenth century and continued to do so for more than one generation, otherwise the name would probably not have survived. It may well have been that they were the first to use the mill as a fulling

Fig 27 The stables (AAW)

Fig 28 The barn (AAW)

mill and that it was from them that the Drewetts took over (see p 147). Samuel Drewett was the last of his line to have a mill and when he died in 1791 it was let for a time by his widow.

The Dowdings

By the time that J W Dowding bought the mill, it had been converted to a paper mill and was operated by Henry Garner who lived at Widdenham, where Walter Garner ran another paper mill. In 1841 Henry was 64 and Walter 35, so it is probable that they were father and son. Chapps Mill and Chapps Farm were then separately run. Robert Wheatland, aged 70, was the head of a family at the farm, but he was described as an agricultural labourer so he may well have been a part-timer, in view of his age. His son George, aged 40, was the farmer. He was unmarried at that time and six other people lived at the farm, Ann 35, Jane 25, John 25, and William 9, all Wheatlands, and Aaron Bence 20 and Martha Holder 15 completed the household.

When the next census was taken Robert was no longer on the list. George had married Mary Ann May of Thickwood, and they lived at Smith's Close. He was still a farmer, but his sister Ann was then farming at Chapps assisted by one man and a lad on the 40 acres there. Jane was still living there with her sister, both of them unmarried. Brother John had married and was at Colerne Down farm with his wife Emily.

The first record of anyone living at the mill, as distinct from the farmhouse, is in 1861. At that time Richard German, a 29-year-old paper-maker born in Slaughterford, lived there with his wife Elizabeth, 27 years old and born at Duncombe, and Celia, their baby daughter.

At Chapps Mill cottages lived William Gaye, labourer, with his wife Harriet, six-month-old son Albert and his mother-in-law, 58-year-old Hannah Ford from Shiplake. She was employed as a paper-sorter. The Smith family were at the cottages too. The forename of the head of the household is difficult to read. He was 34 and hailed from Calstone, near Calne. He was also a paper-maker and lived with his 33-year-old wife Jane and their five children.

The census returns from 1841 to 1861 indicate that J W Dowding never lived in the parish of Colerne, but the paper-mill must have had a measure of financial success, since it appears that the erection of workers' cottages was considered necessary. During this period, a number of workers lived in Slaughterford, as might be expected since Chapps Mill is not much more than a stone's throw from the village. The nineteenth century status of Rag Mill, on the Slaughterford side of the river, is not known; but the Slaughterford registers show that at least six families described as clothiers lived there in the 1820s, so it could be that Rag Mill was still a fulling mill at that time.

The Slaughterford records also indicate that Chapps Mill was a paper-mill at least as early as 1813, for Sarah Moules was baptised in July of that year and her father was a paper-maker. Three children of Robert Whitland [sic] whom we have seen at Chapps Farm in 1841, were baptised at Slaughterford during the second decade of the nineteenth century: Jane in 1814, John in 1817 and Bridget in 1818. There is no record of Bridget in the 1841 census for Chapps Farm, so she had either married and moved out or she had not survived. Robert was described as a paper-maker in all three baptismal entries and it was said that he lived in Slaughterford. It would have made sense for him and his family to go to Slaughterford church rather than take the much longer walk to Colerne.

There is clear evidence that Chapps Mill expanded substantially during the fourth quarter of the nineteenth century. Certainly the work-force increased to the point where the paper-mill became the biggest single employer ever to be seen in the parish of Colerne excluding the Air Ministry and Ministry of Defence. By 1891, Slaughterford provided eighteen workers and Biddestone ten. It is rather unfortunate that the population of Colerne received little benefit; the penalty of living on a hill is, of course, that one is some distance from the river in the valley.

The census of 1871 tells us that Richard German's place at the mill had been taken by Samuel Dowding. He was then 62 and described as a paper-finisher and a native of Westbury, Wilts. His wife Eleanor, ten years younger, came from Reading. Also living at Chapps Mill was John Griffin, aged 48, a paper-maker and like a predecessor, William Gaye, a native of Shiplake. His wife Jane, aged 40 and a paper-sorter, had travelled somewhat further than her husband, for her birthplace is given as Australia. Their teenage children also worked at the mill, Jane as a paper-finisher, and John, a labourer, had been born at Hurley, Berks. The youngest children, Sarah, William, and Frederick, were all born at Marlow, Bucks.

The Griffins' neighbours at Chapps Mill cottages were George Neate, his wife Rebecca and their four young children, Mary, George, Ann, and John. The father was 29 and a steam engine driver at the mill. It would obviously have been convenient for him to live on the spot, since he would be needed to make an early start and get up steam before the rest of the work-force arrived. Although it is clear that steam power had arrived, it is quite possible that the water wheel was still in operation, as it was obviously in the square building standing on its own, separated from the nineteenth century extensions to the north.

Surprisingly, the farmhouse was still in existence, separated from the new extensions only by a narrow yard. Ann Wheatland and her sister Jane were still there and so were James Hillier, a 60-year-old farm bailiff, and Frederick Paul, the same age, an agricultural labourer.

Samuel Dowding (of Colerne) died in August 1873 aged 65. He was buried at Slaughterford which points to him still being in residence at the mill at the time of his death. His wife, Eleanor, who lived in Colerne after his death, outlived him by 26 years and was also buried at Slaughterford, 23rd December 1899, aged 81.

By 1881 William Dowding was in charge. He is described as a master paper manufacturer. He was a 35-year-old bachelor, living at the mill and employing 31 hands there. He had taken over the farm, the Wheatlands having departed, and employed another two hands to farm the 150 acres in his occupation. Being a bachelor it was necessary that he should have a housekeeper, Helen [surname illegible], 48 years old, who had the assistance of a seventeen-year-old domestic servant Louisa Helsfine(?) from Derry Hill. Whether or not the two women were really needed is beside the point. Helen and Louisa could act as chaperones for each other and thus be protected from any breath of scandal.

This census makes no reference to Chapps Mill cottages. It may be inferred that they had stood to the north of the mill and were demolished to make way for the new buildings. Samuel Dowding junior, aged 32, lived at Vale View (see p 15). His three children were baptised at Slaughterford and on each occasion Samuel's trade or profession was given as paper manufacturer. By 1891 William Dowding was married and had moved to Elmsleigh; his wife Laura, 32 years old, was a native of Reading. They had two children, William John and Mary Gwendoline, born in 1885 and 1887, respectively, and both baptised at Slaughterford. It is clear enough that the Dowding family, resident in the parish of Colerne for well over a hundred years, had a strong affinity with Slaughterford, and in particular with its church, having their children baptised there and being buried there when death came. The church had been in ruins for two hundred years, following bombardment by Cromwell's forces in the Civil War, but had been rebuilt and re-opened (in 1823) by the time the Dowdings arrived on the scene.

At Elmsleigh in 1891, in addition to William Dowding's family there were a governess, a cook, and a domestic servant.

Meanwhile, down at the mill was George Henry Dowding aged 39 and timekeeper there. He is noted as having been born in Erie County, New Jersey, America. His 37-year-old wife, Jane, was a native of Canterbury, Kent. Their eldest child, Emily, aged eleven had been born at Holloway, London and the three younger ones, Ernest, Winifred and Gladys, had been born at East Dulwich. George had obviously travelled about a great deal, as had, presumably, his parents. With George and his family, was Kate Bush, from Colerne, a domestic servant aged seventeen. Jane had another daughter, Dorothy Sarah, born 1st December 1891, and baptised at Slaughterford 21st February 1892.

The census enumerator referred to 'Wheatlands Farm' in the preamble. The Wheatland family had obviously lived at Chapps Farm long enough for their family name to be substituted, but there was no longer anyone living there although, unlike the cottages it was, and still is, in existence.

The Dowdings were to continue at Chapps Mill for many years. Children were still being baptised at Slaughterford, and William John, son of William John and Marjorie Kingsford Dowding was baptised there 1st January 1920. The register states that his parents were resident at Slaughterford and Batheaston. William John senior and junior were both buried at Slaughterford, the elder who lived in Bath at the time of his death, was buried 11th November 1931 aged 85, and the younger died at Frenchay Hospital in 1949 and was buried 21st March. He was late of Farleigh, Pickwick Road, Corsham.

The mill buildings

The original mill, or at least the one run by the Drewetts, and probably Chapps before them, appears to have been the rather square building, the remains of which stand astride the mill-race on the southern end of the site. The upper storeys have not survived and older stonework at the base is now topped by an unattractive hotch-potch of breeze block and other modern materials. Inside the building the only notable feature is a splendid iron spiral staircase. On the east side of the building a wrought iron gate gives access to a narrow overgrown spit of land separating the By Brook and the mill race, a mere shadow of what it must have been a hundred years or more ago. Some documents refer to the By Brook as the Wavering stream hereabouts and no doubt this gave the next mill down the river its name, Weavern Mill.

Between the old mill block and the nineteenth century extension there is a wagon track covered by a structure clad with rusty corrugated iron sheeting which was painted a prussian blue colour before rust took hold. The south end of the Victorian block may well have been the boiler house, and a brick tower, obviously supporting a water tank, separates the two sections of the extension which is constructed mainly from stone with red brick window arches and frames. The corners of the building are also of brickwork. The extension was no doubt needed to enable Dowdings to cope with an expanding trade. The *Postal and Commercial Directory of Wiltshire*, dated 1865, tells us that John Dowding was a paper manufacturer at Slaughterford at the same time that William Perren was carrying on the same trade at Widdenham, though Perren was also a farmer. We know from the census returns that Dowding's work-force grew rapidly towards the end of the nineteenth century and directories about that time confirm that George Dowding was at Slaughterford and that the firm then manufactured paper and paper bags. In 1915 they are listed as being manufacturers of paper bags but there is no mention of paper in its own right. By that time Henry Arthur Bolwell had been taken on as mill manager and overseer and he remained as such, living at the mill house until at least 1931. After the first world war the mill was added to by erecting another block to the west side of the existing buildings. This was constructed in red brick and the date 1920 is inset on a rectangular stone lozenge just below the eaves, between the tops of two of the blind arches which are an architectural feature of the building. Stone was no longer used, no doubt because of cost and

Fig 29 Iron spiral staircase (AAW)

Fig 30 The wagon track looking east with the old mill building on right (AAW)

Fig 31 Victorian extension with later water tank (AAW)

Fig 32 Blind arches of the 1920 block (AAW)

because the quarry in Slaughterford had probably ceased producing stone. The extension in the previous century had probably used the stone from the old cottages; it would certainly not have been wasted.

None of the directories makes mention of the rag mill at Slaughterford although it is known that for a number of years, until the mid-fifties, it was operated in conjunction with Dowdings Paper Mill. Cotton rags were shredded and boiled, together with chemicals that assisted in breaking them down into fibres. The pulp so produced was then transported in wagons along a narrow-gauge tramway to Chapps Mill. The former name of the rag mill is unknown. It was certainly a fulling mill before it became associated with the manufacture of paper. Mr John Perkins of Slaughterford recalls that, when the rag mill ceased operations, he saw a large vat the contents of which were agitated by an enormous cast iron hand, complete with thumb and fingers. Presumably this was why the late Mr Ponting of Honeybrook Farm, just a short distance from Chapps Mill, referred to the mill at Slaughterford as Blackhand Mill. Chapps Mill was further extended, apparently after the Second World War, by the addition of what looks like larger than standard Nissen huts to the north end of the Victorian building. Extension of the 1922 building was impossible without first demolishing the farmhouse, the old stables and the small barn. The extended mill buildings had encroached on the heart of the farm to the point where it was almost engulfed.

It is very sad that what was once a prosperous, thriving, and historic mill, was allowed to become an eyesore during the past twenty years. As the last paper mill in the county, it surely ought to be worthy of preservation and rehabilitation as part of the county's industrial heritage instead of being considered a possible site for a housing development, as is the present case.

Footnote. In 1867 W J Dowding was noted as being a paper manufacturer of Quemerford, near Calne, in addition to Slaughterford. In 1840–7 Thomas Dowding was a brewer at Causeway, Chippenham, and in 1850, James Bailey Dowding was a baker in London Road, Chippenham. He must surely have been related to Samuel Bailey Dowding who was at Vale Vue House in 1881.

No 8 Market Place

A New College (Oxford) map of 1767 and the 1787 Inclosure Award map both show a building on this site. It is described as "late Smith house and homestead." We, however, are concerned with the present building which in 1804 when it was sold to the leaseholder by Charterhouse was described as "new erected." It is known that the leaseholder had been in residence since 1794.

This building immediately catches the eye because of its large and unusual roof. This is a gambrel roof which was a construction style much favoured by maltsters, brewers and clothiers because it gave secure storage for raw materials or finished goods, as well as good working space. The leaseholder mentioned above was Thomas Perren, a maltster.

Fig 33 No 8 with its gambrel roof (AAW)

Fig 34 Rear of the older building showing slight curvature where the walls meet (AAW)

Because the history of the building is well documented we know that to the rear of the present house there were much older buildings. There were stables at the back of what is now the Spar grocery shop and there was a long narrow barn with a steeply pitched roof with its axis at right angles to No 8. The northern end of this barn was incorporated into the house occupied by Thomas Perren. The present house still retains these rooms, one on the ground floor and one on the first floor. The floors and ceilings of these rooms are nearly two feet lower than the main house and a blocked up doorway in the upper room once led into the rest of the barn.

The barn itself was converted into living accommodation earlier this century. This separate dwelling had living rooms at each end with a long room in the centre section. This room is said to have been used at one time as a parish room.

In recent years during the construction of modern houses behind No 8 more features of the original complex came to light. A three-sided well was discovered under a timber covering. It was about 40 feet deep with stone facings to the head. In addition to this there was a large iron water tank under what would have been the bakehouse in the barn. This was filled with water piped off the roof. Being softer than well water, it was better for brewing.

The wall of the small attached out-building (now the kitchen, but at one time a china shop, hence the large window) is curved at the side and rear and it would seem that this must have been purpose-built to enable wagons and carts both to make a turn at an entrance to the barn and also to allow goods to be hoisted directly from the back of a wagon to an upper storey. It is still possible to see the intersection of the house with the remains of the old barn. It is unusual in that the walls do not meet at right-angles. Obviously the end wall of the barn was curved. Traces of this curve are visible both outside and inside the house.

The original house almost certainly had a stone-tiled roof overall – only a small area of this remained when the whole of the house was re-roofed in 1983.

Occupancy

In 1794 the premises were occupied by Thomas Perren of Colerne who was a maltster. He lived there under the terms of a lease dated 6th May 1794, valid for 21 years with a covenant to renew at a yearly rent of one guinea.

In 1802 an Act of Parliament was passed which gave power to 'Bodies Corporate and Companies' to sell a competent part of their Manors and Messuages, etc, for redeeming their land tax. As a consequence, in 1804, Thomas Perren was able to buy from the owner, Charterhouse, the messuage, malthouse, garden and hereditaments for the sum of £80. In addition to this he had to pay five shillings to the Governors of Charterhouse in redemption of their land tax owing to the Land Commissioners. The property extended to about a third of an acre.

Thomas Perren died on 2nd December 1836 only eight days after making his Will. The terms of the Will, which are set out later, give a clear indication that Thomas had become a prosperous man. He is described as a farmer, but this would have been compatible with malting as he would almost certainly have grown his own barley.

The census of 1841 lists Thomas's wife Grace, then 70 and independent, as living in the house next to the White Hart (now No 2, two doors away). On the other side lived James Burnett, curate. This indicates that Nos 4 and 6 were not yet built.

Between 1841 and 1851 Grace Perren had moved into Trimnells Farm to live with her son James. She died in 1852 and James in 1853. In 1851 her grandson Frederick was living at No 8 with his wife, family and servant, but by 1861 Frederick had moved to Trimnells and his widowed mother Caroline (James's wife) was living in the house.

In 1866 the house was still occupied by Caroline, but the malthouse was being used by William Webb, a farmer from Thickwood. That same year Frederick, who now owned the property, mortgaged it to a widow, Sarah Reeves of Kington St Michael, for £450, with interest charged at 5%. This was the beginning of the end of the ownership of No 8 Market Place by the Perren family. By 1870 he had raised a further mortgage of £200 with Sarah Reeves. The previous capital had not been repaid but interest payments had been maintained. His increased loan of £650 was still charged at 5 per cent. Frederick was apparently a man of some standing but like many farmers, especially those who were mainly engaged in arable farming, it seems that he had serious financial problems. The repeal of the Corn Laws resulted in cheap corn from abroad being imported. This was bad news for farmers, but the situation deteriorated even further when there was a succession of bad harvests between 1871 and 1880. From 1879 cheap grain flooded in from America and many arable farms in this country failed and were vacated or sold.

By 1889 Frederick was in real financial trouble – no capital repaid and in arrears on interest payments. The executors of Sarah Reeves (now dead) put the property up for sale by auction. The property had been in the Perren family for almost 100 years.

The sale took place at the Six Bells on Wednesday 9th October 1889. The following description was given:

> An excellent Substantially built and Commodious DWELLING HOUSE containing Parlour, Kitchen, 4 Bedrooms, 2 large Attics, 2 large arched Cellars, Back Kitchen, Brewhouse, Bakehouse, Pantries, Coal-house, Stable, and Pigstyes, with large Walled-in and productive Garden.
>
> Also an Excellent 12 Quarter MALTHOUSE, in full Working Order, with large Storehouse, Kiln, and convenient Premises adjoining the Dwelling house. The whole Premises are exceedingly well situated fronting the main street, in the centre of the village, and contain altogether 1 rood, 11 perches, or thereabouts [about one-third of an acre].
>
> The dwelling house, Garden, and Premises are in the occupation of Mr. W. A. Phillips, Schoolmaster, at the annual rent of £12, and the Malthouse of Mr. William Webb, Maltster, at the annual rent of £11.

The property was purchased for £335 by the Revd John Joseph Strutt Bird of the Vicarage, Colerne. The property was vacant by the time that the Indenture was issued conveying the property to him later on in 1889.

It is interesting that at the time of the sale the auctioneer was instructed by Mr F H Phillips, Solicitor, of Chippenham. Was he perhaps related to the schoolmaster who was renting the house?

In 1891 it was let to a farmer, Daniel G Beer, and in 1899 the Revd Bird sold the property to Thomas Hunt, baker, of Batheaston for £320.

The dwelling next changed hands in 1920 when it was bought by James Bence of Bath Lodge, Colerne [at Lucknam House, see p 38] for £500. However, on the day following the purchase, 28th August, James Bence mortgaged the property to the vendor, Thomas Hunt, for £400 at an interest rate of 8 per cent. This mortgage was redeemed in 1928. At that time the property was described as 'The Old Malthouse.'

In 1934 Mr Bence assigned the property to the Midland Bank as security for credit. It was re-conveyed by the bank to Mr Bence in November 1940.

There have been many changes in the last decades, and the house has been modernised. A Mr Warren, who occupied the barn after its conversion, had a grocery shop on the Spar site, which has been considerably enlarged and rebuilt in more recent years by Mr Norman Knight.

The Will of Thomas Perren

The Will of Thomas Perren makes interesting reading in that it informs us about the Perren family in Colerne and also about other farms and properties in the village.

Thomas appointed his friends William Howell of The Full Moon, Bath, Thomas Browning of Box, miller, and Henry Garner of Widdenham Mill, paper maker, his Executors and Trustees. To his three brothers, Samuel, Edward and Henry, he gave five pounds each. To his widow he gave £50 and an equal sum to his daughter-in-law Ann, the widow of his son Thomas.

He left a close of land called Vineyard Tyneing and other buildings thereon to his Trustees with instructions to pay his wife an annuity of eighteen pounds, to be paid in equal, quarterly amounts. Also that the land and house to be held on trust for his son William. The Executors were directed to lay out £100 for the completion of "the house on the land at Vineyards."

To his Trustees he gave his freehold messuage, malthouse, garden and all out-buildings then in his occupation and to pay to his wife an annuity of £35 payable by equal, quarterly amounts. This property was to be held in trust for his son James, and thereafter for his grandson Frederick Perren.

All his debts were to be settled from the sale of wheat on his farm and from monies due to him for malt, and for malt in stock and money in the house.

Furniture and other effects were left to his wife, while stock on the farms which Thomas rented and all his other estate and effects were to be disposed of by the Trustees and delivered to his sons James and William on condition that they sign a bond in the penalty of £500 to provide his wife with a further annuity of £47, making a total of £100 a year.

His Executors and Trustees were directed to set aside and invest £700 and to pay the interest to his daughter Elizabeth Wiltshire for life, and thereafter it was to be divided between such children of his daughter, lawfully begotten.

A further sum of £500 was to be invested for the benefit of his grandson Thomas, the son of Thomas and Ann. Thomas was an infant at the time and the interest was to be added to the principal and paid to him when he reached full age of twenty three years. Provision was made to cover the possibility of Ann dying or re-marrying by charging the Trustee with the responsibility of applying the interest for the maintenance and education of Thomas, and to provide £100 when he attained the age of fourteen in order that he could be apprenticed.

Thomas Perren was clearly a caring 'family man.'

Thickwood and Euridge

Thickwood and Euridge are both ancient manors, and Roman remains have been found at Euridge and Colerne Park (between the two), but they have never expanded as Colerne village has, and there seems to be rather little information about them in the records. This account, therefore, should be seen as little more than a background sketch of the available information, in the hope that a fuller study can be provided in a future volume.

Thickwood

The Manor of Thickwood appears in the Domesday Book as 'Ticoode', but it was smaller than Colerne then (see *V on H* p 8) and has never grown to any size. Nevertheless it did once have a shop and a chapel and there was a bakery. Towards the end of the nineteenth century a maltster Thomas Latham lived there, though no evidence has come to light that he had a malthouse at Thickwood. A shoemaker, Samuel May also lived there. Traditionally most of the male inhabitants were farmers or worked on the land as agricultural labourers. In 1875 the manor was owned by Madam Fisher of a Worcestershire family, and later it came to a relation of hers, John Oseland. During the last hundred years the hamlet has experienced two stages of development, three if one includes the period 1939–45. Late last century Thickwood was very much affected by developments at Lucknam. Laundry cottages were built, a new stable block and other buildings were erected at Thickwood Farm and a pair of handsome semi-detached houses (now Honeysuckle Cottage), were built, one of which was occupied by the coachman to Lucknam and the other by a laundress. Another laundress lived at Laundry Cottages.

According to the census of 1861 the chapel, after which Chapel

Cottages must have been named, was a Primitive Methodist Chapel. It has been said that it was a wooden building. It was pulled down about a hundred years ago and there are no remains. It is not known when Chapel Cottages were themselves erected. They were presumably built to house agricultural workers, probably when other Lucknam-inspired building was taking place.

Somewhat surprisingly, development in Thickwood was restricted to just one side of the road until the Second World War. During that period an RAF site, housing members of the Women's Auxiliary Air Force, was established on the south-east side of the road, and extended from a point a few yards east of the present telephone box for 20–30 yards towards Colerne, past the junction of Thickwood Lane and the footpath (once the main road) to Colerne. This was one of a number of sites in the area for airmen and airwomen from RAF Colerne.

We know from the 1891 census who occupied the three Chapel Cottages at that time. William Wicks lived in one of the larger, four-roomed, pair with his wife Sarah, and in the other lived George Pocock with his wife and three children. Both men were agricultural workers, as was Frederick, the eldest of the Pocock children, aged sixteen. Thomas Latham the maltster lived in a two-roomed cottage next to the Pococks.

As the census enumerator walked towards Colerne from Chapel Cottages, the next house he came to was St Martins. This is a substantial residence which was at one time two cottages. The National Monuments Record at Swindon holds particulars of sale for the property in which the house is described as about three hundred years old with a modern wing constructed in 1936. The house was sold from the Lucknam estate early last century. It is built of local stone under a tiled and part slated roof. There are stone mullioned windows. The large dining room was originally two rooms and as a result there are two fireplaces, one at each end, one of them being a fine old original open fireplace with a natural stone chimney breast. "There are exposed ceiling beams, a recessed display alcove . . . The main old oak staircase leads off from this room." A covenant protected the views over the valley in front of the house by prohibiting the erection of any buildings on the ground opposite the house.

Next to St Martins in 1891 lived Charles Hemmings and his wife,

Fig 35 Honeysuckle Cottage (AAW)

Fig 36 St Martins (AAW)

both of them aged 62; he was an agricultural labourer. His neighbour William Bright was a baker and grocer who had his shop on the premises. He was 32 years old, ten years younger than his wife Mary. They had four children and a fifteen-year-old domestic servant, Harriet Baker, living in the house with them. Jeremiah Fry and his wife Frances (Fanny) lived next to the bakery. He was then 81 and living on his own means. Frances was 76 and was his second wife, his first wife having probably died at the time of his youngest child's birth or soon after, as the 1841 census reveals that his household then included five children, a 60-year-old female servant Hannah Walter, and Thomas Tiley, a 25-year-old agricultural labourer, but no wife. The eldest child was Fanny, nine years old, and the youngest was Jane, two years of age. Ten years later in 1851, the eldest daughter was no longer living at Thickwood, but Jeremiah himself continued to live there, probably in the same house. As the years passed, the children continued to depart so that by 1871 the only other occupant of the house was his unmarried daughter Jane, a domestic servant. She too had disappeared by 1881 but by this time Jeremiah had married again. He was listed as having been born in the parish of Colerne and the records show that he lived at Thickwood for at least 50 years.

In 1891 the enumerator's next call was at Honeysuckle House where the coachman James Poldren (?) lived with his wife Mary and three children.

Thickwood Farm (now Thickwood House) came next, with the Gifford family headed by Alexander, a native of Alveston, Glos. He was 66 and his wife Sarah was 60. They had been in Thickwood for a relatively short time, since William Webb was listed as being at the farm in 1881. All of the Gifford family had been born at Alveston and all three sons, George, Joseph and Alexander were described as farmers, like their father. Walter J King, a thirteen-year-old nephew from Wotton-under-Edge was also in the house.

In 1861 the census lists Crooks Farm, separated by just one residence from Thickwood Farm itself. The latter extended to almost 300 acres whereas Crooks Farm, then occupied by Edmund Tanner, amounted to only 34 acres. It seems that, at that time, Crooks Farm was attached to the old farmhouse at Thickwood.

In 1891 the laundry housed two laundry maids, Elizabeth Coe from

Fig 37 Thickwood House and barn (AAW)

Fig 38 The old farmhouse, Thickwood (AAW)

Fig 39 Remains of wartime dining hall found at Thickwood Estate (AAW)

Audley End, Essex, and Fanny Gaisford born in Colerne, and Alfred Rowe, a three-year-old visitor from Hungerford. In the same terrace, next to the laundry, was Edwin Wicks, 35, gas maker (at Lucknam), his wife Grace, also 35, and five children.

After the cessation of hostilities in 1945 the WAAF quarters mentioned earlier were demolished leaving the way clear for the previously undeveloped side of the road to receive the residences there at the present time. At about the same time the RAF and WAAF communal site No 2 which had included a dining hall and a NAAFI was cleared so that houses for RAF personnel could be built (now Thickwood Estate). It is interesting to note that the foundations of at least some of the wartime buildings still exist beneath gardens on the estate.

Hall Farm

Recent research suggests that Hall Farm may have been the original manor house of Thickwood. Owned over the years by the Governors of Charterhouse, Oseland, and Paul Cobb Methuen, it is one of several outlying farms in the parish. Like No 8 Market Place, the house has a gambrel roof. There does not seem to be an accepted reason for the name. One theory is that it is named after the Hall family of Bradford on Avon, but it may well be that the original farmhouse, if not the present one, had a hall similar to that which Trunnells farmhouse probably had. In the barn there is said to be a number of iron rings set into an internal wall at various heights above the floor. Local legend has it that Hall Farm was a stopover for prisoners being taken to Bristol Docks after being sentenced to transportation. Even if this is only another myth, at least it joins the rolling stones of Eastrip and the Colerne donkey as part of our parish folklore.

Euridge Manor

The Manor of Euridge cum Yatton has a long history and it is clear that the Romans were on or near the site of the manor house since fragments of pottery, coins and tiles of Roman times have been found nearby. It is now accepted that a Romano-British temple once stood at Euridge, a significant find there being a small altar stone. It is presumed that the temple was attached to a residence although evidence remains to be found that there was a villa of any size at Euridge.

The Manor became the property of Malmesbury Abbey but was confiscated by Henry VIII at the dissolution of the monasteries. Somewhat later the Manor was granted by Elizabeth I to Sir Walter Raleigh, presumably in order that he would benefit from the income generated on the estate. When the estate was put up for sale in 1980, the particulars of sale stated that "It is recorded that he lived there prior to his last trip to America", but we are not aware of any evidence of this.

Some of the farm buildings have the appearance of being significantly older than the house itself which has been modernised by successive owners, particularly in recent years. As is the case with the manor house in Colerne, there must be little of the original fabric still recognisable in the building.

Country manor houses were, almost without exception, associated

Fig 40 Euridge Manor House (AAW)

Fig 41 Old barn and entrance gates, Euridge Manor (AAW)

Fig 42 Euridge Manor cottages, front and rear views (AAW)

with considerable areas of farmland. The manor farm is a commonplace in the country but there are many cases where the gentry who were lords of the manor employed a steward to look after the farming and accommodated him in a separate establishment. This appears to have been the case at Euridge where substantial stone-built cottages were erected a short distance away from the manor house. These cottages, which bear the monogram RW [Richard Walmesley], were built in a style which was popular in this area in late Victorian times and they were surprisingly well appointed, having two sitting rooms with a kitchen, three bedrooms, a bathroom and w.c. Each cottage had a garden and outhouse. Even today it could be said that a builder copying the design would have no difficulty finding purchasers, although he would hardly provide so many chimneys!

When the farm was sold in 1980, by direction of the Trustees of Lt-Col Count Peter de Salis, the buildings had obviously been adapted and added to in order to accommodate up-to-date machinery and equipment. Not all of the buildings are as aesthetically pleasing as those which were built over a century ago, but nearly all farms in the area have modern additions to enable them to perform a utilitarian purpose. The unit to the north of the house was described as a "Modern Dairy Unit with a covered yard, built of a concrete portal frame, concrete block walls and corrugated asbestos cladding and roof", but a renovated traditional building fronted the yard and there were said to be two fine, drive-through barns. At some distance from the main buildings, Ashley Field Barn had become more than slightly dilapidated by 1980 and stood in a very sorry condition for a long time afterwards but it has recently been renovated. Adjoining this old barn is an open-fronted cattle shed.

The Village Centre

The whole of the central part of the village is a conservation area and a number of the buildings are listed (grade 2). In this section we describe some of these buildings and people who have lived in them in the past. The section is arranged in the form of a short walk, starting at Quarry Lane, through the north and west sides of the Market Place, along the north side of the High Street as far as Daubeneys, with a diversion up Silver Street, and then back along the opposite side of the High Street, down Tutton Hill and back to the Market Place.

Quarry Lane

In 1875 the furthest buildings from the village on the east side of Quarry Lane were what is now known as Old Martins Croft, Martindale, and the other cottages in that area. The census of 1841 seems to indicate that none of these was then in existence. By 1851 this group of cottages appears in the census as 'New Town' and residents in four of the properties were Thomas and Mary Ann Tiley, Thomas and Elizabeth Gibbons and their three young children, Aminta and Harriet Perren and their sixteen-year-old son Amariah, Ann Box and her five children plus a niece and a visiting relation. Another house was recorded as being uninhabited. All six men of working age living at New Town were agricultural labourers. In Quarry Lane itself three families are listed: Florence Moules and four children, Joseph and Sarah Tiley and four children, and Richard and Elizabeth Mullins and their daughter Jane.

In 1861 the Perrens and Tileys were still in residence at Martins Croft (previously New Town). James Bence, a stone mason lived at what is now Martindale. He was born at Biddestone. His neighbour was Henry Jenkins who was a quarryman. Curiously, the wives of both men hailed from Middlesex, Elizabeth Bence from Aldgate, and Matilda Jenkins from Cripplegate [both parts of London]. It was probably James Bence who embellished his house with a number of stone carvings which still remain as a tribute to his skills. For a time New Town/Martins Croft, was known as Maidens Croft.

The 1875 map clearly shows that there were no buildings between the two cottages, now Old Martins Croft, and the entrance to the Manor House. Walking from these cottages towards the Market Place one would have passed the large quarry from which Quarry Lane derives its name. This quarry was then owned by John Hippesley of Lucknam and was occupied by William Webb, a farmer who lived in Thickwood Farmhouse. Webb occupied other property at Thickwood belonging to Hippesley, as well as owning property in the High Street, including a shop occupied by Lucy Willis. Quite why he should have wanted the quarry is a mystery. The Ordnance Survey Maps of 1900 and 1921 indicate that the quarry was then well overgrown and that there were trees of some size growing in it.

Immediately past the entrance to the Manor House there was a pair of cottages, clearly marked on the 1875 map but they had gone by 1900. Presumably they had fallen into disrepair by the time that Walmesley had taken over the Manor House and he had them demolished. The whole of the Manor House boundary wall was rebuilt following the removal of the cottages. In 1881 the first cottage was uninhabited but the second one housed the Gale family, Dorcus, 41 years old and born at Box, his wife Ann, 42 years old and a pupil teacher, born at Colerne, and their four children, the eldest of whom, fourteen-year-old Bessie was also a pupil teacher. Ann's 75-year-old mother, listed as a pauper, was also resident. Attached to this second cottage was the 'Engine House' owned by the parish. This was where the fire engine was housed before it was found a new home in Watergates, presumably when the cottages were demolished.

Market Place

The Tithe Award map of 1875 shows a plot on the north side of the Market Place, opposite No 8, on which stood the ruins of a brewery and shop, then occupied by James Butler and in the ownership of W. H. A. Poynder. This was presumably the brewery which is said to have been called 'Sumsion's Folly.' An old painting (perhaps itself

Fig 43 Martindale (AAW)

Fig 44 An impression of Sumsion's brewery as viewed from Quarry Lane. From an old painting in the village.

somewhat fanciful) shows a massive building which has sometimes been taken to be a castle!

On the west side of the Market Place, Nos 1 and 3 are obviously buildings where a medieval wing, with a jettied upper storey, had another house built on to it at a much later date, even though it is by no means modern. It appears that the newer part was a separate residence rather than an extension to the older building. A small, two-light window in the wall of the older part where the two buildings join would have been partly obscured by the newer building if the stonework of the latter had not had a slanted recess built into it. In 1861 James Butler lived there. He was a carpenter and wheelwright who had come to Colerne six or seven years previously. He had been born at Atworth. Whether or not he was in occupation of the ruins of Sumsion's Brewery at that time, as he was in 1875, is not known. No doubt even a ruin and the land surrounding it would have been of use to him in his trade. His wife Emily originally hailed from Chippenham and she was a shopkeeper. They had four children, of whom the eldest, Julia, aged eight, had been born at Box, but the others were all born at Colerne. Elizabeth Mullings, a Somerset girl of thirteen, completed the household; she was a domestic servant. In 1875 the property, incorporating a house, buildings and garden, was owned by Poynder and must have formed part of the Trimnells estate.

High Street, north side

Moving towards the Six Bells public house, the next building is the new surgery built on the site of the old Trimnells farmhouse before it was replaced by the one built by Poynder. The old farmhouse was demolished between 1871 and 1881.

Between the surgery and the Six Bells, set back from the road behind the car park, is Pollards, a house with very distinctive windows. This bears W H Poynder's monogram, showing that it was yet another part of his extensive rebuilding programme at Trimnells.

The Six Bells is itself a relatively old building and has retained its name in spite of the fact that the church has had eight bells since 1877. The building is probably very early eighteenth century built on an earlier core. It is certainly older than the suggested date "circa 1774"

Fig 45 Jettied end of No 3 Market Place (AAW)

Fig 46 Junction of Nos 1/3 Market Place showing recessed wall to accommodate the window of No 3 (AAW)

on one of the signs outside, which has also been carved into the large fireplace at the west end of the bar. The building, though clearly not the name, could well pre-date the installation of the fifth and sixth bells in the church tower in 1737 (see *V on H* p 100). During the Second World War and after, it was favoured by personnel from the airfield and was popularly known as 'The Clangers.'

Next door to the public house, and attached to it, is a pair of cottages, now a single residence. They too probably date from the early eighteenth century. They were originally of the 'one-up, one-down' style with a nineteenth century addition running across the back of both. The pitched roof on this extension is a 1985 addition. Previously it had a corrugated asbestos (perhaps originally iron) roof of very shallow slope, with wooden boarded ceilings, which have been retained, immediately beneath it. The various stages through which this extension passed are visible on the end wall of No 29. The two cottages were evidently built separately and No 31, which is clearly the older, has been much altered over the years. Within No 29 is an interesting example of recycling of older materials. A wooden door at the foot of the winding staircase has an old oak core, about 5ft 6ins by 2ft 6ins, which has been made to fit its present position by nailing on newer strips at one side and along the bottom. The original oak has the name "Michl Sumsion" branded into it in three places, once upside down. At least one Michael Sumsion was a brewer and it looks as though this may perhaps have been the trap door of his cellar, on which he tried out the branding iron for his barrels.

The Baptist Chapel built in 1867 is a good example of the small Independent chapels of that period. It stands back from the street in its own grounds. Regrettably it is now disused and its future unknown. On the 1785 map a building is shown on the site and set back a house depth from the street. Unfortunately neither the owner's nor the occupier's name is listed in the schedule to the map. Immediately to the west of this building is where the great fire of Colerne (1784) is believed to have broken out and the map shows some ruins still existing at that time. There can be little doubt that they represent only a small part of the area ravaged by the fire a little more than a decade earlier. A number of properties would have been rebuilt within a year or two.

Fig 47 Pollards (AAW)

Fig 48 The Six Bells (AAW)

Clyst House (No 27 High Street) may have been such a rebuild with an up-market face-lift to the front in 1893. A datestone above a garden door on the west side of the house carries the date 1744 and may have been salvaged from a house that was destroyed in the fire. Beyond Clyst House, in the entrance to the yard, stood the old 'blind house' or lock-up, but there appears to be no surviving evidence in the form of photographs or drawings to show what it looked like. It was probably similar to the one which still exists at Box, and others in the area.

A little further up the street stands a house which has apparently been converted to two separate dwellings since its original construction, Nos 23 and 25. The form of construction of the west elevation and the old windows in that wall are not in keeping with the front wall, and it is clear that this was one of several houses which were upgraded as far as their facades were concerned, pointing to a prosperous period having been enjoyed at the time, at least, by the then owners of the properties.

Standing back from the street is the Old Fox and Hounds. Now a private residence it was sold off by the brewers between the wars, together with Box Brewery and a number of other properties. The well-named Francis Beer was the licensee in 1861 and when he died his widow continued until at least 1891. Susan Beer was then 65 years old and although her two eldest children, William and Emma, were no longer with her, she still had the younger pair, Mary a dressmaker and Albert a gas-fitter. Also in the household in 1891 were two of her nieces, Emma and Charlotte Tidmarsh, together with a fourteen-year-old domestic servant, Harriet Box.

No 17, Forge Cottage, is a modern house which was built on the site of a smithy. In 1891 the village still had several blacksmiths. At No 19 Charles Bence lived with his wife Sarah and their three sons, the eldest of whom, fifteen-year-old Hubert, was his father's apprentice. The family had moved to Colerne from Marshfield some time after Hubert was born, and before the second son Gilbert had appeared on the scene. Next door lived Thomas Dixon also a blacksmith. He and his wife Miriam, both born at Iron Acton, had four children all born at Colerne. Aubrey, seventeen, and Maurice, fifteen, were both blacksmith's apprentices and Robert, fourteen, was apprenticed to a tailor. Thomas, the baby of the family, was only six. The two daughters,

Fig 49 Nos 23/25 High Street showing old stone work at west end (AAW)

Fig 50 The Old Fox and Hounds (note decorative ridge tiles, unusual finial and regular quoin stones in relief) (AAW)

Fig 51 Doorway of Ashby House (AAW)

Fig 52 Shell hood at Charterhouse (AAW)

Caroline and Bertha, who would have been nineteen and eighteen respectively, were no longer living with their parents in 1891.

Ashby House with a date over the door of 1738 and the initials J.S. was owned and occupied by John Sumsion of Colerne in 1787. If he was J.S. then he must have been well into his sixties, if not older, when the schedule to the 1787 map was made. The building may, of course, have been erected by his father. John seems to have been a name passed from generation to generation in this branch of the Sumsions. The 1841 census recorded that a John Sumsion, then aged 75, lived at the house which stood next but one to Charterhouse. He was listed as being independent and in the house were another John Sumsion, 25, a thatcher, and Mary, aged 10. The census also recorded a third John Sumsion living there, with his wife Elizabeth. This third John was also described as 25 and a thatcher, so one must question the validity of this entry. The Sumsions were thatchers for several generations (see *V on H* pp 68–71).

On the east side of John Sumsion's house and homestead in 1787 was a vacant plot of land, listed as being Thomas Smith's garden plot. On the other side another vacant plot belonged to Samuel Long and was the "Scite [sic] of a house and garden." The next building before Totts Lane, now Silver Street, was called Moxham's House and is now known as Charterhouse. It was one of several properties owned by the Governors of Charterhouse, and two hundred years ago the homestead attached to it was of no mean size and included all of what is now Charter Square. Joseph Pinchin may have been a tenant of Charterhouse and Charterhouse Farm. According to the map and schedule he certainly occupied or owned two houses and homesteads one of which is now the Old Malthouse, the other being attached to the east wall of Charterhouse. Pinchin also had a garden and pigsty in Totts Lane. This was in a triangular plot which shared its southern boundary with Daubeneys. A garden plot further up Totts Lane and just a few yards before what is now the entrance to Grocyn Close completed Pinchin's holdings in the village. One of the houses on the corner of Totts Lane opposite Daubeneys was occupied by John Sumsion of Marshfield in 1785. Whether or not he was related to his near neighbour, John Sumsion of Colerne, has not been ascertained.

Silver Street

Higher up Silver Street, on the far corner of Grocyn Close, is a house, No 10, which appears to have been built as an above average dwelling for its time. One suspects that there was a homestead attached to it when it was erected as it then backed on to open fields and the now blocked-up pigeon entrances in the front upper storey wall echo similar features found in farmhouses locally. The single storey extension on the end furthest from Totts Lane was a later addition.

The earliest record of this property seems to be an indenture dated 15th December 1786 between Paul Methuen of Corsham House and William Ricketts of Colerne which confirms the sale of "All that messuage or tenement and garden adjoining and belonging situate and being in or near the North End of a certain place called Totts Lane in the parish of Colerne . . . now in the occupation or possession of William Ricketts." The purchase price was £10. Together with the indenture is a declaration to the effect that William Ricketts took possession of the property on 19th December 1786.

In 1840 the property was mortgaged by Samuel Ricketts to William Fox, Esq. It is assumed that Samuel had inherited the property and followed the not uncommon practice of taking the opportunity to raise money using his inheritance as security. The census of 1841 indicates that he was not residing in Totts Lane, but a Sam Ricketts, 50-year-old shoemaker, with his wife Edith, sons William and Frederick, both of whom were masons, and his fifteen-year-old daughter Ann lived in The [High] Street (at No 31).

By 1851 Samuel had moved to Totts Lane, presumably at No 10. His wife Edith, a monthly nurse, and his daughter Ann were still with him. Ann was now described as a "servant out of employment." Ten years later Samuel was still in Totts Lane, but by then he was a road labourer, living with his wife but all his children had left home.

In 1870 William Henry Ricketts conveyed the property, then described as two messuages, to Charles Osborne, who had the grocer's shop at No 6 Market Place in 1871. William H Ricketts appears in the census of 1891, living in Totts Lane. He was a widower aged 43 and a shoemaker, who had seven children living with him. Only Mary the eldest daughter, 21 years old, had been born in Colerne. Arthur,

Fig 53 No 10 Silver Street (AAW)

Fig 54 'Tanners Jubilee Provision Stores' (AAW)

seventeen, was born at Pimlico, Charles, fourteen, was born at Maiden Bradley, William H junior, twelve, at Westbury, Edith, ten, at Chapmanslade, Albert, six, at Bradford on Avon and Hellen, five, at Box, obviously en route back to Colerne.

It is possible that William H senior was the son of Frederick Ricketts, mason, who lived in Tutton Hill in 1851, and grandson of Samuel and Edith.

High Street, south side

Returning to the High Street, opposite Daubeneys is a public house, the Fox and Hounds. In 1875 another Joseph Pinchin owned the Fox and Hounds Beer House, which was then run by Francis Beer. Pinchin was a farmer aged 77, according to the census of 1871, and had Charterhouse Farm, with a total area of 300 acres. He employed eight men and four boys. He had a malthouse which was probably at the rear of the Old Fox and Hounds. His holdings in the village were considerable for a man of his apparent status. Apart from the properties noted above, he owned at least seven cottages in his own right, several gardens, the site of a cottage and, together with Mary Pinchin, a house, as well as a house and court.

Turning back towards the Market Place, one cannot fail to notice the large building which still proclaims, though now indistinctly, on the string course below the upper windows, that it was at one time 'Tanner's Jubilee Provision Stores.' Keystones over two of the upper windows carry faint dates and it seems that business was brisk enough to warrant an extension.

Further east the Liberal Club building sits rather uncomfortably next to Nos 24 and 26. It has no pretensions to grandeur being constructed in rough stone, and made up of two cottages. Its neighbour is resplendent with large ashlar stone blocks, a clear indication that whoever built those cottages wanted to be seen to be fashionable. On the other side of Chapel Path stands No 28 and one can imagine the original owner making the point that this was the kind of building that someone of importance would want to live in. Not only is the more expensive ashlar stone in evidence but the house boasts a parapet as its crowning glory.

From a point at the entrance to the yard by Clyst House and looking towards the Market Place one sees that the buildings on the south side of the High Street seem to shout out their individuality. Style, size, height, the pitch of the roofs, all different. None of the straight line terrace nonsense there, only a range for which the term higgledy-piggledy seems to be appropriate. A number of these cottages and houses were shops during the nineteenth century and indeed continued as such well into the twentieth.

Tutton Hill

The house at the very top of Tutton Hill, with blind windows on the eastern gable-end was owned by Paul Methuen in 1785. He also owned the first two cottages down Tutton Hill. Below the terraced cottages near the top of the hill is a detached house with steps up to the front door and a simple hood supported on equally simple brackets. The date 1711 over the door does not really fit with the architecture of the building as a whole and it may have been that of an earlier building on the same site. In 1785, a house on this site appears to have been in the occupation of George Hilbert, and by 1875 the property was owned by Ann Woodman and occupied by William Tyley.

A little further down the hill stands No 19, a very substantial old building with a number of blocked up windows immediately suggestive of the effects of the window tax. Some modern windows have been inserted, and above and to the right of the front door the two sets of first floor windows are surmounted by a curiously long hood mould indicating, perhaps, that somewhat larger windows may have been there originally. If this was the case then it seems possible that this was once a weaver's house and that weaving was carried out on the upper floor. However, the stonework between the existing windows exactly matches in regularity the rest of the stonework in that end of the house and there is no other sign of a larger window. On the other hand, the stonework in that part of the house furthest from Tutton Hill is not quite so regular, especially immediately to the left of the window over the door. There must be a suspicion that the house was extended on at least one occasion, and possibly two. If that is the case, then the extension(s) must have been earlier than 1785, as the

Fig 55 Higgledy-piggledy High Street (AAW)

Fig 56 Paul Methuen's house on the corner of Tutton Hill (AAW)

Fig 57 No 19 Tutton Hill (AAW)

map produced at that time shows the layout of No 19 and the adjoining property on The Bank as being exactly as it is now. The end wall of the house, with its old blocked-up mullion windows, is actually founded on the bedrock and this is probably the only building in Colerne where such construction can be observed.

Back at the top of Tutton Hill we have Parsonage Farmhouse and its yard. In 1785 the property was described as a house, barn and homestead. Under the heading of proprietor we find that it is termed Glebe property, belonging to the church, hence the name which has come down to the present time. For several decades in the nineteenth century Elizabeth Weeks, or Wicks, was the occupier. In 1851 and 1861 it was referred to as Glebe Farm, but it was known by its current name from 1871, apart from 1881 when it was referred to as Vicarage Farm. In 1875 the owner was listed as being John Weeks and the occupier Mary Weeks, though it appears that Robert, her brother, was the farmer. The size of the farm varied from about 30 to 45 acres according to the census returns. The 1891 census tells us that the

Fig 58 Western wall of No 19, founded on bedrock (AAW)

household consisted of Robert Wicks aged 52, his sister Mary, 54, and Mercy another sister aged 47. The Wicks family had a boarder, appropriately a Clerk in Holy Orders, 50-year-old William Lloyd, a Welshman from Cardigan. It is apparent that the farm buildings which back onto the High Street once had windows and entrances which have been blocked up for many years.

Market Place, south side

No 2 Market Place was at one time the White Hart and in 1841 it was occupied by Isaac Pointing, described as a victualler, his wife Catherine, and Elizabeth Ford an 80-year-old, possibly Catherine's mother. There were seven lodgers with them, all labourers, including one who was only twelve years old. Ten years later William Lewis was the victualler. He was 40 and like his 36-year-old wife Ann, was a native of Marshfield. They had a son, seventeen, and a servant, 37-year-old Jacob Cainey from Cold Ashton. Samuel May, baker and sometime cordwainer, had moved in by 1861, at which time it appears that the premises were no longer used as an inn. Samuel May and members of his family continued to occupy the premises for many years. By 1891, Mary J May was there with two young nieces, and the premises are referred to as a baker's shop. The frontage has been altered in recent years but two blocked-up windows below the west gable point to the building being of some age.

Nos 4 and 6 Market Place are not as old as No 8. The houses are marked as being a little out of the ordinary by the attractive shell hood between their front doors and linking the plain, flat, shelters over those doors. The map and schedule of 1785 indicate that at that time Daniel Davis had the house and homestead which was to become the White Hart, and also had adjacent property (the site of No 4). On the site of No 6 stood S Sumsion's house and homestead, the property of Charterhouse, as was late Smith's house and homestead next door (see No 8 Market Place).

In 1851 Thomas Tiley, woodcutter, aged 45, lived at No 4 with his wife Eliza, 40, and four children, Thomas, thirteen, Henry, eleven (both agricultural labourers), Sarah, nine, and John, two. Eliza was born at Buckland, Somerset, the rest of the family were born in Colerne. At No 6 lived Isaac Webb from Tormarton. He was a butcher aged 30 and he and his wife Elizabeth had three children. None of these children was born in Colerne and, as the youngest was only five years old, it seems that the Webb family had only been in the village for a short time. Ten years later, the residents of the two houses had changed again. Thomas Proctor, a police officer from Rowde, with his wife and nine-year-old son were at No 4, while at No 6 was Charles Osborne, grocer, and his wife Ann, both born in Colerne.

James Tiley and his family had moved into No 4 by 1871. He and his wife Jane then had two children, but the family grew over the years, with an additional four children by 1881 and another daughter by 1891.

Charles Osborne remained at No 6 until at least 1881 when he was 59 years old. He was a grocer throughout the twenty and more years that he was there. Henry Butler, a carpenter, was the next resident there and it seems that it was still a grocer's shop as his wife Georgina was a grocer. They had four young children and a thirteen-year-old domestic servant, Kate M Snell from Castle Combe. Henry and his family had all been born in Colerne.

General

A visitor may remark on the fact that there is no thatch to be seen and this in spite of the fact that up to 1861 there were two thatchers in the village, though there was only one from 1871 to 1891. There is clear evidence that many older buildings have been re-roofed on at least one occasion, and it is known that one old farmhouse has a thatched roof which is now hidden beneath a modern one. Some buildings have traditional Cotswold stone tiled roofs and these were probably original. Other houses would have been thatched originally but the great fire of 1784 may well have resulted in thatch being replaced by fire-resistant material.

A walk along the High Street and some of its offshoots leads one to think that the window tax was the reason for many windows to be blocked and remain so to this day. Why were so many left in that state when the tax was repealed? Could two people walk separately round the village and count those sightless windows and arrive at the same number? How many buildings with rubble and random stone end walls have been subject to face-lifting by rebuilding the facade with ashlar stone and perhaps re-styling at the same time with Georgian or Victorian windows?

Artefacts and Extras

We seem to take it for granted that what we can see today we are likely to be able to see tomorrow. Earlier in this part of the book it has been pointed out that this is not the case when the time-scale is extended from days to decades. The lock-up and the stocks are long gone and more than a handful of buildings have been demolished or rebuilt in the last 40 years. There are many who do not mourn the passing of any reminders of the past. On the other hand, Colerne is a village with a significant history and it behoves us at least to record what we have now, accepting that it is not always possible, nor in some cases desirable, to preserve all our old buildings and other artefacts. In this section we offer a pictorial record of a few of the smaller features of our village buildings.

First, the pump and trough in Tutton Hill, which no longer serve their original purpose. They are often obscured by the luxuriant growth with which nature seeks to impose itself over disused man-made objects (see *V on H* p 150).

Likewise, at Watergates, at the top of the green, stands a reminder of times long past. Could this really be the sole surviving lamp post in the parish? Though it must be many years since its gleam showed the way down to Eastrip it would have been regarded as a miracle of 'modern' times when it was first lit. Although there were foundries at Chippenham and elsewhere in the vicinity, it can be seen that the column had to be brought all the way from Bristol where it was cast by Edward Crawford.

Colerne had its smiths but never a foundry. However, a manhole cover in the pavement a few yards west of the Post Office, was cast to the order of a Colerne builder as can be readily seen.

Back at Watergates we have the frequently photographed well and its attractive cover. Old maps indicate that the spring here, long before it was capped, overflowed across the road, as a stream, into the village

Fig 60 Base of old gas light column (AAW)

Fig 59 Pump and trough, Tutton Hill (AAW)

Fig 61 Manhole cover near Post Office (AAW)

Fig 62 Overflowing spring at Watergates (AAW)

Fig 63 Rear of Elmsleigh (AAW)

Fig 64 Hitching ring on stable wall at Solar (AAW)

Fig 65 Wattle and daub at Daubeneys (AAW)

Fig 66 Former poorhouse, Watergates (AAW)

pond. In the very wet winter of 1994–5 the spring could not be restrained from behaving as it did centuries ago.

Elmsleigh has a history which goes back much longer than one might imagine as one sees it from the Market Place. The large Victorian building has a rear section which is obviously older. Was this, though, the original Elm Villa?

In 1787 the ruins of Michael Sumsion's brewery stood next to Elm Villa and now The Solar has an old stable with a pitching hole handily placed to receive hay from a cart in Quarry Lane. An iron ring remains attached to the wall, a reminder of the time when the horse was the only means of transport other than one's feet. There is another such ring in the wall of the Six Bells.

There are many other reminders in the village of the days of horse-drawn wagons. Where these had to negotiate an entry from a main road the corner of a building was frequently curved up to the height of a loaded waggon and this, together with a large stone at the base of the corner, served to protect the building from damage.

The interior walls of medieval buildings were largely constructed of wattle and daub and roofs were thatched. No doubt the two together account for the widespread destruction caused by the great fire of Colerne. In *Longhouse on the Hill* reference is made (p 37) to wattle and daub walling, and a section of this has been preserved.

Looking towards the south-east across the churchyard, one sees the backs of a row of cottages, some with recent extensions. On the chimney stack of one of the houses there can be seen clear evidence that the house had a much steeper roof line originally. The house also has coping stones following the pitch of the roof but standing well proud of it. According to the 1787 map, this was one of three 'poor houses' in the village, the others being in Totts Lane (now Silver Street).

Conclusion

The foregoing accounts represent only a small sample of buildings in the parish which can be considered as being of historical interest. The Wiltshire Buildings Record will no doubt carry out further surveys in the parish from time to time, and possibly more old papers and even photographs may come to light. It is known that only a few years ago a large number of old photographs were consigned to a garden bonfire without the slightest thought as to their historical value. One of these photographs was said to be of the towering brewery, otherwise known as 'Sumsion's Folly', which once stood in the garden of Elmsleigh. Was there also, one wonders, a photograph of Noah's Ark, or the village lock-up, or the old Trimnells farmhouse next to the Six Bells, and so on?

Is it just a romantic notion that the gazebo might have seen young ladies, perhaps of the Drewett family, reading, sewing and even painting village aspects of the late eighteenth century and that their efforts may still exist, waiting to be discovered?

Recent years have seen a remarkable increase in the pursuit of family history. Perhaps the penny will eventually drop, that local history, including the history of buildings, goes hand in hand with family history, and that there will be a great deal more in the way of cross-fertilisation in the future.

Acknowledgements and sources

Thanks are due to those who have made personal contributions to this section on buildings, and to those who have made information freely available such as Barbara Collins, Gordon Maynard, Pam Slocombe and the Wiltshire Buildings Record, and to all those who have kindly given permission to take photographs of their property.

Apart from documents in the possession of individuals, the principal sources of information have been the Wiltshire Buildings Record,

R and B Harvey (*History of Lucknam*), the national census returns, and *Kelly's* and *Post Office Directories*. A number of other publications and documents held in the Local History Library and the County Records Office at Trowbridge have also been consulted.

Apologia

It is inevitable that a wide-ranging contribution such as the foregoing is likely to contain some errors, whether they be of fact or interpretation. Apologies for any such errors are given in advance together with a plea for anyone who notices any which are significant to bring them to the attention of Colerne History Group in order that the record may be put straight.

AAW 1995

Glossary

Our descriptions of village buildings contain a number of architectural terms which may not be familiar. Some of these are explained below.

bolection moulding, covers a joint between two different surfaces
cornice, a decorative moulding along top of building, window etc. or around a ceiling
coving, large arched moulding at junction of wall and ceiling
cyma moulding, has a double curve
gambrel roof, high roof with a double slope (see fig 33)
hood moulding, above a window or door to throw off rain (also known as a dripstone)
jetty, projecting floor of building, to increase space above (see fig 45)
lancet (window etc), narrow, with a pointed arch
mullion, upright of stone or other material dividing a window into lights
ovolo moulding, convex moulding, usually quarter-round or quarter-ellipse
pediment, structure, triangular or arched, above a doorway, window or niche
quoin stone, stone (usually dressed) at corner of building
roll moulding, in form of a half (or more) cylinder
saddlestone, stone at apex of a gable
stops, projections, usually decorated, at the ends of a moulding
string course, projecting moulding along surface of a building
trimmer, short horizontal beam across an opening, such as a hearth, to take ends of joists

The Walmesleys of Lucknam

Simon Garrett

Much has been written about the lives of the Walmesleys during their short tenure at Lucknam Park. The purpose of this article is to try to explain who they were and where they came from: why Lucknam was an important acquisition, designed to help them 'better themselves', and why their plans were doomed to failure.

When the Walmesleys came to Colerne they were finally realising an ambition to achieve social status which had brought them south from their native Lancashire a hundred years earlier.

An old Lancashire family

The first written reference to the family comes in the Domesday Book. A Sir Roger [Richard?] de Warmeslegh came over with the Conqueror and was rewarded with lands in Lancashire.

Their next known appearance (or at least, like everything else in this article, the next known to the author) is in 1506 – the twenty-second year of the reign of King Henry VII. Various Lancashire sources of the seventeenth and eighteenth centuries name Sir Thomas Walmesley of Sholley in the county of Lancaster as marrying Elizabeth, daughter of William Travers Esquire of Neatey in the same county. Sir Thomas's descendants are easily traced up to about a hundred years ago. They intermarried with several landed Lancashire families, notably the Braddylls, Shaws, Dimmocks and Gerards. The Walmesleys of the Hall of Ince, as the Lucknam family was known, believed they descended from a mysterious individual named Henry Walmesley – 'the common ancestor.'

The liberal use of the descriptions cousin, sister and brother in documents referring to the line which eventually came to Wiltshire makes it infuriatingly difficult to calculate precisely where they descend from the 'senior' branch of the Walmesleys. They are frequently called a 'cadet' branch of the Walmesleys of Sholley, Westwood House (also in Wigan) and Inglewood, Berkshire. The relationship to the main Walmesley line cannot have been very distant because of the inheritance of the Ince estate later.

The Walmesleys were one of the plotting Catholic families of the seventeenth and eighteenth centuries.

They were involved in Jacobite rebellion. Bonnie Prince Charlie stayed in a Walmesley home in Wigan during his military adventure in England. A handkerchief passed by him to Lady Catherine Walmesley as a token of affection still existed in this century. The family adhered to their faith until long after it became safe so to do. Then, perversely, they became protestants!

This unusual religious history left an equally odd legacy. At the Parish church of All Saints in Wigan, near to the Ince estate, there is a family chapel, founded by the Gerards of Ince in the early middle ages. By the time of the Reformation in the sixteenth century this was known as the 'Walmesley chapel'. Despite the church's adoption of the new 'English' faith, this family-funded chapel within the building remained Catholic. A Papist chapel in a Church of England building may have been unique. Certainly it was not used by the rector of All Saints until a Colonel Walmesley relinquished his rights over it in 1955!

The basis for the wealth of the Walmesleys of Lucknam was an estate which had passed to their forebears in the fourteenth century. Ellen de Ince married John Gerard despite a family relationship. "This marriage required a papal dispensation, for the contracting parties were related to each other in the fourth degree of consanguinity, which was granted in 1 Hen IV (1399–1400)" (*Ince Hall or Hall of Ince* by the Hon and Revd Canon G T O Bridgeman MA).

The Walmesleys and Gerards had already been joined in marriage more than once. That they shared similar political instincts is highlighted by the military career of Colonel Richard Gerard (b October 1613). After fighting for the King of Spain in the Low Countries, at the outbreak of the English Civil War he went to Charles I's Queen, Henrietta Maria, who was trying to raise support in Holland. He raised a regiment of foot guards at her behest and together they successfully besieged Burton-on-Trent. He was wounded but later waited upon the King while he was imprisoned in Hurst Castle. At the Restoration he was made cup-bearer in ordinary and waiter to Henrietta Maria, then the Queen Mother.

This is where it gets complicated! Colonel Gerard's great-granddaughter, Mary, inherited the estate via a convoluted route in 1743. She married John Walmesley of Wigan, himself the second son of a Walmesley and a Gerard. At some stage it appears John and Mary disposed of the Ince lands to yet another cousin of them both, also confusingly known as John Walmesley of Wigan. This was the great-grandfather of Richard Walmesley of Lucknam.

There is, however, a slightly divergent view. A history of Lower Ince and Spring View compiled for St Mary's church in Wigan claims Mary's father, Richard, had already sold the estate a generation earlier, in 1716, to the father of the John I have described as the buyer.

John Walmesley I (my numbering), the buyer's grandfather, was known as John Walmesley of Blackburn (the location of Showley or Sholley Hall, the ancestral seat of the senior Walmesleys). His son, the buyer's father, was also John (II) and married Mary Hearle [Herle, Earle] before his death in 1726.

John III, the buyer of Ince, married the daughter of another dynastic Lancashire family, Ann[e] Brad[d]yl[l]. The Braddylls had been influential in Ribblesdale from the reign of King John.

The Hall of Ince estate was located at Ince in Makerfield, near Wigan in South Lancashire. The Hall itself was a fine half-timbered mansion. Older records call it Tudor; St Mary's historian describes it as seventeenth century (both could be right; after all, the Tudor dynasty only ended in 1603). It was "surrounded by a moat, but about 1900 the timber frame at the back was replaced by brick, and the rest covered with stucco." The job cannot have been done so well. By the early part of this century the Hall was visibly crumbling and regarded as uninhabitable. "A three-storey gabled hall with a roof of old stone slates, it was, in later years, divided into three dwellings and was finally demolished in 1970."

Ince land was above part of the Lancashire coalfield. Profitable tenant farms were interspersed with even more profitable mines. In most cases, rather than work them themselves, the Walmesleys rented out the collieries, in return for a basic lease and a commission for every barrowload of coal brought to the surface. The family's wealth burgeoned thanks to the Industrial Revolution. Lancashire coal was needed to power the new creations of the age of steam.

By 1894, some land had been sold at healthy profit to the London and North Western Railway, the London and Yorkshire Railway and for construction of the Leeds and Liverpool Canal. There was more than one brick works, a wagon works (horse-drawn rather than rail), clay pits - even an iron works. Apart from the wagon works, which by the late nineteenth century was beginning an inevitable decline, they were all substantial money-spinning concerns of their day.

Legal papers relating to Richard Walmesley and his son Johnnie describe a variety of tenants and also people to whom land was sold. These included The Pearson and Knowles Coal and Iron Co. Ltd., Hall of Ince Farm, Moss Side Farm, Elias Dorning and Sons (Civil and Mining Engineers) and Dallan Forge. Pearson and Knowles leased mine workings on the estate from 1901 to 1927 for £464 5s 11d per annum.

Money was all very well but it did not buy 'class.' It did, however, provide the means to achieve strategic marriages over a period of years. These were more easily to be found in the south. It was a migration designed to acquire an aspect of gentility which would never be accorded to northern mine owners.

Moving south

John Walmesley III died in 1749 leaving a nine-year-old son John (IV). He married Mary Shaw and became High Sheriff of Lancashire. It was this couple who moved to Bath.

On 28th December 1775 they had a son, surprisingly named John (V). His first wife, Hannah Conron was from County Cork, his second, Ellen Moss Long, a daughter of Wiltshire. Hannah Conron bore John three sons and a daughter. Her first son John (VI), (b 1793 or possibly 1799) was a pupil at Eton. He matriculated at University College Oxford on April 3rd 1816, and graduated BA in 1820 and MA in 1826. He became a barrister, joining the Inner Temple in 1824, but he died in Boulogne in 1832. Hannah's second son, William of Ince (b 1800), inherited the estate for just a short time on his father's death. A third son, Christopher (b 1808), lived to go to Oxford (matriculated at Trinity College, 13 May 1826) but also died young. The family fortune and name therefore passed from William to his half brother, Richard Walmesley (b 31st July 1816), later of Lucknam. (Richard had a full older brother who also came to an untimely end. He was the Revd Edward Jones Walmesley, rector of Hilperton and Whaddon, who was born 9th June 1814, died 23rd October 1847 and is buried beneath the church at Whaddon, also the site of the Long burial vault.)

Richard's mother was a member of the Long family of North Wraxall and Steeple Ashton. The families hunted and worshipped together. Ellen Moss Long was the daughter of Richard Godolphin Long who came from a long line of Wiltshire gentry, MPs and High Sheriffs, who can trace their ancestry back to the pre-conquest Welsh Princes of Powys. They were known as the Longs of North Wraxall and Dolforgan Hall in Montgomeryshire, their Welsh seat. Ellen therefore represented a perfect wife for Richard's father within the family plan.

Richard's father lived to the remarkable age of 92 (d 1867), outliving most of his children. Much of his wealth had already passed to William (it was a not uncommon practice for a father to hand over much of his property to his son before death), and thence to Richard following William's death (after 1875).

In 1849 Richard married Anne-Eliza Donaldson (b 19th July 1827) at the parish church in Langton in Dorset. She was the daughter of William Donaldson, a landowner of some means at and around Littleton and Charlton Marshall in the same county.

Little is known of what Richard did and where he was living between his marriage and the move to Lucknam. He qualified as a barrister-at-law, and was listed as living at the Hall of Ince on his son Johnnie's birth certificate (22nd July 1861). The same document describes his occupation as "landed proprietor."

Immediately prior to buying the estates at Colerne and Euridge, Richard Walmesley was living at Standerwick Court near Frome in Somerset. He was there long enough to register it as his address in Walford's *Landed Families of the United Kingdom* (1872), but was

Fig 67 Interior *c* 1900, showing Richard Walmesley's harp and family portraits (SG)

probably only renting, as the house is believed to have been in the continuous ownership of the Edgell family for some years on either side. *Kelly's Wiltshire Directory* confirms Lucknam Park as his address in 1875.

Lucknam Park: a country seat

Richard bought the Lucknam lands from the estate of John Christian Boode who died on 1st February 1870 (aged 64 years) and is buried at Colerne. The *Wiltshire Echo* of 24th September 1873 reports Lucknam Park had been sold to a Mr Malmesy [sic] of Frome for £62 000.

Although his half-brother, William, was still living at this time (at Ince), Richard was already possessed of sufficient wealth to make the purchase. His mother had brought to her marriage some land in North Wraxall. This may be relevant to his position by 1870. His motives, apart from the obvious need of somewhere to live, may have included the desire to be close to his mother's home. He undoubtedly believed the estate might make a good investment. He fancied the Somerset coalfield might extend as far as Colerne. R and B Harvey report in their *History of Lucknam Park* that a trial bore of 773 ft was sunk but no deposits were found.

Richard appears to have been a man of model Victorian rectitude. His donations to worldly as well as spiritual causes are evidenced by the family crest adorning the old village school in Colerne. His good works stretched back to the traditional family haunts in Lancashire. On 29th May 1872 he laid the foundation stone of Whalley School in Wigan. He was also involved with Messrs William and Thomas Walls in founding a new school at Castle Hill, Hindley.

His spending on church restoration in Colerne is well documented. R and B Harvey tell how "one of his first acts of benevolence was to join with Mr Poynder of Hartham in restoring Colerne Church which was reopened in 1877." He also restored Euridge Manor Farm and built the farm cottages in 1876–7.

He contributed to other places of worship too. A window, paid for by Richard and installed in 1868, can still be seen on the west side of his mother's family's church at Steeple Ashton. It is tempting to believe, as has been suggested, that it depicts his mother, Ellen, and her sisters. At the same time he also paid for removal of the church's old music gallery and replaced it with a 'modern' organ.

In later years Richard's health was not good and he spent much of the winter in southern France. But duty was everything and just months before his own death he was discharging the stipulations of his father's will. On 13th April 1893 he paid Gregory Rowcliffe and Co (family solicitors of many years standing) £12 6s 7d for conveyancing 12 Walcot Parade, Bath, to Bath Orphans Home. This bill was paid by Richard from 4 Queen's Square, Bath (another Walmesley address?).

Richard attained the office of High Sheriff of Wiltshire (1877) and was a Justice of the Peace. He was a member of the National Club (SW) and a lover of art and literature. His will is very telling. To his wife Anne-Eliza: £11 000 within one month of his death. Also:

> My harp and other musical instruments and also all my furniture plate and plated articles china glass books linen prints pictures (except the Adoration of the Magi by Carlo Volce which I expressly bequeath to my dear son John Walmesley) and other articles of domestic use and ornament and all my horses carriages saddlery harness and stable furniture except those horses carriages saddlery harness and stable furniture which my dear son John Walmesley shall be hunting and using for and as his own which I bequeath to him. I also bequeath to her all wearing apparel jewels and ornaments of the person belonging to me (including apparel jewels and ornaments of the person used or worn by my said wife) I bequeath to my said son an immediate legacy of one thousand pounds ... and also all monies which at the time of my death shall be standing to my credit at the Consolidated Bank of London.

The will was signed 1st January 1890 (proved 9th August 1893). The effects totalled £67 277 6s 7d.

The Trustees were Anne-Eliza, Johnnie and William Rowcliffe (solicitor). The Executors were John Clavell Mansel Playdell (Esq.), Whatcombe, Dorset, Revd John Sparling, Petton Park, Shropshire (probably a first cousin; Richard's father's sister, Emma-Elizabeth Walmesley, had married William Sparling of the same address), and William Rowcliffe.

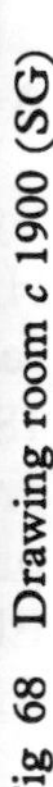

Fig 68 Drawing room *c* 1900 (SG)

A trust was established in Anne-Eliza and Johnnie's names. It relates to Snape Farm, Westleigh, Lancs, and other unnamed land in Lancashire and elsewhere.

Other legacies included payments of £1000 each to Richard's surviving sisters, Ellen Mary Henrietta Walmesley and Ann Katherine Emma Soltau; to Mary Ann Whitehead "who was wet nurse to my son", £150; to Edward Wiles son of Sarah "who was nurse to my son", £150. The executors received £100 each.

He died at Lucknam at the age of seventy-six after eight days of pneumonia. Here was a clue to his piety, evidence that it was genuinely felt. He ordered that the "funeral shall be a very plain and simple one and without hat bands or scarves."

A wayward youth

By the time Richard died the survival of his family seemed assured. His son, Johnnie, after a wild youth, had apparently settled down to a respectable marriage. His wife had been delivered of a male heir in 1890 amidst great sighs of relief. But young Richard, named for his grandfather, was not Johnnie's first child. The relationship which had produced the little boy's elder sister had caused Richard and Anne-Eliza substantial embarrassment and concern, and probably indignant fury! It was a scandal they must have tried very hard to keep quiet.

It seems Johnnie was brought up in a loving, if rather strict and overtly pious environment. Propriety was drummed into him as a boy. He was born on 22nd July 1861 at 16 Cadogan Place in London. In 1867 at the age of just six his father gave him a present, a very dry scientific catalogue of the various wild grasses to be found in the English countryside. Hardly the kind of gift to set this little boy's pulse racing, I suspect, even in the days before television! As he grew up he became rebellious. Once he tried the high life he developed a taste for it.

He had an affair with a teenage girl. How he met Lydia Rose Powell is not known. She may have been in service at a house he visited. He may have met her while revelling with friends in London. She was born on 21st February 1867 at 10 Victoria Terrace, Holloway in London. Her father was a principal warder at 'the model prison.' I have always thought of Pentonville as the model prison and he may have worked there. However, Holloway is nearer. Then a men's prison, it was run by the local authority. In the nineteenth century several London prisons passed from local authority control to that of the Home Office. He retired as a civil service pensioner so probably worked through the transition. His title denotes a rank not dissimilar to a senior NCO in the army. He will have carried significant authority (almost total in the case of the prisoners and the junior warders) and no little responsibility. But he will have been on a strictly cap-doffing "yes, sir – no, sir" basis with the governor and other white-collar staff.

In 1887 the nineteen year old girl from a small terraced street of identical houses fell pregnant by the rich young Johnnie. He apparently put up little or no resistance to the claim of paternity and a house was bought for the mother-to-be in Paddington. There at 15 Portsea Place, on Christmas Eve 1887, a girl was born, Lydia Eve Walmesley Powell. (Her birth certificate carries no father's name although Walmesley is included as a forename.)

What happened then would be regarded today as worthy of the more lurid Sunday newspapers. In the last years of the nineteenth century it was remarkable, romantic and downright scandalous! Far from 'putting away' his lover and baby daughter, it seems that Johnnie moved in with them. In the 1891 census returns at 27 York Terrace, Johnnie Walmesley is listed as living with his (unnamed) wife and three-year-old daughter. The possibility that this was a coincidental overnight stay is made less likely in that when Lydia Rose Powell died five years later he is listed on her death certificate as the informant of death and the occupier of the house. Describing Lydia Rose as his wife, lying on the census form, was the smallest of his misdemeanours. For when the census was taken in April 1891, Johnnie had already been married, for a year and a half, to another woman.

The prodigal's conditional return

On 4th December 1889 (rather interestingly just a month before his father's final will was drawn up and signed), Johnnie took a wife. His bride was a girl of twenty-three, Violet Louisa Haworth-Booth. Five years younger than her new husband she was the daughter of Colonel

Benjamin Blaydes Haworth-Booth of Hullbank House and Rowlston Hall in the East Riding of Yorkshire. From a significant landed family, Violet Louisa was a good catch, especially for a young man who had gone so wildly astray – or so it seems his father thought. It is possible she was chosen from a northern family (the first northern bride for three generations) explicitly because she would not know of the scandal surrounding her prospective husband.

The pious Richard cannot have been overly impressed with his errant son's unexpected arrival at fatherhood. His will stipulates the marriage with Violet Louisa as a prerequisite for his son's inheritance. Couched in the sweetest of terms it states that the estates of Colerne and North Wraxall will be run on Johnnie's behalf by William Rowcliffe and Warner James Halsey of the Bank of England, a trusted family friend. The contract between the family members and the professionals was drawn up on 3rd December 1889 – the day before the wedding! It makes Richard tenant for life "at Lucknam" of lands in Lancashire. It also points out that Lucknam was mortgaged at the time for £11 450.

Possibly connected with this, also in Richard's will, there is a cryptic mention of "the two policies of assurance in the West of England Assurance Society for securing certain sums of money payable on the deaths of certain persons", to be shared between widow, son and solicitor.

What sort of a relationship Johnnie and Violet Louisa had is a matter for conjecture but they hardly got off to the best of starts. She was reputedly of a no-nonsense disposition. She was young and of some standing. Yet here she was a virtual pawn in a deal brokered between a feuding father and son. Worse still her new husband was living a double life, sharing his time between his lawful wife and a girl of no class or position and their bastard daughter. Did she know about Johnnie's other family when they married? Surely she must have discovered the truth almost at once.

Despite all this, whether through love or duty, on 21st November 1890, at 14 Norfolk Square, Paddington, she was delivered of a son, Richard. He was the flower of his family's hopes – the next generation. As it turned out, neither he nor his sister would have the chance to fulfil the Walmesley master-plan.

Fig 69 Group at Lucknam, 1904. Eve is towards right of photograph (SG)

On 2nd January 1896 Lydia Rose Powell died. She suffered from asthma, and it eventually contributed to her death at the age of twenty-eight. The main cause of death is listed as "acute pulmonary tuberculosis." Her name reads, "Lydia Rose Powell aka Mrs Walmesley." Now the way was clear for Johnnie to return to Lucknam full time. His problematic daughter came with him.

The dynasty that never was

Life for Eve, as she was always known, was transformed when she moved to Lucknam. A greater contrast than that between the grandeur of Lucknam and the London terrace she had previously called home must have been hard for an eight year old to imagine. She was a passionate horsewoman and joined in with the hunting scene almost immediately. She was imbued with the same love for France and all things French as were her father and grandfather (it has been suggested that the Walmesleys owned mines on the continent as well,

Fig 70 Anne-Eliza Walmesley and Madame d'Avenarius, 1924 (SG)

but I have no evidence to support that) and spent much time there at school and with a wide circle of French friends. She was bilingual and some people even felt she spoke English with a slight French accent. She adored her little brother as he did her.

She loved company and horses and animals in general. Her illegitimacy was no secret and because of it she was shunned by many in polite society. There were notable exceptions. She was awarded her hunt button by the Duke of Beaufort at the tender age of sixteen (1904). The Morleys, who lived at 'The Rocks', were one of few landed families to treat her with kindness and dignity. But even that acceptance had its limits. She fell in love with their son. They used to meet at Cheltenham and other race meetings. They planned to marry but his family refused their consent and the relationship was ended. (When she died in 1970 the gentleman in question, by then in his eighties, sent one of his sons with a dozen red roses, cut from his garden, to lay on her coffin.)

Lucknam itself was an impressive affair. Photographs taken in the early 1900s show a sumptuous collection of the spoils of empire. A tiger skin, grand furniture, silver and porcelain ornaments and mirrors from around the world. Portraits of the Walmesleys and the Longs bedecked the walls.

(For those who know Lucknam, one photograph of the large room to the left of the entrance hall showed two large marble pillars, now boxed in. It also had book shelves covering at least the two walls visible in the photographs; see fig 12.)

Possibly as early as 1894, Johnnie and his wife Violet Louisa had become estranged. Young Richard was away from his father and living with his mother. She remarried and by 11th January 1906 she was Mrs Arthur Wartensleben Ewart. A sworn affidavit of that year obliges Johnnie to put aside £5000 of his mother's estate for Richard.

Richard senior's widow, Anne-Eliza Walmesley had died at Lucknam on 22nd May 1905 from "aortic heart disease and heart failure." Johnnie was with her at her death.

Kelly's Wiltshire Directory of 1895 describes her as living at Lucknam as "lady of the manor of Euridge." In the time since her husband's death she had rebuilt Colerne Manor House (1900). The Electoral Register for 1900–05 lists her as an occupation voter entitling her to participate in ballots for county and parish elections.

Her will is very similar in content to Richard's. Johnnie was executor and trustee. Her sisters, Henrietta Anna, Charlotte Harte and Emily Elphinstone Keightley received £200 each and £50 for each of their daughters – in all cases for their own use and not that of their husbands.

Young Richard received £5000 to be paid when he reached twenty-one (1911). Other bequests included £100 to Mary Anne Bishop, head housemaid at Lucknam, and £50 each to James Tildren, coachman, Richard Weeks, farm steward, and William Hitchenough, gardener. Head laundry maid Elizabeth Coe was left £25. A £50 annuity for her maid Elisa Nicolet was to be payable half-yearly and administered by Johnnie. All other domestics of a year or more of service and not under notice received £10 each.

On top of the exact same list as given for Richard's will Johnnie was to get "my watches jewels trinkets personal ornaments and wearing apparel and all my wines liquors and consumable stores and provisions . . . and all my plants and garden tools and implements and farming stock both live and dead."

The document was completed 15th May 1900 and proved 31st August 1905.

The family vault

Lucknam and Colerne were a source of pride to the Walmesleys. The land gave them a sense of belonging in the south which they felt was necessary for respectability. They wanted to feel tied to it and interdependent with it, and so immersed themselves in local society and the community. It is possibly with that in mind that the burial vault was sunk. Initially part of the grounds of Colerne Manor the land was eventually given to the church with the stipulation that it was to be maintained. The four modest if remarkable heavy bronze doors which criss-cross each other on top of the excavation do not betray the scale of what lies beneath. If you stand looking at the vault from the front, the low metal rail covers perhaps two thirds of its width and half its length. Fifteen shallow, six feet wide stone steps lead almost straight down. The vault measures nine and a half feet from floor to ceiling at its highest point. The roof is curved to the centre and falls to eight feet four inches high at either side. The ceiling and walls are covered in small ceramic white tiles which, along with the roof shape, make it feel, with no disrespect intended, not unlike a cross between a public convenience and an underground station.

On either side four massive stone shelves have been carved out, giving twelve bays including four on the floor. In the middle on the right-hand side rests the coffin of my grandmother (Lydia) Eve (Walmesley Powell) Garrett. It bears a Catholic crucifix. She and her husband both converted to the Roman faith before they were married.

On the left on the floor is the coffin of Anne Eliza (Donaldson) Walmesley. A plate on the top is inscribed "Anne Eliza, Wife of the Late Richard Walmesley Esquire of Lucknam Wilts. Born 19th July 1827 – Died 22nd July 1905. Blessed are the pure in heart for they shall see God."

Immediately above her lies her husband Richard. His coffin is inscribed "Richard Walmesley Esquire of the Hall of Ince, Lancashire and Lucknam, Wilts, JP for Wilts, Sheriff for Wilts 1877, Born 31st July 1816 Died 26th May 1893. God guide thy people."

Both their coffins have a darker hue than my grandmother's and heavier solid brass handles. By ironic contrast on the shelf above sits a sagging old cardboard box, tied together with string. Inside are the ashes of Johnnie Walmesley. There is nothing to identify them or mark their interment.

The part of the Manor grounds containing the vault was handed over to the church when Johnnie sold the house. The church still considers it 'family' property. The scale of the vault shows it was clearly intended as the final resting place of a dynasty. It was not to be. There is still space for eight more family members. Servants were sent in the time following Richard's death in 1893 to dust the coffin and lay flowers on it – a job they did not relish!

On a lighter note a letter from a Mr H S Perrin, the Superintendent of the Abbey Cemetery in Bath, reveals a previous intention to be buried there. He wrote to Rowcliffe's, solicitors, on 27th July 1927 asking about the possible sale of a double vault which had been bought by Richard in 1877. It remained unused and Mr Perrin had received an offer of five pounds for it. He asks if the sale meets with family approval, and if so would he be entitled to a commission.

Johnnie's son

One family member who never made it to the vault was Johnnie's son Richard the younger. By the time the First World War broke out he was living at Melton Mowbray in Leicestershire. He became a Lieutenant in Alexandra, Princess of Wales, Own Yorkshire Regiment, The Green Howards. The regimental history tells how on August 6th 1914, two days after war was declared, Second Lieutenant Walmesley was among reservists from the third Battalion who joined the second in Guernsey. They sailed for Southampton on Friday August 28th and thence to Belgium a short while later, where they took part in the first, ghastly battle of Ypres.

> On the morning of the 20th the German artillery commenced to shell the positions very heavily and about 10.30 am General Capper sent forward two battalions from both the 20th and 21st brigades towards Gheluwe and Terhand respectively. These came under heavy fire and were shortly ordered to fall back whence they had started, and the Germans then followed up and an engagement spread southwards along the whole front of the Division. The Germans were driven back by fire: but at 4 pm they

made another attack – it was also repulsed, but the enemy got within fifty yards of the British trenches at one place, and continued his attempts to advance until well into the night.

The official history quotes the Battalion correspondent of *The Green Howards Gazette*:

> "That day was our first experience of shell fire and though we had only shrapnel against us it was not very pleasant. The enemy's snipers came into action too, and wonderfully good they are in utilizing ground for cover . . . There was a certain amount of shooting on the left during the afternoon, and when dusk fell we were able to get out of our trenches and found out what had happened generally. We were told that among the casualties in 'D' Company, Walmesley had been killed.

Various other sources suggest he died on 21st or 23rd October and not 20th. Either way, his father and half-sister were devastated. Richard had his own house by that time at The Manor House, Kirby Bellars, Melton Mowbray in Leicestershire. His mother was granted probate on December 21st. Of effects totalling £11 178 6s 2d, three thousand pounds was left to his god-daughter, Cordelia Howard, daughter of Mr and Mrs Kenneth Howard of Eden Lodge, Ellerden, Brough, East Yorkshire. His mother, Mrs Ewart, received all the rest.

After the war there was a row over the memorial in Colerne, involving Richard's mother. She had promised a sizable donation towards the memorial, but squabbling split the village into two camps and she threatened to withdraw her donation if they did not get on. The result was that Colerne has two war memorials, one in the market place and the other in the church. Some names are missing from one, but Lt Richard Walmesley is named on both.

For Eve, Richard's death was the first in a seemingly never-ending roll call of the boys she knew, sacrificed in a war which scarred her like many of her generation. She said later that virtually all the men of her own age she had ever met were killed. But his loss was most keenly felt for he had accepted her in a way few did. Her name was conspicuous by its absence from the wills of either grandparent. She was a constant living reminder of Johnnie's wayward youth, and never quite allowed to forget it.

Eve's marriage

In the intervening years between her disappointment over her first love and the death of her brother, Eve had married. In that most delightfully formulaic way of those days she had dropped her handkerchief and Reginald William Burnham Garrett had picked it up.

'Reggie', was a history lecturer at Cambridge University. His forebears had been London-based importers of olive oil who had diversified into wine. Eve spent many happy days travelling with her father-in-law to France, helping him conduct deals. He thought it was rather beneath his dignity to speak in a foreign language and she was a willing companion and perfect translator.

The Walmesleys regarded the Garretts as 'trade' and therefore not quite nice; but then Eve was illegitimate and previous experience showed they could not be too choosy in the matter. Eve and Reggie married in August 1911 and their first child, Judith, was born a year later.

Many photographs survive from the next four years, most of them of Cambridge. But Eve never enjoyed the city, and when Judith contracted meningitis and died in June 1916, she could bear it no longer. She and Reggie moved to the Manor House in Colerne for a period of convalescence.

Having a young husband who was not at the war was in Eve's mind a mixed blessing. He had been certified as suffering from angina and therefore exempt from service. Eve was of course glad he was spared the conflict which had taken her dear brother. But it seems there was always a feeling at the back of her mind that her husband's ailment might just have been rather convenient. She was glad to have him, but worried that he was shirking his duty.

The death of ambition

Johnnie, meanwhile, had married again (25th October 1911). Marie Bernard was a young Belgian who was very kind to Eve and apparently loved by the staff of the estate and household. This union was childless, and although it lasted longer than Johnnie's first marriage they were divorced in 1925.

The affairs of the Ince estate in Lancashire were beginning to run into difficulty. The Hall itself was in a poor state of repair. By the 1920s the walls were crumbling and it was beyond restoration. There were disagreements over renewals of mining leases. Johnnie appears to have procrastinated to the extent that deals with companies which had existed in his father's youth lapsed. He asked mining engineers to inspect a flooded shaft. The water appears to have breached the diggings because of inadequate maintenance by a neighbour, going back many years. It was too late for legal redress and too expensive for the mine to be made workable again.

It was inevitable that the sell-off of Ince land for railways, canals etc, while producing instant capital, significantly reduced the income generated by the estate.

Financial pressures rarely seemed to cramp Johnnie's style. As well as their grand lifestyle at Colerne, he and Eve persisted in the expensive round of hunt meetings throughout the south and west. They rented houses and entertained and kept the necessary string of horses and attendant staff to take part in the 'pursuit of the inedible.'

Family photograph albums filled with snapshots taken between 1900 and the departure from Colerne show lavish hunting parties picnicking on trestle tables in the middle of fields (undoubtedly heaved over land by horse and cart and human hands). Other local families like the Morleys are prominent. Also Johnnie's lifelong companion Jim Whelpley who lived with him at Colerne, his mother Anne Eliza Walmesley, the cricketing Drs Grace and many others.

Johnnie is described, as was his father before him, on electoral registers as a "scholar at home." What a wonderful life that simple title must have indicated. They were surrounded by wealth and dazzling company, constantly wining and dining, untroubled by the worries of work which were the daily lot of the rest of the local inhabitants. But the product of the two lives could hardly be more different. The father contributing to good causes and instilled with a sense of social responsibility that he felt his station demanded, the son generous to a quite debilitating fault and dedicated to hedonistic pleasure. Both were men of their time.

Fig 71 Johnnie Walmesley and Madame d'Avenarius, 1924 (SG)

After Colerne

Richard the younger's death finally put the dampers on Johnnie's gaiety. By 1918, family and local legend has it that he was under the spell of a pair of emigrée white Russian ladies. They were sisters named Claudia d'Avenarius and Vera Borrisoff.

They were the daughters of Sergei and Vera Balago who had presumably escaped the revolution in their homeland with their lives but not too much else. Claudia, like Johnnie, had been married and divorced twice before (divorced Michael Sedkoff 1908, divorced Nicholas d'Avenarius 1924).

She became the third, official, Mrs Walmesley in March 1926. No one I have spoken to has known much about the Russians. But none has had a good word for them. The suggestion is that they were not well liked – used him for his money and position. They went with him to France and were with him until the time of his death at the age of 75 on 9th January 1937.

Some evidence from the Russian side of the family would surely furnish us with a more balanced view. Who knows what hardships they had suffered in escaping their own post-revolutionary country? What status and wealth had they lost? People might be more sympathetic if more was known.

Madame d'Avenarius had a son who adopted his new step-father's name becoming Alexis Walmesley de Sedkoff. He died in Cornwall on 8th June 1973. In his will he is styled simply as Alexis Walmesley. But neither he nor his step sister Eve is named in Johnnie's will, which is a curious document. Written in 1935, it gives his address as "The Conservative Club, St James Street in the City of Westminster." Did Johnnie return temporarily to England to tie up the loose ends of his business or was he sharing his time between the two countries? Certainly he was emphatic about his "domicil." The will declares "my domicil and origin is and always has been English and that I have never had and have not now any intention of changing such domicil and that however much I may in future reside abroad I intend that my domicil shall be and remains English until my death."

His entire estate was left to his sister-in-law, Vera Borrissoff, who survived him, eventually dying in 1976. Even had she not done so, there was *still* no mention of his daughter or step-son. In that case a third of the estate would have gone to Vera and Claudia's mother, the rest being shared between the grand-children of his aunt Henrietta Harte (his father's sister) and the children of his friend Colonel Hugh Clutterbuck of the Orleans Club, London, the widower of Margaret Long and thus Johnnie's mother's great-nephew by marriage – hardly a close relative!

Confusion surrounds even Johnnie's instructions regarding his own burial. In the will proper he requests to be "cremated at the Golders Green Crematorium or at some other Crematorium near to the place where I shall die and that my ashes be deposited in my father's tomb at Colerne in the County of Wilts." The will was dated 10th March 1935. A letter later attached to it contradicts the instruction.

St Germain en Laye 1st July 1935.

Dear Rowcliffe
Under my will I ask to have my ashes taken to Colerne.

> I write this to tell you that I have changed my mind and that to save trouble and expense I wish my ashes to be put into a common urn and deposited in the Colombarium at the Pere La Chaise cemetary in Paris
> Yours sincerely,
> Johnnie Walmesley

> When my body has been cremated and my ashes have been deposited in the urn in the Colombarium at the Pere La Chaise cemetary in Paris then but not untill [sic] then please announce my death in The Times and in The Post – John only child of the late Richard Walmesley of Lucknam, Wilts. I am pretty well for me but very old & feeble.
> JW

Why that final request was ignored and the original instruction followed is not known.There is one last, tantalizing instruction in the will. It suggests that Johnnie, in his final years, decided he wanted his bizarre, some would say shameful, past to be hidden forever.

> I bequeath all my private papers letters and documents to my Executors upon trust to examine the same and to destroy all of them except such of them as they may consider it necessary or proper to keep and I declare that it shall be in their entire discretion whether to show or disclose the same or the contents thereof to any other person.

It seems, despite his return to The Conservative Club in 1935, Johnnie largely turned his back on Wiltshire and England in 1918. The household effects were sold off or given away and he left for France. It is said he could stay no longer because he was haunted by memories of his dead son. However, he had managed to live at Colerne for four years after Richard's death. What is therefore more likely is that the end of the war meant he could at last go abroad, something the hostilities had prevented. He could undoubtedly live there far more cheaply as well, a factor which may also have been significant.

Johnnie's last known address at 1 Ter Rue d'Alger, St Germain en Laye, is today a suburb of Paris, to the west of the city straddling the banks of the Seine.

My father, Eve's son, was seven years old when Johnnie died but never met him. It has been suggested to me that his remains came back to Colerne by post. But the date has been put at varying times from 1937 to 1946!

No death certificate was issued in Britain, and French records are somewhat different from our own. Fifty-three boxes of documents relating to the Walmesleys sit in the lightless vault in the Lancashire County Record Office in Preston, virtually undisturbed since they were donated by Gregory Rowcliffe & Milners, as the solicitors are now known. The few papers I have had the chance to examine seem to suggest that income from the family estates at either end of the country had peaked during Richard's lifetime. Johnnie has always been blamed for frittering the fortune on "slow horses and fast women" (with apologies for a lack of political correctness – it is a family saying about him) but the rot may already have set in.

When my grandmother, Eve, died in 1970 she was the last of the Walmesleys of the nineteenth century. She had three daughters and three sons, although in 1994 only the boys survive (along with numerous children and grandchildren).

The Walmesleys' tenure in Colerne was to be their undoing. Extravagance and short-termism in Wiltshire were matched by lack of control and eventual ruin in Lancashire. Their status and position, so important to them that they moved and married for it, are all gone. They were a family of the old order whose time, thirty years into this century, had passed. But they did leave their mark. Several churches and other institutions benefited from their generosity and are still to be admired; and when I look at my great-great-grandfather's monument in the market place at Colerne, I cannot help but feel just a little proud.

Fig 72 Richard Walmesley's monument *c* 1900 (SG)

Printed sources:

International Genealogical Index, Lancs, Wilts, London Middx etc
Registers of Births Marriages and Deaths
Census Returns: 1841, 1851, 1861, 1871, 1881 and 1891
Burke's Landed Gentry – various years
Burke's Peerage and Baronetage – various years
Debrett's Illustrated Peerage
County Families of the United Kingdom – F Walford (1872)
An History of the Original Parish of Whalley – Revd T D Whittaker (1872)
The Parish Church of St. Mary, Ince – Centenary brochure (1987)
Victoria History of the County of Lancashire, Vol IV – W Farrar
Ince Hall or Hall of Ince – Revd Canon G T O Bridgeman
Ince-in-Makerfield Rate Book – April 1838
Leigh Journal – 5th August 1910
APWO Yorks Regt, The Green Howards – Regimental History
The Green Howards' Gazette – Vol XXII, November 1914
The Green Howards Roll of Fallen Officers
Last Will and Testament – Richard Walmesley (1893)
Last Will and Testament – Ann Eliza Walmesley
Last Will and Testament – Richard Walmesley (1914)
St George's Visitation – 1900
Pedigrees of Lancashire Families – Joseph Foster (1873)
Journals of the Harleian Society – various
Portfolio of Fragments relative to the Duchy of Lancaster – Matthew Gregson (1869)
OS Map W461.06 Lancashire (1894)
History of Leigh – John Lunn
History of Lucknam Park – R and B Harvey
The Ancestor (1902)
Dictionary of National Biography
Who's Who of British MPs – various years
The History of Lancashire Vol II – Corry (1825)

The Colerne Drewetts

Adrian Wood

It is known that the Drewetts were in Colerne for about 250 years. During that time several branches of the family attained prosperity and status. Some of them were clothiers and at one time or another they had Chapps Mill and Widdenham Mill as well as a dye house near Sewell Springs. They had farms and shops in Colerne and elsewhere, and Vale Court, Easton Town House (on the site of Elmsleigh), a house on the site of the present rectory, and Boys House near Star Corner, were all residences which have been occupied by members of the family. Tutton Hill House was actually built by Anthony Drewett in the late eighteenth century.

Fig 73 Tutton Hill House, built by Anthony Drewett (AAW)

Origins

From parish records dating back to the early sixteenth century it is clear that the largest concentration of Drewetts in Wiltshire was at Edington and the surrounding area. A second, substantial cluster was to be found at Box and Colerne with a few over the county boundary, in Somerset.

Ann, the daughter of Anthony, was baptised at Colerne in 1630. They are the first of the Drewetts to appear in the Colerne registers. Some thirty years passed before the next entries were made, John 1666, Anthony 1667 and Thomas 1668 were all buried at Colerne. There were three baptisms, Daniell 1663, Peter 1665 and John 1668. These were the children of Anthony and Mary, whose family name is unknown. There were also two marriages at this time, Elizabeth marrying Samuel Millard in 1676, and Anne marrying Thomas Carrington of Holt in 1687. A certificate dated 15th July 1690, to the effect that the house of Joan Hooke, widow, was a meeting house for Quakers in Colerne, was signed by a number of villagers including Anthony and Peter Drewett. It seems likely that they were father and son.

Daniell 1663–1729 and Peter 1665–1732

The records tell us quite a lot about these sons of Anthony and Mary. It seems likely that Daniell married twice, for Ruth, wife of Daniell, was buried 5th June 1701, less than a week after her daughter Mary was baptised. Mary did not survive long and was buried 24th July 1701. Daniell married Lydia White at Kington St Michael 26th May 1702 and they had one child, also Daniell, born 20th December 1706 and buried 29th October 1723. Daniell the elder died in 1729 and left a will in which he bequeathed all his property to Lydia. When she in turn died in July 1750 she made three small bequests to friends: "her brown silk gound [gown] and her blue silk pettycoat" to Mary Mode of Comb, her largest dish of pewter to Sarah Gingell, and her Snap Reel to Hannah Bull, an indication that she was probably used to spinning wool. (There are a number of snap reels to be seen in the museum at Trowbridge; they were devices used to measure the length of woollen yarn automatically as it was wound onto the reel.) The rest of her estate, including a house occupied by her nephew, was left to her brother Ayliffe White.

Peter can be considered as the founding father of the Drewett clothiers of Colerne. He and his wife Joan had six children between 1696 and 1707. They were Thomas, Anthony, Peter, Daniel, Mary and Ann. When Peter died he left a will in which he describes himself as a clothier. He left his copyhold lands etc in the parish of Colerne to his wife, as well as his brewing furnace and brewing vessels. The lands which he leased from the Governors of Charterhouse, he left to his eldest son Thomas for their unexpired terms. To Anthony he left his largest brass pot on his wife's decease and on similar terms he left his silver tankard to his grandson Peter, the son of Thomas. To his daughter Mary, who had married Robert Powell 6th July 1732 he gave one guinea, to his son Daniel he gave £5 and to his unmarried daughter Ann he gave £400 together with his second best bed, the latter going to her only after the decease of Joan. Though the lands and properties are not identified it is likely that the copyholds which went to his wife were the property of New College and may well have included Vale Court, while the Charterhouse properties were Chapps Mill and the farmstead.

Thomas 1696–17??

It would appear that it was Thomas, the eldest son of Peter, who had a daughter Mary, baptised 9th October 1719. Joanna, his wife, was buried 19th December 1719. Thomas then married Mrs Mary Fido 9th July 1725 and they had five children during the years 1726 and 1732. John, the eldest died within a year but Thomas, Peter, Helen and Mary all appear to have survived for some years. Mary, the second wife of Thomas, was buried 8th November 1733. Recalling that Peter, the father of Thomas, was a clothier, it is almost certain that Thomas himself was the drugget maker who had Chapps Mill in 1737, having taken over on his father's death. We then find a Thomas Drewett of Colerne, drugget maker, marrying Mrs Mary Walters, of Batheaston, widow, although it must be noted that the entry in the register of marriages does not refer to Thomas as being a widower. In any event it is clear that the marriage to Mary Walters was very advantageous, for a marriage settlement dated 21st August tells us that Mary brought with her considerable rights to lands at St Catherine in Batheaston as well as lands at Yatesbury. The former lands had been inherited from her father Thomas Clements and the latter from her late husband. There was one child of the Drewett–Walters marriage, Samuel, baptised at Colerne 15th August 1744.

Samuel 1744–1791

Although he was only 46 years old when he died, Samuel had managed to extend his interests, particularly at Yatesbury. A previous lease there had been granted to Samuel and Mary his wife, together with Peter the son of Thomas Drewett, drugget maker. On 1st March 1776, a new lease for the Manor and Prebendary of Yatesbury was granted to Samuel, Mary his wife, and Thomas their son, and the yearly rent was set at £3 6s 8d. This was for 88 acres of farmland, 120 sheep leazes, a farm and twenty dwelling houses of various descriptions. A list of tenants of a number of fields at Yatesbury reveals that four other Drewetts had interests there, namely Anthony, Peter, Thomas and George. With their involvement in the woollen trade in a variety of forms, it is likely that the Drewetts used land at Yatesbury and Batheaston, as well as Colerne, for pasturing sheep for the wool.

Samuel also had property at Seend which he quit in 1790 in favour of Nathaniel Bliss, Mary his wife, Mary Drewett, widow, and Ann Drewett, spinster. Samuel, now described as clothier of Batheaston, was buried at Colerne 27th May 1791. He left his widow, Mary, who was one of three daughters of Thomas Whitaker of North Bradley, and four children, Samuel Clement, Peter, Anne Cecilia, and Eliza. He left a will in which all his cash and monies were to be divided between his four children, but his property, messuages, land etc were to go to Johnathan Noad, clothier, Nathaniel Alsop Bliss, clerk (vicar of Colerne), and his son-in-law Charles Crook, apothecary, of Bath. Samuel was the last of his line to be involved with Chapps Mill, for on his death his widow let the mill to Ward and Duckett who operated it for a time as a papermill.

Anthony 1698–1780

The second son of Peter and Joan, Anthony, obviously made his mark as had his older brother, Thomas. He married Philippa, family name unknown, and they had nine children. The eldest, also named Anthony, was baptised in 1719 and buried in 1721. George, the third child, described as yeoman at the time of his father's death, was granted administration of the estate of his father who died intestate. The last of the children was William, baptised 7th November 1734, who married Elinor Browning at Leigh Delamere in 1760. When George died, he referred, in his will, to his nephew John Browning of Coldhorne [Colerne].

Although Anthony was the *second* son of Peter the clothier, it appears that his status was at least as high as that of his elder brother Thomas. The lands which Peter had left to his wife appear to have gone eventually to Anthony as may be inferred from the section below. His wife, Philippa, did not long survive the birth of her youngest child, being buried 20th November 1734.

Properties of New College 1767

A map and terrier dated 1767 is the earliest source of significant information in respect of property occupation in the parish of Colerne. At that time New College was the biggest landowner, and several Drewetts were their leaseholders or copyholders. Mr Anthony Drewett is listed as having the lease of the Manor House with all the outbuildings and associated farmland, as well as Widdenham Mill with all its land and buildings. He also had Easton Town House and a piece of arable land near "Tutnall Gate", with a house built by him (Tutton Hill House). In addition Anthony leased over 30 other areas of land in the parish, including some in common fields.

Mrs Sarah Drewett was a copyholder of "A large house in good repair with several outbuildings, garden, orchard, close and part of the ground adjoining, containing in all two acres. Situate in Colerne worth together if lett £6 0s 0d." This was the large house which is now Vale Court. Sarah appears to have been the widow of Peter 1700–17??, and the mother of Peter 1733–17??. She leased over twenty parcels of land, some of which were in common fields.

Mrs Elizabeth Drewett is the next named copyholder. She had two messuages with barns, stables etc in Colerne. She also had woodland and fields numbering 38. The messuages were at Star Corner on the site of what is now Catley House.

Mr Peter Drewett had 24 parcels of land, including woodland. In view of his being addressed as Mr it is assumed that he was Peter 1729, the son of Thomas the drugget maker, and cousin of Peter 1733.

Samuel Drewett was probably operating at Chapps Mill but is not mentioned in the terrier as the mill was not New College property.

The Inclosure award 1785

Unfortunately the schedules to the Inclosure award do not list all the occupiers of property. The owners are listed (e.g. New College for the Manor House but we are not told who lived in it). Similarly, Chapps Mill belonged to Wentworth Parsons of Euridge, but we can be fairly certain that Samuel was there at that time. Mr Peter Drewett had the dye house at Sewell Springs as well as Vale Court and 25 parcels of land.

Patience, the widow of George (the yeoman?), had Oakey Leaze. Misses Drewett, Lewis and Jones, had the house and homestead where the present rectory stands. In addition they had fourteen acres of land allotted to them. Mary Drewett had a wood at Westwood and together with Ann had eleven acres. William Drewett, and Miss Drewett, both had houses and homesteads which had belonged to "the late Osland."

Mary and Ann appear again as the occupiers of four more areas of land as well as two houses and homesteads.

Samuel held five acres of land which belonged to C P Wyndham Esq. Finally, Florence, a daughter of Peter 1700, had married Richard Hill in 1764, and Richard was the occupier of Widdenham Mill as well as the house and homestead.

The last of the Drewetts of Colerne

Peter 1758–1817, Anthony 1767–1839 and George 1794–1851, appear to have been the last of the Drewetts to have any impact locally. After his marriage to Frances Woodham of Bath, Peter took up residence there himself. He and his wife had three daughters. Susanna was only twenty years old when she married Thomas Brown, a widower, at Bath Abbey in 1806. The second daughter, Frances had married Thomas Harding by the time that her father died. The youngest daughter Mary Ann did not marry until 1729. She married first, Morgan James Morgan and, after being widowed, remarried, Thomas Arnold Loxley of Hackney, Middlesex, in 1845. She was buried, a year later, at Corsham, aged 54.

Peter, Anthony and George all left interesting and informative wills. Space permits only a brief outline. This Peter was the eldest son of Peter and Mary. His mother was the former Mary Walters and may well have been related to Mrs Mary Walters, who appears to have been his father's stepmother. Peter presumably outlived his wife, for he left the bulk of his estate to his daughters, having already settled £2100 on daughter Frances when she married. On his death she was to receive property in Colerne which was valued at £515. He willed that Mary Ann should receive property in Colerne valued at £1284 as well as £1331 in money. Presumably he considered that Susanna had married well enough not to need a substantial portion of his estate. She did, however, get a third share of the furniture, linen, plate, china, and all else in his house. Thomas Drewett Brown, his grandson, was to receive his large china punchbowl. A particularly interesting clause in the will states "I declare that should my single daughter decline placing a life in my Colerne property for the space of two years after my decease that a child of my daughter Susanna be requested to put his or her life in that the same may remain in my family."

Anthony was the eldest son of William 1734, and Elinor (Browning). He married Mary Greenway in 1791 and they had eight children. Their first child, Philippa, married George Reed in 1814 and George, their second child, born in 1794, married Sarah Tuckey, daughter of a blacksmith in 1829. At least two of the eight children died as infants. Anthony himself died in 1839 at the age of 72 having been a widower for over 30 years. His Will was extended by three codicils and commences "Will of me Anthony Drewett of Colerne otherwise Coldhorne, maltster and baker . . ." In the codicils he styles himself "maltster and brewer." He gave to his son George his house, malthouse etc and the house in which George resided, also the shop etc occupied by Elias Tuckey the blacksmith. Provision was made for his grandchildren, the children of his son Peter 1800–1833. Also to George went his stock in trade, implements etc. Bequests were granted to his daughter Jane, his daughter Mary, wife of Thomas Gough of Bath, painter, and to Philippa the wife of George Reed of Colerne. To Jane, the widow of his son Peter, he gave the house and premises in which she resided for her lifetime and then to his grandson Peter for ever. Jane and his son George lived next to each other, for the will refers to the well shared by both. Whether or not there was some jealousy in the family Anthony thought fit to state, "In the event of any dissatisfaction by any of those named in the will then any bequests to them are declared null and void and their bequest shared between the others."

George and his wife Sarah had only one child, William, born in 1833. The family enjoys the distinction of being the only Colerne Drewetts to figure in the available records of the Census. In his will George described himself as baker and maltster and he left everything to his wife. His estate included his house, bakehouse, malthouse, etc as well as his stock in trade, furniture and so on. On Sarah's death his estate was to go to his son William. George also left his wife a house, garden etc situate on the other side of the street, adjoining Mrs Butler's, the said house, blacksmith's shop etc was to be disposed of as Sarah thought proper. It seems that George and Sarah lived at what is now 38 High Street and that they were flanked by Joseph Smart, grocer, at 36, and Elias Tuckey, smith, at 40 at the time of the 1841 census. Sarah and her son, William, carried on the business after George's death, and William married a woman from Portishead who was twelve years older than he. He lost his wife in 1867, aged 51, to be followed by his mother a year later, at the age of 75. By 1871 he was lodging with Thomas Tuckey, blacksmith at No 32(?). He was still working as a baker but the premises which he previously had were then occupied by Lucy Willis, grocer and draper. William later left Colerne and appears in the census of 1881 at Chippenham, where he was employed as a servant.

The final departure

Although William was the last of the Colerne Drewetts, he was not the last of that name to be born at Colerne in the nineteenth century. That distinction belongs to Frederick J Drewett who was six months old at the time of the 1861 census. He was the younger son of Job, a shepherd, who lived with his wife Elizabeth and older son Henry in one of the cottages at Euridge. Job was born at Edington and the link between that long established Drewett centre and with wool, from which many of the Colerne Drewetts appear to have made a fortune, seems to be a curious coincidence. By 1871 Job and his family had departed for pastures new and in 1881 the family of four was still together at Abbots Leigh in Somerset.

Drewetts Mill

Drewetts Mill lies just across the By Brook in the parish of Box. A watermill appears to have existed on the site since the time of the Domesday survey. It was then in the Manor of Hazelbury and was known as Crok's Mill, later Crook's and yet later Spekes. It is apparent that in earlier times the mill took its name from the Lord of the Manor. In a terrier of Box, in the register of that parish for the year 1783, reference is made to Drewetts Mill, formerly Parkers, otherwise Crooks. Anthony Drewett of Box, seems to have been the man after whom the mill was given the name which it has enjoyed for over 200 years. He left a will which was proved 6th August 1751. He gave to his son Isaac, "All that messuage etc and Water Grist Mill called Spekes Mill, together with closes lands and premises in the parish of Box." The mill etc had been granted for a term by William Northey Esq to Anthony, his brother James, and the son, Isaac, and in any event for as long as any of the three should survive. It does not appear that Drewetts Mill was ever any other than a flour mill. When Anthony died there were still many watermills in use as woollen or fulling mills and surely he would have referred to his mill as a fulling mill had he been using it as such. He was resident in Colerne when he died, and he appointed "my kinsman Anthony Drewett the elder of Colerne, Gent", a trustee for a sum of £300, which was to be invested

Fig 74 Drewetts Mill from the south (AAW)

Fig 75 The old Mill House (AAW)

and the interest used for the maintenance of his daughter, Ann, until she attained the age of 21.

Sources:

Parish Registers of Colerne and Box.
International Genealogical Index 1992.
Wills of the Archdeaconry of Wiltshire.
National Census Returns 1841–1891.
Drewett papers and deeds.
(All the above sources at Wiltshire Record Office, Trowbridge.)
Parish Registers of Batheaston and Bath, Bath Reference Library.
Papers of the Crook Family, including Samuel Drewett's will etc at Somerset County Record Office, Taunton.

RAF Colerne: The Early Years 1940–46

David and Annette Hitch

Can you imagine Colerne before the airfield was built? Most of us would have difficulty visualising Colerne without 'The Camp' and take for granted the effects it has had on the village and the continuing role it plays in village life. A few villagers, however, can still remember pre-camp days. For some the arrival of the aerodrome completely devastated their lives, yet for many others it was a revolution that brought unexpected prosperity and widened horizons.

Danger looming

So why was an airfield constructed beside a small,[1] out of the way, Wiltshire village. The answer may seem obvious. It was built in the Second World War, along with literally hundreds of others throughout the country.[2] Indeed the aerodrome at Colerne became operational at a period when many hurriedly constructed airfields were coming into use. However, RAF Colerne was a little different from most of these other stations and this difference was a factor at least in ensuring that Colerne's airfield was not returned to the plough at the end of hostilities, as was the case with so many. Colerne's gestation period was somewhat longer than that of the mass of wartime emergency airfields, for Colerne was planned as a 'permanent' RAF station.

In November 1933 Adolf Hitler became Reich Chancellor of Germany having been leader of the largest single party in the Reichstag since July of the previous year. In 1933 the Royal Air Force only possessed some thirty-six front line operational squadrons. These operated from forty-three flying stations. In the summer of that year Air Staff planners produced Plan A, a scheme to expand the Air Force

[1] Colerne's population in 1931 was 844.
[2] See page 171 for details of the size of the building programme.

to seventy-six squadrons and to put it on a footing to fight a war against Germany in March 1939 – an uncannily accurate forecast as it turned out! In 1934 the National Government of Ramsay MacDonald[3] accepted the plan and a process that would totally transform the RAF, and Colerne, got under way.

The 'Expansion Plans' (officially at least there was a succession of new plans before the outbreak of war), called for new flying stations to fulfil a variety of roles. Some were to be the glamorous fighter stations and bomber bases, while others were required to house the more mundane, but vital backup units, such as maintenance and storage. RAF Colerne was intended, initially, as one of the latter.

What were these new stations to be like? The first requirement of a flying station at this time was a reasonably smooth and level grass field able to contain a circle of at least 1100 yards from which to operate the aeroplanes – concrete runways were not considered necessary at this period.[4] Concrete areas, or aprons as they are called, were laid down in front of the hangars that fronted on to the flying area. Hangars were used to store aircraft and for second line servicing – first line servicing, tyre checks, fuelling and the like, took place in the open on the apron. Most of the technical accommodation, the offices, the workshops, stores and so on were, in those pre-war days, housed in the permanent lean-to structures along the sides of the hangars. Expansion Scheme airfields were the first to boast purpose-built, brick constructed, watch offices or flying control towers as they were later known, although air traffic control was almost non-existent before the war. To the rear of the technical site was the domestic site. Airmen's quarters were usually of the two-storey H-block type with each wing accommodating forty men. These barracks normally looked out upon the parade square. The Airmen's Mess would be nearby with the Sergeants' Mess further from the airfield. Further away still would be the Officers' Mess. All buildings were of standard type designs.

The Expansion period stations were designed for war and of course

[3] MacDonald was a pacifist and largely left defence matters to his deputy, the Conservative leader, Stanley Baldwin.

[4] At Colerne the construction of the three runways and perimeter track was not approved until 3rd July 1940, a year after the aerodrome was started.

functionality was the prime consideration. However, during the inter-war years the aesthetics of public buildings and works was considered of great importance. For this reason the Fine Arts Commission and the Council for the Preservation [now Protection] of Rural England were requested to advise upon the designs of military aerodromes. The result was architecture of gracious form and simplicity and with strong Georgian overtones. The leading British architect of the first half of the twentieth century, Sir Edwin Lutyens, was engaged to design Officers' Messes.

In 1936 a young Air Ministry civil engineer, Robert Struthers, arrived in Colerne as a member of a three-man team whose task was to assess potential aerodrome sites (the term 'airfield' only came into use during the war). "In the days of expansion when war was coming the Air Ministry was looking for strategically suitable sites where there were large flat acres of land." An Air Force officer looked at the site from a strategic point of view. A Land Officer ensured that the acquisition of the land required would not be too difficult. Finally, a civil engineer assessed the land's suitability to be built upon. Drainage, geology and topography were considered. Mr Struthers, who was to retire from the MOD [Ministry of Defence] in 1970 as Director of Works (Air), recalls this preliminary survey took two or three days to complete and that surveys of this type were by no means top secret with the team lunching at pubs and talking freely with the locals.[5]

Peaceful farms

What would Mr Struthers and his team have found on their arrival at Colerne? The 880 acre site being considered for the aerodrome was broadly contained within a triangle bounded to the west by the Fosse Way, to the east by Doncombe Lane and in the south by a road, known as the 'Back Road', which then ran from Hunters Hall to the present main entrance of Lucknam Park Hotel. Three major estates were adjacent to this triangle, Lucknam Park, owned by Colonel

[5] Mr Struthers remembers that among the other sites surveyed at about this time were Stansted in Essex, Dyce near Aberdeen and Lulsgate Bottom, now Bristol Airport.

Merry, Ashwicke, belonging to Major Pope, and Southern Wood Castle, more commonly known as the Rocks, the property of Darcy E Taylor. The area within the triangle itself was undulating agricultural land, crossed by footpaths and traversed by stone walls. One Colerne farmer was reported at the time as saying that there was not a hundred yards of hedge on the whole site. There were a number of landholders but most of the area was held by the occupants of the three farms on the site. These were, Doncombe Farm to the north, Vineyards Farm near the present restaurant and a further small farm, also situated near the Vineyards.

Doncombe Farm was the largest on the site, covering 400 acres. It was owned by Mr Henry John Knight of nearby Northwood Farm. Henry John had three sons, Henry, Frank and Arthur. Mrs Linda Knight (née May), wife of the younger Henry, recalls, "Grandad [Henry John] bought it to have enough work for the three sons." Henry and Linda married and moved to Doncombe Farm in 1933. Within a couple of years they had a baby daughter, Joyce. "My hubby was a shepherd really. Another old man helped with the night work. Nearly 400 sheep and there wasn't two alike!" In fact Henry Knight was a champion sheep shearer and a water dowser. Peter Sheppard, a schoolboy at the time, remembers Henry as a big, strong man of over six feet and anchorman of the village tug-of-war team. The house at Doncombe Farm had an attached cottage where a carter who worked on the farm lived. The outbuildings included stables for the farm's five large cart horses. Two cows were kept for house milk, hens were also kept, while ducks occupied the large pond. The farm also boasted a tractor! As well as rearing sheep, wheat, barley, rye and oats were grown.

Vineyards Farm, a mixed arable and dairy farm of 102 acres, was farmed by Mr Thomas Pullen and had been rented from the Rocks estate by the family for several generations. Mr Pullen lived on the farm with his wife and their young daughter, Margaret, now Mrs Mortimer. The farm included 59 acres of good arable land, on the future airfield site, on which was grown wheat, barley and oats and a further 43 acres of pasture land sloping away south from the main road. The farm buildings lay just to the west of the Vineyard restaurant. Besides the farmhouse there was a yard barn, a two-bay open shed, a four-stall stable, a loose box, a fowl house, and two pigsties. A plantation to the north of Vineyards Farm was used by Darcy Taylor as a pheasant shoot. Mrs Mortimer remembers their landlord riding through the plantation – he could not walk very well. Mr Pullen once accidentally set fire to this plantation whilst stubble burning. The Pullens were usually given one or two birds each shooting season, although whether this was the case that particular year is uncertain. All of this was soon to disappear for ever. Beautiful white flowers – butterfly orchids – grew in the plantation. These too were lost when the airfield was built.

Mr Pullen's close neighbours along the Back Road were Mr Pope, his live-in housekeeper Miss Hurle and Harold Marsh his employee. They lived in a relatively new house constructed by Mr Ivor Gunning, a one-time owner of Daubeneys, in the mid-1920s. This farm was privately owned and much smaller than the other two.

In the south-west of the triangle, on the other side of Vineyards Farm, there were several fields, owned by the Rocks, and farmed by two brothers and a sister, Billy, Richard and Violet Reed of Hunters Hall.

George Gifford, of Trimnells Farm, owned land in the south-east corner of the triangle that probably extended to the present main Camp entrance. One of his fields, known as 'Six Acres', was used as allotments. Next to the allotments and directly opposite the entrance to the drive of Lucknam Park was a plantation of trees. Jack Hoskins, then a teenager, recalls that this was called 'Strawberry Woods' as this wild fruit grew there. Mr Gifford rented out strips of land to the north of the plantation, to Albert Sheppard of Star Corner, William Hall of Bath Road, who used the land as grazing for his horse,[6] Ted Field of Tutton Hill and Ike Tanner of Ogbourne. Bill Knight of Charterhouse Farm also owned two fields within the triangle, one along Doncombe Lane, a little to the south of Northwood Farm, and the other, known as 'The Tynings', close to the top of Totts Lane.

A hundred years before, the remains of a Roman villa had been discovered in this area. It had originally been revealed in 1834, by ploughmen, in a field then called 'The Allotment.' Because of the lack

[6] William Hall had two steam engines which were used to do the threshing for the village farms.

of local interest the villa site was covered up again until it was excavated in 1854 by Mr Edward G Godwin and the Reverend Gilbert Heathcote, then vicar of Colerne. Although the site had suffered since its original discovery, Godwin's work revealed a fine villa of some twelve or thirteen rooms around a central courtyard. Tessellated floors and a hypocaust were found with painted plaster and tiles. The mosaic floor had disintegrated. Coins of the Constantinian period (308–337 AD) were also found. The then land owner, a Mr Perren, allowed the villa again to be covered and the site was returned to the plough. No remains of the villa can now be seen, but it is said that until the airfield was built the surface of the field, when newly ploughed, glistened with the fragments from the building.

The survey team's report to the Air Ministry on Colerne must have been favourable and this scene of rural tranquillity was not to last.

On 2nd February 1938 members of the Aerodrome Improvement Board visited Colerne. The Board, which comprised a Wing Commander and two Squadron Leaders, was assessing the suitability of the proposed airfield site for the installation of the Lorenz Blind Landing System. This system of overlapping radio beams formed a funnel, enabling an appropriately equipped aircraft to find the correct approach path irrespective of visibility. The Lorenz system was, at the time, being introduced on civil aerodromes and would be used by the RAF during the war. The Board's report on Colerne concluded, "The site would appear to be quite satisfactory although a considerable amount of work will be necessary in view of the undulations [of the site]."

Mrs Knight, of Northwood Farm, saw a good deal of air activity, "These aeroplanes kept coming and swooping down and going all round the house for several weeks. I said to my hubby 'There's something going on I reckon'. 'Oh', he said 'They're only practising.' Never thought they were looking for it to buy."

This was, by the way, far from the first time the people of Colerne had seen military aircraft. It is said that in 1912 a Bristol Monoplane from the School of Army Flying at Larkhill, Britain's first military airfield, landed near the field called the Tyning. Apparently villagers flocked to see this wonder of the age.

The construction

"Site of New Wilts Aerodrome." So read a headline in the *Bath and Wilts Chronicle and Herald* of 20th June 1939. This appeared over a series of photographs and a caption that spoke of the "great new aerodrome, construction of which is about to commence at the hilltop village of Colerne."

In fact it appears that by this time the contractors were already on site. On Monday 5th June Bill Knight recorded in his diary the arrival of the first machinery. Jack Hoskins remembers that June, his first sight of a giant D8 caterpillar tractor, a piece of machinery with which he was to become very familiar:

> One Sunday afternoon we'd been down to Doncombe Bridge. When we came back up the top, by Bill Knight's field, there was one of those big caterpillars on a low-loader. We'd never seen anything like that so we stayed and watched them off-load it. We thought he'd have to take the wheels off. A bloke just twisted it round and drove it off.

A great deal of planning had to be undertaken before an enterprise such as constructing an aerodrome could begin. The provision of services to the station was essential and, at least initially, making available off-site housing was considered important.

The Air Ministry had been in discussion for some time with Calne and Chippenham Rural District Council on the matter of water supply and of sewage treatment for the station. Mains water had been available in Colerne village since the end of 1935, at least to those willing and able to pay, but supplying the aerodrome was a matter on another scale. At a Council meeting on 24th July 1939 a sub-committee, appointed to consider the question of water supply for the new camp, submitted a report recommending the Council should seek to obtain water rights to six springs at Collett's Bottom Woods, which lay just to the east of Colerne parish. As for sewerage, the Council wanted the Air Ministry to contribute towards a greatly enlarged version of their own works already planned to be built at Watergates. The Air Ministry was reluctant to join this scheme because of the additional cost to them of a drain of considerable length, plus a pumping station.

BATH AND WILTS CHRONICLE AND HERALD. TUESDAY. JUNE 20, 1939

SITE OF NEW WILTS AERODROME

Left, Mr. Pope's house, and, right, Mr. Tom Pullen's farm, which are to be demolished to make way for the great new aerodrome construction of which is about to commence at the hilltop village of Colerne, in Wiltshire, seven miles from Bath. Below, a view from the road of part of the 880 acres which the aerodrome will cover. The site is skirted on its western border by the Fosse Way, running northward from Bannerdown, and in its centre is Doncombe Farm. The aerodrome will be on a tableland, 550 feet above sea level, surrounded on all sides by trees or valleys. The land undulates a little and is traversed by stone walls which split it up into fields. According to one Colerne farmer there is not a hundred yards of hedge on the whole site.

KILLING NOISE

"FLOATING" ROOMS SOLUTION TO

Fig. 76

The Air Ministry was also in discussion with Bathavon Rural District Council, although here the subject was the provision of married quarters. The Council was told that the Ministry was seeking assistance in erecting a large number of houses for use by married staff who were to be stationed at Colerne from early 1940. Despite hearing that there would be difficulty in obtaining suitable land and water supplies for housing, the Council, at its meeting on 16th August 1939, decided to continue discussions with the Ministry. However, all such matters were quickly rendered unimportant, for in little over a fortnight war was declared. In the event, RAF Colerne was not to get its married quarters, nor Colerne village its sewage works, for many years to come, but the Air Ministry did construct its own sewage treatment plant, despite its earlier reservations, at Watergates, to the eventual advantage of the whole community.

The Air Ministry employed, as their main contractors at Colerne, the firm Allan Fairhead and Sons Ltd of Enfield, Middlesex. However, the first task, that of clearing and levelling the site fell to another firm, B Sunley and Co of London. Today the clearest evidence of this levelling is to be seen on the airfield side of the road running from the Vineyard towards Hunters Hall. Here a high bank is formed from material moved from the higher parts of the site. Before the airfield was built the land here was at road level. The large companies working at Colerne brought their own skilled workers with them. Several villagers remember two of the first Sunley men, Dick Eldridge ("a proper cockney") and Tom Byne who lodged with Lena May at No 23 High Street.

The firms also recruited locally. Jack Scrivin, who was himself employed on the construction work, recalls his father, Ernest, along with Harry Brain and Elliot Bass "was the first on the books." Some three weeks after the start of construction Tom Kent, then a twenty-five year old gardener at Ashwicke, was in the Fox and Hounds when he met Sunley's foreman, Mr Armstrong, who was looking for recruits. When asked if he knew of anyone out of work in the village he replied "Yes I do; me." And so started a career on the camp which lasted forty years. In September 1939, Jack Hoskins, together with Maurice Whale, went to the site to seek work with Fairheads but was told that, at that early stage, the firm did not require extra labour.

However, Jack's brother told him that Sunleys were looking for workers. At that firm's site offices, in what had been Bill Knight's field off Doncombe Lane, Sunley's agent, a Mr Smith, said he was looking for a mate to work on the D8 caterpillar tractors. Mr Hoskins remembers he started work on the Sunday. His pay at Gaisford's nurseries had been a respectable £1 17s 6d a week. His starting pay with Sunleys was a shilling an hour, with Sundays at time and a half. Pay day was Tuesday and although he had worked only three days he took home over three pounds. "I said to my mother and brother 'Look at this – Rothschild'." He was employed at the northern end of the airfield, cutting out roads and hangar sites, although the first work, it seems, was carried out in the south, alongside Totts Lane. Here three L Type storage hangars were built.

Mr Hoskins remembers the construction methods used. "The airfield was marked out with profiles – crosses for levels. Banksmen walked around with boning rods. All the top soil was stripped off and stacked in mounds, the ground levelled and the top soil replaced." The actual levelling was carried out by enormous scrapers towed by the D8 caterpillars. Sunleys had twenty D8s of their own and hired two more from a firm called Rayners. Jack Hoskins, who initially worked as Dick Eldridge's mate, eventually was given a D8 machine of his own and reached the full rate of 1s 8d an hour. Where solid stone was encountered other means were employed. "They had a big machine, like something out of the ark, big iron wheels with great big teeth on, what they called a rooter. It broke up the stone so we could pick it up." Small Alice Charmer tractors were used for harrowing the relaid top soil and for re-seeding with grass. Hired lorries were used, including those belonging to Harry Reed from the village. 'Navvies' were employed for general labouring tasks such as trench digging.

Other Colerne men were taking advantage of the high wages now on offer. Horace Guy worked for Fairheads as a carpenter producing shuttering for concrete hard standings. When working for the builders, Merretts of Box, the top rate was £3 2s 6d a week, now he earned five or six pounds. For a teenager like Jack Scrivin the airfield work could bring an even greater change in fortune. Farm work at Eastrip had brought in only a pound a week – now it was four or five pounds. Young Jack was put on unloading bricks – London Brick

Company fletton common bricks and holly chrome yellow-coloured facing bricks, for the outside of buildings, from Kingswood, Bristol. He recalls that the brick lorries would arrive six or seven at a time and that the loads would be dumped, with no time to stack the bricks properly.

Mr Scrivin also recollects the large number of men brought from great distances to work at Colerne. "Geordies came down to work. Hundreds of men came down from the north-east of England who hadn't worked for years." Frank Champion, an apprentice plumber, started working for Fairheads at Colerne in February 1940, pipe-laying to get water into the camp. Frank who had been living in London but had relatives in the village remembers how the workmen were bussed in from Bath, Chippenham and Corsham. "There was a big car park made where they used to arrive and get off. Everything was checked in and checked out like miners. I presume a lot of it was to do with security at that time. It was all pretty well organised."

To the youngsters of the village all this activity was a cause of great excitement. Norman Alford recalls as a boy being given rides on the D8s by Bert Jenkins. Tom Kent's wife, Anne, also remembers the children having rides, "They were in their heaven."

The dispossessed

For a few, however, the construction of the aerodrome was anything but heavenly. For Henry Knight senior, of Northwood Farm, it was especially distressing, as his daughter-in-law Linda Knight recounts:

> Nearly broke grandad Knight's heart because he bought [Doncombe Farm] thinking he could keep the three boys together.

At Doncombe Farm itself things were fairly miserable for Linda and her family:

> They did everything they could to annoy us when they started. They started digging out right up to the house for their runway for their planes. When I was indoors it all started vibrating. That's why we came to turn out and go to grandad's. They wanted to get in the house because we left a petrol stove [sic] and of course they had nowhere but like outside in a

caravan or something. As soon as ever we moved out they moved into the farmhouse to sleep, and meals.

Doncombe Farm had been unoccupied for two or three years before it was purchased by the Knights. It had been in a dreadful state and a great deal of time and money had been spent on improvements. Although compensation was received, the Knights were not adequately reimbursed for the improvements they had made because, as Mrs Knight recalls, "They didn't have dilapidated put on the deeds or they'd have got a lot more from the Air Ministry."

Henry, Linda and five-year-old Joyce moved to Northwood Farm towards the end of 1939. "There wasn't room for all the furniture, we had to stack it in the shed and stable. We had to live together." As well as Mr and Mrs Knight senior, Northwood Farm was already home to the older Mrs Knight's sister, plus the other two sons. "Grandad wanted us to stay and finish the threshing – three weeks threshing still to do." But perhaps not surprisingly the younger Henry wanted to "get a place of our own." In April 1940, after a six month stay, Henry and family were on the move again.

The Air Ministry, however, had not yet finished with the Knights – they would go on to buy up Northwood Farm as well. Henry John died there soon afterwards. "It was a great blow to Grandad."

Tom Pullen's daughter, Mrs Mortimer, too recalls this traumatic period for her parents:

I was about thirteen when the news came that the airfield was to be built. All the correspondence went to my father. I can remember the shock horror. I think it was in the summer holidays or something and my mother said "Oh they're going to build an airfield here." I think it was about two years before it was built – something like that. We knew well in advance. [There was] a lot of surveying. We were visited by various people. Sometimes I was at school and didn't know who exactly came. I remember later on the bulldozers came in and the excavators and tore up the land and eventually the house was demolished.

It seems Mr Pullen resisted eviction almost to the very end:

He was very reluctant [to leave]. He was 68 and I think he was rather ill-advised. Various people said you don't have to get out – you can hold on.

I mean you couldn't because you were compensated. He received compensation – not as much as if he'd been the owner – but he did receive compensation and it was a very awkward situation. Eventually we had the excavators going through the garden on about the day we were leaving with our furniture. It was a very bad situation I suppose, but I was very young. I think these things bounce off you when you're as young as that.

It was a very bad winter, really bad, with snow and ice and everything. We couldn't get through the little driveway down into the road when we moved out with our things because of the excavators. I suppose they were determined to get us out, they'd gone through the garden, across the path and anyway there was all the snow and ice. I remember the lorry had to go through the Home Field then we got out through a gateway onto the road out there and eventually made our way to Thickwood. Yes, that was rather bad.

And there was a chestnut tree, which my grandfather planted, and the excavators gouged a great piece out of the trunk as they went by. It was very sad for my father you know. I'm sure there's a plot for a good novel in all this if I was able to write it.

We found accommodation with some friends at Thickwood [Jim and Nita Payne], another farmer, who offered to put us up as it were and we were there from about January to September [1940].

It fell to Tom Kent to tell the D8 operators to knock down the Pullen's farm, "The sad part was Tom [Pullen] was a great friend of Colerne people . . . it had to be done."

Mr Pope's house was not demolished. Instead it was used by Sunleys as offices. Jack Scrivin remembers how refreshments were provided, "Bert Jenkins, he used work up there for them. He used to make tea in a chamber pot because he couldn't get a tea pot." Some of the out-buildings were also retained for a while and Sunleys used these as workshops. They also put up a temporary covered way. Beneath this a night shift serviced the machinery to make it ready for the next day's work.

The new aerodrome resulted in another family losing their home even though they did not live on the airfield site. Andrew Hurcombe, a Lucknam estate worker, and his wife lived at the estate's Bath Lodge. This was situated to the left of the main entrance to Lucknam Park.

Being so close to the flight path of aircraft using the main runway the lodge had to come down. The Hurcombes moved to Tutton Hill.

Flat out against the odds

With war now declared, rapid completion of the new aerodrome was a priority. Jack Hoskins and the others were working flat out, "We started a long shift, 6am to 11pm, but we couldn't cope with that for long – we only had [black out] lights with slits. It was mainly twelve hour days."

But various factors were conspiring against the builders. As we have heard from Mrs Mortimer, the winter of 1939–40 was severe. (In fact this was the worst winter in living memory – the sea froze over at Boulogne.) Jack Scrivin confirms this, "The winter of 1940 was the worst I've ever seen – telegraph wires were breaking with ice – boughs breaking off – like guns going off." Jack Hoskins remembers the D8s lined up in the morning with icicles hanging from the tracks and the practical effect this weather had: "In the Plantation we could not get the trees out because the ground was too hard. The D8s wouldn't touch them. The ground was so hard the rooter just slid over it, even on top soil." Later the site turned very mudd, which caused further problems. Even the wind hampered construction. Cyril Rogers, then an airman, newly arrived in Colerne, remembers the difficulties the constructors had with one of the two L Type hangars being built near Bath Road. It seems the arching was up but not all the ties were in place, "There came up a powerful wind and it went down like a stack of dominoes. Everyone thought Colerne had been bombed."

Other problems were besetting the work at Colerne. These were the supply and transport of materials and the shortage of suitable labour. Never had the demands on the building and construction trades been greater. The airfield construction programme was vast. By the time of its virtual completion in 1944 some 570 airfields had been built and at the height of construction a labour force of some 60 000 was employed. Material requirements were on the same scale. A typical Type A airfield such as Colerne needed, for instance, 130 000 tons of hardcore, cement and tarmacadam for the 40 000 square yards of

Fig 77 Airfield site, February 1940 (FC)

Fig 78 Outbuildings at Mr Pope's farm used as workshops (FC)

Fig 79 Telegraph wires broken by the weight of ice (FC)

Fig 80 Sunleys' storage tank (FC)

Fig 81 D8 caterpillar tractor (FC)

Fig 82 Tractor and earth scraper (FC)

runways, taxiways, hardstandings, roads and pathways. Much else was of course required for what in effect was also a small self-contained town.

As early as 19th July 1939 the *Bath and Wilts Chronicle and Herald* reported that Fairheads were to build an aerodrome at Lyneham but that, "Labour shortages were apparent with no casual labour in the district." In May 1940 a second enormous and competing construction programme began. With Britain facing invasion, 'stop-lines' consisting of hundreds of miles of anti-tank obstacles, and ditches were begun together with a planned 17 000 pillboxes. At this time of course, the forces had a priority call on fit young men. Frank Champion saw the effect of this at Colerne: "These were all experienced men, bricklayers, carpenters and all the other associated building trades. Once you took one man away you depleted the gang – this was happening all the time. They got a date for when they had to report, and that was it, they were off and gone."

The Air Force seemed to have been unaware of these problems affecting their new aerodrome. What's more they now had much grander plans for Colerne – it was to be a major fighter station.

The maintenance units

Meanwhile, on 1st January 1940, with building hardly begun, Colerne was opened in its intended maintenance role by No 41 Group, RAF Maintenance Command. It seems the first unit at Colerne, No 39 Maintenance Unit, arrived even earlier, on 1st November 1939, but did not open until 18th May 1940. At this point too, Colerne saw the appointment of its first commanding officer, Squadron Leader Chalmers. No 39 MU's function was that of Aircraft Storage Unit, but there was much more to this role than the title suggests, as Wing Commander Wooliams, the unit's CO from 1942 points out:

> No 39 MU's job was to take aircraft from the [manufacturers] and to carry out modifications to save time at the factories. We did such things as synchronising guns, fitting wireless equipment and carried out any modifications. The aircraft were prepared ready for testing. I had two test pilots and if the aircraft passed the tests they were allotted to various

> squadrons. We had to report certain aircraft were ready, then the girls, mostly girls [of the Air Transport Auxiliary] came and flew the aircraft away. They used to come in an Anson and then they'd fly the aircraft away to various units.

Before the runways were built aircraft operated from a grass strip to the north of the camp, where the sports fields were later sited. During the war aircraft were often flown to holding airfields until they were required by the squadrons.

> I had two landing grounds, one in Blenheim Park and another one near Bicester. We used to fly aircraft there and park them under the trees in their dispersal sites. These came under 39 MU. They were called my satellites.

No 39 MU was to remain at Colerne, fulfilling basically the same role, throughout the war and beyond.[8]

As we have heard, women of the ATA were often seen at Colerne. This civilian organisation was formed in 1939 from experienced pilots who were ineligible for the RAF, and that of course included all women pilots. They did various second-line flying duties including ferrying aircraft from the factories to the airfields and the work described above. Horace Guy recalls seeing the most famous ATA pilot sitting beside the runway at Colerne. This was the celebrated pre-war aviatrix Amy Johnson.[9]

Alongside No 39 MU, in these early days, was No 4 Aircraft Assembly Unit. This unit was controlled by Lord Beaverbrook's Ministry of Aircraft Production (MAP) and was concerned with the assembly of Curtiss aircraft shipped in crates from the USA.[10] The first type the unit dealt with was the Hawk 75A, dubbed 'Mohawk' by the British. The RAF received 227 of these aircraft as a result of outstanding contracts to supply the French Air Force being hurriedly transferred to Britain following France's defeat. In the event, these

[8] No 39 MU operated at Colerne for over thirteen years, finally closing down in October 1953.

[9] Amy Johnson crashed in the Thames Estuary, on 5th January 1941, while flying for ATA. She was probably shot down by the British.

[10] It is said that, as well as aircraft, these crates sometimes contained food parcels and other treats packed by sympathetic Americans.

Fig 83 Bell Airaçobra, an American aircraft type assembled at Colerne (IWM CH 3728)

already obsolete fighters were held in reserve at various RAF maintenance units until the end of 1941 when they were shipped to India, for use by the Indian Air Force, to South Africa and to Portugal. The USA quickly supplied Britain with more modern Curtiss Hawk P-40 types – the Tomahawk (some of these were also intended for France) and Kittyhawk. These later aircraft were used widely by the RAF, especially in North Africa, and supplied to other countries, notably the Soviet Union.

In 1941 a repair facility operated by the British Overseas Airways Corporation moved into some newly completed hangars to the north of the airfield. Alex Sleap was an aircraft engineer working for BOAC and ATA at Colerne during 1941 and 1942. His job was servicing aircraft on 'Flight Sections' – outside the hangars. The aircraft he maintained were Curtiss Mohawk and Tomahawk and new Bell Airacobra fighters. Mr Sleap also remembers working on Lockheed Liberator four-engined bombers for the Return Ferry Service from the USA and Canada, including Winston Churchill's personal

Liberator. He recalls the involvement of the Americans, well before their entry into the war, "There were two US test pilots both majors and they were also twins, one named George. Also several US ground engineers from the Curtiss and Bell aircraft corporations with their lovely tool kits, the like of which we had never seen before, which enabled us to do the jobs twice as fast."

Soon the BOAC unit also began assembly work. Here the aircraft was the Bell Airacobra fighter. This type too was originally intended for the French Air Force, but in April 1940, 675 were ordered for the RAF, with the first machine reaching the UK on 3rd July 1941 for testing at Duxford in Cambridgeshire. Colerne's Station Diary entry for 8th July states "Major Price US Army Air Corps[11] tested first Airacobra aircraft to be assembled in the United Kingdom." A considerable number of defects and faulty installations were found on the aircraft when they arrived and this delayed assembly. The Airacobra was found to be definitely inferior to the Hurricane and Spitfire and was dogged by a number of problems. However, by the end of September eleven aircraft had been delivered to No 601 Squadron and this unit undertook strafing operations, from Manston in Kent, along the French coast, the following month. In the event many of the Airacobras were sent to the Soviet Union and, following the start of the Japanese war, to Australia.

In March 1942 a new unit, No 218 MU, manned by RAF personnel, took over the Airacobra work from BOAC. In June, 61 aircraft were assembled against an already high target figure of 50 aircraft in May. For their efforts the unit received a personal message of congratulations from Colonel Llewellyn of the MAP. In July the MU assembled 81 Airacobras against their target of 70 aircraft. During that month three Soviet ground technicians inspected the assembly operations. In August Airacobra work came to an end and No 218 MU was 're-formed' to carry out special installations. Initially this meant fitting aircraft with airborne radar, but later the work included a variety of one-off modifications to many types of aircraft.

[11] In fact the US Army Air Corps had become the US Army Airforce on 20th June 1941. The US Air Force did not come into being as a separate service until 1947.

No 10 Group

For operational purposes RAF Fighter Command was organised on a regional basis into Groups. For the first ten months of the war No 11 Group, based at Uxbridge, had been responsible for the defence of the whole of Southern England. However, even before the start of hostilities plans had been made to form a new Group for the South-West, thus freeing No 11 Group for the defence of London and the South-East.

Accordingly, construction of RAF Rudloe Manor, a non-flying station near Box, and some four miles from Colerne, was begun in February 1940 as the headquarters of the soon to be established No 10 Group RAF Fighter Command. In July 1940, with his Fighter Operations Room in the old Manor barn and the station still mainly a tented camp, the new Group's first Air Officer Commanding, a genial and distinguished South African, Air Commodore (soon Air Vice Marshal) Sir Quinten Brand took control of all fighter operations in the south-west of England and part of Wales.

Fighter Groups were further sub-divided into sectors with their headquarters usually at the most important aerodrome in the sector. These sector stations would control minor satellite airfields. When No 10 Group first went into action Brand took control of three sectors with headquarters at Pembrey in South Wales, Filton near Bristol and St Eval in Cornwall. He had only four fighter squadrons to divide between his three sectors. The Group gained control of a fourth sector, with its headquarters at Middle Wallop, in August.

To add to No 10 Group's problems, by July neither radar nor Observer Corps cover was yet complete. Additionally, Brand lacked good aerodromes, especially permanent sector stations. His sector headquarters and fighter squadron at St Eval, for example, were 'lodger units', courtesy of Coastal Command, while Filton was only a stopgap until his new permanent station was ready – at Colerne.

Sector Station

So what was a Fighter Command Sector Station? First, it was an important base, normally the most important in the sector area, from

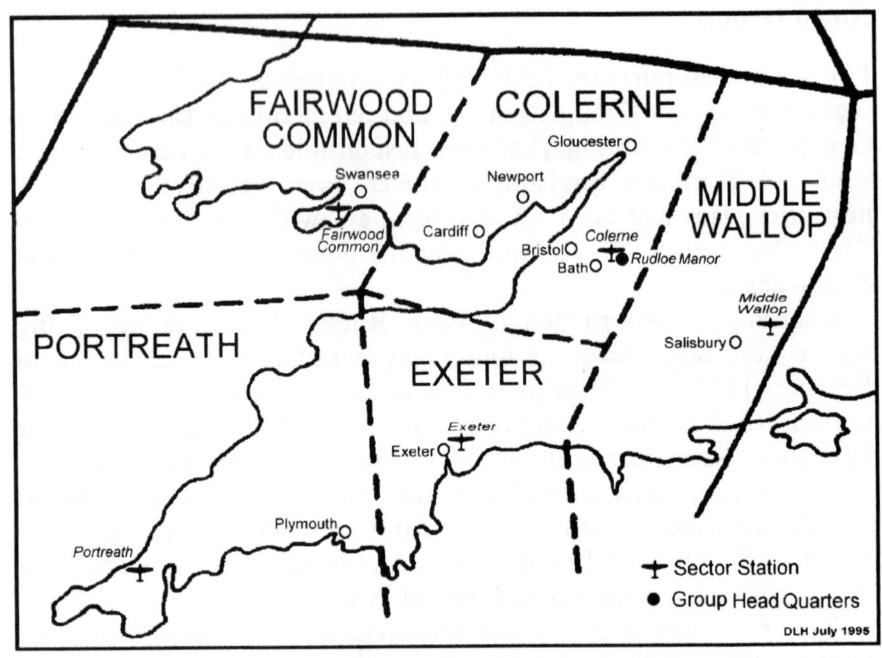

Fig 84 No 10 Group and its Sectors, April 1941

which the fighter squadrons operated. Second, the station's Commanding Officer was also the Sector Commander and responsible for the administration of other stations and units within the sector. Third, this station normally housed the Sector Operations Room, a vital link in the system of command and control of the aircraft operating within the sector. When Colerne opened as a Sector Station it was one of fifteen throughout the country.

By September 1940 a chain of Radio Direction Finding, or radar,[12] stations covered most of the coast of Britain, looking out to sea to provide an early warning system, enabling fighters to be 'scrambled' (ordered to take off) when notified of the approach of hostile aircraft, rather than having to maintain costly, continuous patrols. Having detected any aircraft, the radar station would telephone estimates of the position and strength of the force to the 'Filter Room.' Originally

[12] The term radar – radio direction and ranging – was coined in 1942 by the US Navy.

there was only one Filter Room, at Fighter Command HQ, but with the establishment of No 10 Group a separate Filter Room was set up for the Group area. Others were later established for each of the other Fighter Groups. In the Filter Room, WAAF (members of the Women's Auxiliary Air Force), in direct contact with the radar stations, plotted reported aircraft movements on the plotting table. This information was 'filtered' by validating the aircraft position, providing an estimate of height if possible, and adding the all-important identification as 'friendly' or 'hostile.' The filtered information was then passed to the Group and Sector Operations Rooms. In these 'Ops Rooms' the controller and his staff sat on a balcony with batteries of telephones before them, and below them was again a plotting table. WAAF received plots over their headsets and moved coloured counters with croupier's rakes – red representing enemy formations and black friendly aircraft. Arrows on the counters indicated direction of flight and numerals showed height and strength. The controllers above would decide on the action to be taken on the basis of what was already known from intelligence sources and Royal Observer Corps sightings or what they saw on the plots below them. The Group decided which sector should deal with the raid and the resources to be committed. The co-ordination of fighter movements with the operations of anti-aircraft guns was also controlled at this level. It was for the controllers in the Sector Operations Rooms, like the one at Colerne, to order the squadrons under their command to various states of readiness or to scramble them into the air. If fighters were sent into action the Sector Controller, or his deputies, used the radio telephone to 'vector', that is direct, the fighters towards the enemy. For the system to work, the controller needed to be able to follow the position of his own aircraft. To allow this, each sector had three direction-finding stations that took bearings on the automatic transmissions of fighter pilots' radio-telephones.

This system worked well enough to help win the Battle of Britain, although only just, as it was far from foolproof. In daytime, in poor weather conditions, British fighters and their intended quarry could pass through the same square on the plotting table without either side seeing the other. By the time Colerne became fully operational the main threat came at night and here successful interception, even with the co-operation of searchlights, was little more than a matter of luck. The introduction of AI (Airborne Interceptor) radar to large twin-engined night fighters, mostly Beaufighters and later Mosquitos, was an important first step in changing this. However, Mark 4 AI had a maximum range of only three or four miles, while at best the Sector Controller could only bring a fighter within five or six miles of the enemy – still a vast difference in this deadly three-dimensional chess game. The problem was at last solved with the introduction of new inland ground radar stations called Ground Controlled Interception Stations, or GCIs for short. Night interception now became a four-phase operation. First, the Sector Controller would scramble the fighter or fighters and direct them towards the enemy. Second, the controller at the nearest GCI station would take over and bring the interceptor to within one to two miles of the quarry. Third, the navigator/radar operator in the fighter would direct the pilot close enough to obtain a 'visual', 1000 to 1500 feet on an averagely dark night. Finally, the pilot would position the aircraft for the 'kill'.

Fighter station

On 1st September 1940, while the Battle of Britain was being fought out in the skies over southern England, RAF Fighter Command, from its headquarters at Bentley Priory, in Middlesex, issued instructions for the forming of a new Sector Station at Colerne under No 10 Group. No 39 Maintenance Unit already at Colerne, along with No 4 Aircraft Assembly Unit, was to become a 'lodger unit' at the aerodrome. Arrangements were made for forming Colerne's opening up party. This was to assemble at Filton.

Two days earlier Fighter Command had informed the Air Ministry in London of its opening-up programme for Colerne. This was a five-stage process intended to have the aerodrome ready to receive its first fighter squadron on 15th October. However, an internal Air Ministry note of 2nd September shows the urgency there was to open Colerne. "Tell [Fighter Command] that the Air Staff want to move the squadron from Filton as soon as possible. I suggest that the opening date might be 1st October." On 5th September amended opening instructions were issued to comply with the Ministry's suggested date.

On 15th September Colerne's new Commanding Officer, Squadron Leader Beamish DFC, arrived at Filton to head the start-up party. The following day the Station Headquarters was formed – at Filton – there was not accommodation at Colerne. It was not until 23rd that Beamish, now promoted Wing Commander, was able to move his HQ staff to Colerne, but even then numbers had to be kept to a minimum. The officers and men involved, some 35 in number, moved into the only available building, Barrack Block A.

The Station Diary records that during September the only flying at Colerne was the ferrying of aircraft to and from No 39 MU and No 4 ASU and that of No 10 Group's Communication Flight, now based at the airfield. It also states that the 'old aerodrome', that is the grass air strip at the Doncombe end of the station,[13] was used by day and the "new aerodrome by night." The strength of RAF Colerne on 30th September 1940 was put as follows:

Officers	Senior NCOs	Other ranks	Total
9	2	270	281

Of these 109 were at Filton.

Thus RAF Colerne officially came into being as a fighter station on 16th September 1940, only one day after the date later to be commemorated as Battle of Britain Day. Yet Colerne was to play no real part in that battle or any other for several months, except, that is, an inter-departmental Whitehall battle.

Recriminations

No 10 Group appears to have been shocked by what they found on taking charge of their new Sector HQ. On 9th October Air Vice Marshal Brand wrote to Fighter Command explaining why the move to Colerne of No 56 and No 87 Squadrons had to be cancelled.

> The deferment of the move of the above Squadrons was necessitated by the state of the aerodrome at Colerne. It was found that the previous day's

[13] One of Norman Alford's first memories of the aerodrome is of a squadron of Gloster Gladiator biplane fighters landing on this strip, which later became part of the station playing fields.

> rains had so softened the ground adjacent to the runways that it was impracticable to taxy aircraft to and from dispersal points, and there was considerable danger that pilots would wreck their machines if they ran off the runways. It was for the above reason also impracticable to land elsewhere in any direction but on the one finished runway surface.

Brand attached a very detailed report on the state of the buildings and runways as of 9th October. The brickwork of the Officers' Mess had reached a height of ten feet, while that of the Sergeants' Mess and Quarters was complete but only one wing had been plastered and had windows installed. No plumbing or ovens had been fitted. The Airmen's Mess and Institute was more advanced but far from finished. Of the six barrack blocks, one was complete, a second almost complete and a third could be used but still required considerable work. Only the brickwork had been completed on the other three blocks, each of which was intended to accommodate 150 men. The Motor Transport garage still had no floors and could not be used, in any case, as the lack of any roads, apart from a single one to the centre of the station, made it inaccessible to vehicles. None of the other buildings, such as the Station Headquarters, workshops and stores, was finished, and some, including the WAAF Quarters and Sick Quarters, had not been started. Construction had started on one hangar for the fighter squadrons. Water had now become available and was installed in one barrack block, but there was no lighting or mains sewerage although these were expected to be available within the next few days. A central heating station was to have provided heat and hot water to the Station but this was two or three months away from completion, besides which the boilers for it were presently unobtainable. In the meantime arrangements were made for hot baths for airmen – 120 per week – at the public baths in Bath!

The real problem lay, however, with the airfield itself. One runway (NE to SW) was complete but drain laying along the runway edge had brought fresh clay to the surface and this was soft even in dry weather, impassable if wet. Elsewhere the ground had only recently been sown and the surface was not yet knitted and would seriously rut if crossed. A second runway (N to S) was two-thirds complete but had open drains along its sides. Work had started on the third (E to W) runway and it was thought it would be completed in three months. The perimeter track would probably not be complete for four to five months. The report concluded:

> To sum up, except in fine weather aircraft must land and remain on the runway and even in very fine weather it is undesirable for aircraft to operate from and consequently damage the unknit grass surface. The surface should be in good condition by next spring. A considerable number of trees will have to be cut down to allow the approaches from the East and South to be used or allow aircraft to take off from the runway in the Southerly or Westerly direction. The trees are off site and action through the Lands Office No 12 Area is being taken to have them cut down.

It was suggested that Charmy Down, a satellite station of Colerne and very near completion, should be used to base a squadron. Only accommodation was lacking, but it was believed wooden hutting could be provided.

Fighter Command forwarded Air Vice Marshal Brand's letter, together with the report, to the Air Ministry and in their own covering letter remarked, "On the face of it, it would appear that the Air Ministry have rather rushed us into Colerne at least a month too early." But being even-handed in criticism added, "Why No 10 Group allowed this opening-up programme to go on, and even make all the arrangements to move a squadron in on the 8th October is beyond my comprehension. It would appear that AVM Brand did not really know the position at Colerne until a few hours before the squadron from Boscombe Down was due to go into Colerne."

The response from the Air Ministry was not sympathetic. "After all, Fighter Squadrons were operating on one runway last winter and [the Ministry] does not see why they shouldn't operate at Colerne now. As regards accommodation, we never promised anything more than 'picnic' accommodation for one squadron by 1st October 1940." However, questions were now being asked as to the reason for this state of affairs at Colerne and a report was prepared.

The Air Ministry report highlighted three reasons for the delay in Colerne's completion. The severe weather conditions in January and February 1940 had caused unavoidable delays, difficulties in obtaining transport in that part of the country had been great, thereby affecting the amount of material that could be brought to the site, but above all the problem was labour.

The report stated that the contractors had repeatedly asked the Ministry of Labour, who had powers to direct workers to anywhere in the country, to supply the necessary men to enable the completion of the contract on time. These requests had met with little success. Sunleys, the runway constructors, had asked for a minimum of 320 men but were having to make do with fewer than 200. The quality of labour supplied was also remarked upon. When Sunleys were finally supplied with 40 men from the north of England, from a promised total of 100, it was found the majority were from the distressed areas in Sunderland and Newcastle and had not been in employment for periods varying from several months up to twelve years. "In fact one of the men sent to this job, according to his own statement, had been on sick benefit for twelve years previous to arriving at Colerne and was unable to commence work on arrival." Finally, it was said, many men employed from distant locations were inclined to leave for their own districts after only a short period on the site. When this happened the contractors retained the men's insurance cards to indicate to the Labour Exchange (controlled by the Ministry of Labour) that the men were still required. Instead of having the men returned, the Labour Exchange had, on such occasions, demanded the contractors forward the men's insurance cards.

The Ministry of Aircraft Production, who used one of the hangars at Colerne for the assembly of Mohawk fighters, was also expressing concern that construction work they needed to avoid production delays was unfinished.

A number of minutes and notes were exchanged within the Air Ministry to establish how best to proceed in what was now clearly an inter-departmental dispute. By this stage the frustration within the Air Ministry is clear. "This job has from the start been short of labour and all our efforts to effect the necessary increase have been unavailing." After some hesitation it was decided to go to the top and the political head of the Air Ministry was asked to intervene. On 25th November the Secretary of State for Air, Sir Archibald Sinclair, wrote to his opposite number at the Ministry of Labour, Ernest Bevin.

Dear Bevin,

We are having trouble at Colerne where the completion of the RAF station and landing ground has been seriously delayed. The job has from the start been short of labour and all our efforts to effect the necessary increase have been unavailing. There is still a considerable amount of work to do and not enough men to carry it out as fast as we want. It is the worst case we have had.

The Ministry of Aircraft Production have asked us to give special attention to the approaches to and other work in connection with one of the hangars which is being used for the assembly of Mohawks. Non-completion of this work is likely to delay production of these aircraft but we cannot promise them immediate assistance because of the urgent need for concentrating the labour on the landing ground and the accommodation for fighter squadrons. The sooner the station and landing ground are complete the sooner shall we be able to give Bristol the scale of defence which we want. Can you help us?

Yours sincerely

Archibald Sinclair

It is doubtful whether before, or since, Colerne has been the subject of correspondence between such senior government ministers.

Bevin's reply, on 12th December, acknowledged that there had been labour shortages at Colerne although he blamed the contractors for not asking for all the labour they needed. Almost all that had been asked for had been supplied, he said, but added, "I need hardly say that the Local Office is fully aware of the importance of completing this contract, and that every endeavour is being made to cope with the increased labour demand."

Documents make it clear that the Air Ministry did not agree with Bevin's version of events but the last word on the matter, at least on record, came from a senior official on 29th December 1940, ". . . this does not seem entirely satisfactory, but I do not think we can harry him further. I hope that the correspondence will at least stimulate the M. of Labour to greater efforts."

Defending the airfield

On 23rd December 1940 the new Station Commander took over responsibility for the defence of the aerodrome from No 39 MU's commanding officer. At this time, when invasion appeared a real possibility, the handover was more than a mere formality. Cyril Rogers remembers his arrival at Colerne the previous month,

> As we came to the camp there was no organisation at all. They made us ground gunners, we didn't come into our trades, I was a butcher by trade. There were pill boxes round the Camp. We had twin Lewis guns [First World War vintage .303 machine-guns]. We had a rare old time of course. I'd be a country bumpkin. I used to catch all the rabbits round the perimeter track, and hares, and everyone used to be ringing up on the field telephone for rabbits.

At the end of October the Station Diary records that Colerne's defences included a detachment of the Staffordshire Regiment, quartered in Ashwicke Park, and a section of two three-inch anti-aircraft guns and one thirteen-pounder field gun on the aerodrome.[14] In November a Major Frazer was posted to Colerne and he became the first in a series of Army officers appointed to co-ordinate the ground defence of the station. Other army units recorded at Colerne, in the defence of the aerodrome, included a detachment of 70th Battalion Dorset Regiment, No 19 Company Pioneer Corps (five officers and 261 men) and 6th Battalion Suffolk Regiment. Royal Artillery units also manned the searchlights and anti-aircraft guns. On 28th May 1941, 85 Light AA Battery RA relieved 128 Battery. Also arriving that day, the Station Diary records, were two modern 40-millimetre Bofors anti-aircraft guns, "making a total of six guns on the Station."

Also involved in the airfield's defence was the Colerne platoon of the Home Guard. The platoon was commanded by Lieutenant Thompson, a First World War officer and pilot of the Royal Flying Corps. Lieutenant Thompson lived at the Vineyard, then a private

[14] The three-inch AA gun was of First World War origin while the 13-pounder was developed from the lessons of the Boer War and can still be seen in the musical rides of the King's Troop Royal Horse Artillery.

cottage, on the very edge of the airfield. He died there on 5th December 1944 and the RAF paid tribute to "an extremely keen and efficient Home Guard Officer."

By 1941 defences were on a firmer footing and in September a major two-day defence exercise was held involving Army, Home Guard and Air Force personnel. 'Attacks' were made on the airfields at both Charmy Down and Colerne, with aircraft participating on both sides. Umpires considered the two airfields successfully held.

As the war progressed the RAF took on more responsibility for its own defence. Cyril Rogers was involved briefly:

> The RAF Regiment was formed [on 1st February 1942 to specialise in airfield defence]. When it formed here I got into it. I was only in about six months and they sent me for a colour vision test which I failed. So I was back to my old trade, as I'd been mustered, and I was Station Butcher on the camp for two and a half years.

The squadrons

On the 27th November 1940 No 87 Squadron finally arrived from Exeter with their black Hawker Hurricane fighters. "The Squadron on duty from dawn 28th..." So states the Station Diary, and thus No 87 had the distinction of being Colerne's first fighter squadron. But it is not an honour they seem to have savoured, for on the day following their arrival the squadron's B flight departed for night flying duties at Charmy Down. On 11th December the whole squadron was at Charmy Down after a stay at Colerne of less than a fortnight. The other squadron due to move to Colerne at the beginning of October, No 56 Squadron, never did come; instead it eventually went to Middle Wallop in Hampshire.

It was only on their move to Colerne that No 87 Squadron went over completely to night fighting. This they continued at Charmy Down, but in the new year, as well as defending the Bristol Channel towns, a detachment operated, very successfully, from St Mary's in the Isles of Scilly. This arrangement continued when the squadron had a second spell at Colerne, from August 1941 until the following January. During the latter part of this second visit No 87's Commanding Officer was Squadron Leader D G Smallwood, many years later to

Fig 85 A Defiant with its power-operated gun turret facing rear (IWM CH 3448)

become Air Chief Marshal Sir Denis Smallwood, KCB CBE DSO DFC Air Officer Commanding-in-Chief Strike Command, the successor to both Fighter and Bomber Commands.

During the spring of 1941 a number of squadrons spent a short period at Colerne. No 256 Squadron had been formed at Catterick in November 1940 and was still working-up with their Boulton Paul Defiants when based at Colerne during February and March. At this time, however, a detachment of the squadron was operational at Middle Wallop. At the end of March No 256 Squadron left and was replaced by No 307 Squadron. This was the first Polish squadron in the RAF to become night-fighters and they too were equipped with the Defiant. This two-seater aircraft had its entire armament in a bomber-style, power-operated machine-gun turret behind the pilot's cockpit. The type had some early success, when the German pilots mistaking them for Hurricanes attacked from behind only to receive a withering concentration of machine-gun fire. However, as soon as the Luftwaffe modified its tactics the Defiant was forced to withdraw from

Fig 86 Spitfire of 501 Squadron at Colerne, May 1941 (IWM CH 2821)

Fig 87 Spitfires of 501 Squadron on patrol at Colerne, May 1941 (IWM CH 2826)

Fig 88 S/L D G Smallwood and officers of No 87 Squadron at Colerne, Nov 1941, (on far right, F/O John Strachey, post-war Minister of Food) (IWM CH 4249)

Fig 89 Sergeant Pilots of No 87 Squadron at Colerne, Nov 1941 (IWM CH 4248)

daylight operations. The type subsequently equipped thirteen night-fighter squadrons, when again some success was achieved. No 118 Squadron was briefly at Colerne in April, a period when it was exchanging its Spitfire Is for a later marque. From the same month through to June, No 501 Squadron was at Colerne exchanging its Hurricanes for Spitfire Is, aircraft formerly belonging to No 66 Squadron.

On 24th April 1941 Colerne's Operations Room finally became fully operational and took over Sector Control from Filton. Also in April, with the runways completed at last, No 307 departed and Colerne received its first fully operational squadron, No 600 (City of London) Squadron. The Commanding Officer of this Bristol Beaufighter IIF squadron was Wing Commander G H Stainforth, who as Flight Lieutenant Stainforth had been one of the pilots in the British Schneider Trophy team of 1931. On 29th September of that year, at Ryde on the Isle of Wight, Stainforth set a new world airspeed record and became the first man to exceed 400 mph by flying his Supermarine S.6B at 406.94 mph. It seems that a decade later his love of speed and daring remained undiminished. The story is still told in the village of men, working on a hangar roof, threatening to down tools unless Stainforth ceased buzzing them as the finale of his unofficial aerobatic displays. It is also said that villagers had to take care when Stainforth took to the road in his sports car.

No 600 Squadron had been operating in Scotland and was partly equipped with Bristol Blenheim IFs, a type it had used since September 1938, and partly with the newer and highly successful Beaufighter. Before the month was out No 600 had scored twice, downing a Junkers Ju 88 and a Heinkel He 111, while on 7th May two more He 111s were accounted for. On 8th May a further Ju 88 was damaged but on the following night one of No 600's aircraft was shot down by another British fighter. This was the sort of accident that was all too easy in the pitch dark and without effective electronic IFF (Identification Friend or Foe) equipment being carried.

No 316 'City of Warsaw' Squadron was formed at Pembrey, South Wales, on 15th February 1941 and soon their Hurricane Is were busy patrolling the Bristol Channel and on convoy duty. In June the squadron moved to Colerne where it began to receive mark IIa and

Fig 90 Black Beaufighters of 600 Squadron based at Colerne, 1941 (IWM CH 17265)

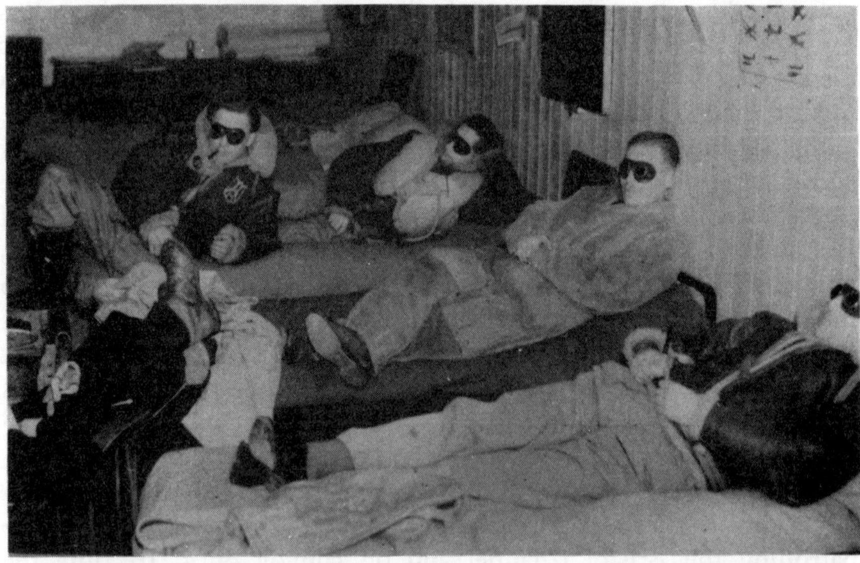

Fig 91 Crews of 600 Squadron resting before patrol. The dark glasses are to improve night vision. Colerne May 1941 (IWM CH 2820)

IIb Hurricanes to supplement their earlier machines. Convoy patrols remained No 316's staple diet, but on 24th July the squadron escorted Handley Page Hampden bombers on Operation *Sunrise*. This was an attack on the German battle-cruisers *Scharnhorst* and *Gneisenau*, and on the heavy cruiser *Prinz Eugen*, then at Brest and La Pallice. The operation was a failure with neglible damage to the ships for the loss of seventeen British aircraft. However, No 316 was able to claim a Messerschmitt Bf 109E destroyed. In August the squadron left Colerne for Church Stanton, Somerset, a station that had only opened on the first of that month and, as the home of No 2 Polish Fighter Wing, was soon to be known as *the* Polish airfield. A second Polish Hurricane squadron, No 317, visited Colerne briefly in June.

A number of new fighter squadrons were formed at Colerne during the war, the first being No 125 on 16th June 1941. The squadron spent several months working-up on their Defiants, first at Colerne, then, from August, at Charmy Down. In September No 125 moved again, this time to Fairwood Common, near Swansea, where on 27th it at last became operational. Over the following months the squadron scrambled to intercept night raids on the towns and industry of the Bristol Channel area, but without success. In January 1942 No 125 returned to Colerne and became non-operational while awaiting conversion to Beaufighter IIFs. It was ironic that No 125's first victory was gained by one of the squadron's old machines when, in the early hours of 26th April, Pilot Officers White and Gavegan scored a probable He 111 over Bath during the blitz on that city – more of which later. Now fully equipped with Beaufighters, No 125 returned to Fairwood Common in May.

One of the schemes developed in an attempt to overcome the relative inefficiency of early British night fighters was the use of airborne searchlights. The idea was that a fairly large aircraft of the American Douglas Boston or Havoc type carried the 'Turbinlite' to illuminate the enemy while an accompanying Hurricane made the kill. To this end, ten Air Target Illumination Units were formed during 1941, each to work with a particular fighter squadron. Two of these units were formed at Colerne: No 1454 Flight on 4th July and No 1457 Flight on 15th September. In November No 1457 moved to Predannack, Cornwall, while in the following January No 1454 moved to Charmy

Down to work with No 87 Squadron's Hurricanes. In September 1942, in an attempt to improve the co-ordination between illuminating aircraft and fighters, the ten Turbinlite flights were expanded into full squadrons, incorporating their own Hurricanes. The flights that had been formed at Colerne became, respectively, No 533 Squadron and No 536 Squadron. The whole Turbinlite experiment, however, proved a failure and in January 1943 all the squadrons were disbanded.

No 600 Squadron had been kept busy patrolling the West Country but from the middle of 1941 the squadron found little action, with the Germans pre-occupied with the war on other fronts, and flights moved to Predannack and Fairwood Common. When the squadron finally departed from Colerne for Predannack in October 1941, it went with a new commanding officer. No 600's former CO, Wing Commander Stainforth, stayed to command No 89 Squadron. This squadron, formed at Colerne on 25th September 1941, was a night-fighter unit destined for the Middle East and equipped with Beaufighter IF aircraft. By November 1941 the last elements of the squadron had left Colerne.[15]

January 1942 saw the arrival from Charmy Down of No 263 Squadron with their elegant Westland Whirlwind twin-engined, single-seat fighters. The Whirlwind, which equipped only two RAF squadrons, had proved troublesome with engine and cannon problems together with a rather high accident rate. Despite this, No 263's pilots successfully turned their hands to a wide range of duties. These included low-level attacks over the Continent, bomber escort work and anti-shipping patrols. No 263 even went on to dive-bombing! At Colerne the squadron tried the Whirlwind as a night-fighter but soon gave up and in February left for Fairwood Common. No 263's Whirlwinds were briefly seen again over the skies of Colerne. On 15th August, the squadron arrived from Angle, Pembrokeshire, to rest, having constantly achieved the highest number of operational flying hours in No 10 Group. The squadron departed again the following month.

[15] On the night of 27th/28th September 1942, while in the Middle East, Stainforth and Pilot Officer Lawson were killed when their Beaufighter had engine failure. Both baled out but too low for their parachutes to deploy fully.

Fig 92 A Whirlwind of 264 Squadron (IWM CH 4998)

Fig 93 A Mosquito Mk II (IWM E(MOS) 516)

No 286 Squadron was formed in November 1941 at Filton and its mixed bag of Oxford, Lysander, Defiant, Hurricane, Martinet and Master aircraft provided target-towing and gunlaying training for anti-aircraft defences in the No 10 Group area. This squadron visited Colerne on three occasions, twice in 1942, from April to May and August to October, and again in 1944.

No 417 Squadron was formed at Charmy Down on 27th November 1941 with Spitfire IIa aircraft. These were replaced with the Spitfire Vb before the squadron became operational, which it did following its move to Colerne in January 1942. However, on 12th February, five days before the squadron's first operational patrol, it was put on standby for possible action against the *Scharnhorst* and *Gneisenau* during the German ships' Channel dash. But No 417 was not destined to see any action in the UK, for later that month it moved to Scotland before going to Egypt.

Another squadron re-equipping with Spitfire Vb aircraft at this time was No 402 Squadron (Royal Canadian Air Force). From their base at Warmwell, in Dorset, the pilots of No 402 had pioneered the operational use of the Hurricane as a fighter-bomber during the winter of 1941–2. However, in March 1942, leaving their Hurricanes behind for other squadrons to continue the work, No 402 moved to Colerne to convert to Spitfires. In July, another Spitfire Vb unit, No 19 Squadron, was briefly based at Colerne.

The Station Diary entries reflect the general lack of action at this period, although the 'Baedeker' raids[16] did make something of a jolt:

> The month of April 1942 has again been, until towards its end, very quiet, when the comparative peace of recent months was ended by the violent bombing attacks on Bath, which occurred on the nights of 25th and 26th. The station was not affected further than that some corrugated sheeting on a Nissan hut was moved by one stick of bombs dropped from Hunter's Hall to the grounds of the Rocks. Assistance was rendered to the Bath authorities by the Station transport. The other chief item of interest during the month was the visit of the Higher Officers' Course, who arrived by air

[16] These bombing raids on towns of cultural and historic importance in England were in retaliation for the RAF's destruction of German medieval Baltic towns of Lubeck and Rostock. The Germans were said to have selected their targets from the Baedeker travel guidebook on England.

> from Old Sarum on 10th April to witness the controlling of fighter aircraft in action staged by the Colerne Operations Room and the Middle Wallop Wing [aircraft].

Some people in Bath may have thought that Colerne could have provided more 'assistance' than merely transport. The RAF appeared to have done little to interfere with two nights of raids that destroyed or seriously damaged many buildings, including 1185 houses, and left 417 people dead. In fact aircraft and crews from squadrons at both Colerne (No 125) and Charmy Down (Nos 87 and 317) were very active, if not very effective, during the Bath blitz. Unsuitable aircraft, mostly Hurricanes and Defiants, inexperienced crew and defective tactics all meant the German bombers were able to roam the moon-lit skies above the city largely unmolested. The raiders did not have it all their own way, however. As previously mentioned, Pilot Officers White and Gavegan achieved No 125's first success. This occurred on the first night of the attack on Bath. The same crew destroyed a second aircraft the following night and their CO, Wing Commander D V Ivins, claimed a Dornier Do 17 after a chase over the Avon Valley near Limpley Stoke. Nevertheless, Ivins recorded "the bandit proved a difficult target against an unilluminated background." In all, local fighters claimed four kills, while the Germans probably lost five more aircraft on their return flights. In May the Station Diary stated: "A repetition of the raids on Bath was expected during the [full] moon period, and all available single-engined fighters have been standing-by for a fighter night, but up to date, the Hun has not made another attack on Bath."

1st May 1942 saw the arrival at Colerne of No 264 Squadron. This had been another Defiant unit, in fact No 264 was the first squadron so equipped, flying the aircraft from December 1939. But May was to see the squadron receive a replacement for the Defiant, and a very capable replacement it was, the de Havilland Mosquito NF II. No 264 became operational with these 'wooden wonders' in early June and later the same month one of its aircraft damaged a Dornier Do 217 over Weston-super-Mare.

A few weeks later the Station Diary records another action:

> On the night of 30th/31st July, No 264 Squadron gained their first victory

> with an operational Mosquito aircraft. Squadron Leader C A Cook with his [radar] operator Pilot Officer R E Macpherson, when on patrol at about 0130 hrs were vectored on to an enemy raider. A chase followed, during which the enemy took evasive action. The pilot, however, obtained a visual. He followed for some time in order to identify, and then fired two or three short cannon bursts in quick succession. The enemy immediately burst into a huge sheet of flame, spiralling earthwards and falling to pieces in the air, it finally crashed near Malvern. The enemy aircraft has been identified as a Junkers 88; the crew of four baled out and have all been captured.

However, despite this success, generally there was little action to be found over Britain and in December the squadron began daytime patrols over the Bay of Biscay. Detachments at Trebelzue, and later Portreath, both in Cornwall, flew *Instep* patrols – the interception of German aircraft attacking shipping in the Western Approaches. No 264 also carried out night *Ranger* operations – deep penetration flights into occupied Europe to engage targets of opportunity – and a detachment used Bradwell Bay in Essex as a forward base for these. The wooden construction of the Mosquito did have one disadvantage – the appalling weather during the winter of 1942–3 resulted in the aircraft becoming sodden – at one stage twelve were under repair. The squadron left Colerne in April 1943 for Predannack. No 264 returned briefly in November 1944 with their Mosquito NF 13 but left again in December.

On 24th August 1942 a flight of Spitfires from No 234 Squadron escorted the Liberator bomber bringing Prime Minister Churchill back to Britain. These aircraft had been at Colerne and Charmy Down for the moonlight period of the month.

By 1942 the Hurricane was definitely outmoded as an interceptor fighter, but new roles continued to be found for this versatile aircraft. No 184 Squadron was formed at Colerne on 1st December 1942 and was equipped with the Hurricane IId 'tank busters.' This type was armed with two formidable 40-millimetre cannon, and became the scourge of Rommel's armour in North Africa. No 184 was, however, destined to be the only home-based IId squadron and even that for a very short period before re-equipping again. Not, however, before taking part in one large exercise:

Fig 94 A Typhoon (IWM CH 9289)

> A rehearsal for a Tactical Exercise in co-operation with the Army was held at Silk Hill (near Bulford) to be given on 28th January as a demonstration for 50 Members of Parliament. An Airborne Division at Netheravon took part and Nos 184 and 263 Squadrons gave close air support. The Exercise involved ground strafing, but no firing; laying of smoke screens to cover landing paratroops and landing of glider troops and transport etc.

Having completed its work-up period the squadron left Colerne in March 1943.

Exercises were a constant part of the routine of the station throughout this period. The most common seem to have been *Bullseye* exercises, which involved the interception of mass mock attacks on towns and cities in the Group area. These tested not only aircraft and crews but the whole defence system, including radar stations, ground control and so on.

Early 1943 saw two squadrons with detachments at Colerne. No 124

Squadron, based at North Weald, in Essex, flew in three high-altitude Spitfire VIIIs and No 456 from Valley, North Wales, had a flight of its Mosquito IIs at Colerne in March to fly deep penetration *Ranger* operations. March also saw the arrival of the Hawker Typhoon Ib fighter-bombers of No 183 Squadron. No 183 had been formed at Church Fenton, Yorkshire, on 1st November 1942, but had yet to fly operationally. This came on 19th April when the squadron bombed the Yainville Power Station. Soon after this raid No 183 moved on to Gatwick, but the squadron did not forget their association with Colerne. Later No 183 was to incorporate the rampant dragon of the RAF Colerne station badge into its own badge. The squadron returned briefly during May and June.

No 175 Squadron was at Colerne from March to May, converting from Hurricane IIb aircraft to the Typhoon Ib.

On 30th April 1943 No 151 Squadron arrived and began to intensify the night-intruder raids over France that it had been flying since February. The squadron's Mosquito IIs also flew daytime *Ranger* operations. Until July the squadron was very active but in that month it began to convert to Mosquito NF XIIs. In August they left for Middle Wallop. In November No 151 returned to Colerne and very quickly ended a lean period by claiming a Messerschmitt ME 410 destroyed. On the night of 21st/22nd January 1944 the squadron had a Heinkel He 177 confirmed when the giant four-engined bomber was shot down near Hindhead in Surrey. In March No 151 moved to Predannack, but not before one very successful night when the squadron's Mosquito NF VIIIs were able to claim four kills.

> 2nd March, 1305 hrs, Six aircraft of No 151 Squadron were scrambled for Sopley, Durrington and Worth Matravers Control due to hostile raids approaching Beachy Head. [One aircraft] pilot Wing Commander G H Goodman and navigator/radio Flying Officer W F E Thomas destroyed one Ju 88 and one He 177 under Sopley Control. This aircraft made an emergency landing at RAF Station Ford [Sussex], being damaged by debris from the exploding enemy aircraft and additionally the navigator was injured.

Another of the squadron's aircraft destroyed a Ju 88, while a third aircraft bagged another Ju 88.

Following No 151's departure four Beaufighter aircraft of No 68 Squadron, from Fairwood Common, arrived as reinforcement for 'Night Readiness' but left the following day. No 151's replacement at Colerne was another Mosquito squadron, No 219. On 27th March seven of its aircraft were scrambled to intercept what were thought to be some one hundred raiders heading for Cardiff and Bristol. One of the squadron's aircraft, piloted by Squadron Leader Ellis, destroyed a Ju 88 over Yeovil, but the operation was hampered by the enemy's use of 'Window'[17] and by the bad weather conditions. In early May the unit left for Bradwell Bay, Essex.

Early 1944 saw more squadrons converting at Colerne. In January No 137 Squadron moved in. Six months earlier this had been the RAF's second and last Whirlwind squadron. Now they were exchanging their rocket-firing Hurricane IVs for Typhoon Ibs. By early February the squadron was back on operations at Lympne, in Kent.

The same month saw the arrival from Culmhead (Church Stanton), Somerset, of a Spitfire wing under the command of Wing Commander Denis Smallwood, last seen at Colerne leading No 87 Squadron. The wing comprised No 131 Squadron and No 165 Squadron. On 19th the squadrons moved to Predannack to carry out *Instep* patrols, returning the following day. Two days later No 165 helped provide fighter cover for a No 11 Group *Ramrod.* As well as patrol work and the odd scramble from Colerne the squadron's aircraft and crews were also busy training or on operations from a number of other stations including Bolt Head, Devon, where during a *Rodeo* operation Pilot Officer Haslop of No 165 destroyed a Ju 88. However, four days later the same squadron lost an aircraft on a similar operation. On the last day of March No 131 moved to Harrowbeer in Devon. Two days later No 165 moved to Predannack.

Early in May No 488 (Royal New Zealand Airforce) Squadron's Mosquito aircraft spent a few days at Colerne while problems at their intended base, Zeals near Mere, Wiltshire, were resolved. This was the first appearance at the station of a 2nd Tactical Air Force squadron. The 2nd TAF was the British component of Allied

[17] A mass of aluminium foil dropped by aircraft to confuse enemy radar.

Airforces under General Eisenhower's overall command. The Station Diary remarked with interest on the complete mobility of the unit, in terms of its backup, a key element of TAF squadrons.

May also saw the third appearance at Colerne of the anti-aircraft defence training squadron, No 286. A detachment of a similar squadron, No 587, also visited the station at this time.

The period preceding D Day saw No 39 MU work flat out as their commanding officer Wing Commander Wooliams recalls. "We were very active of course. We were terribly busy getting our aircraft out to equip squadrons, to make sure all the squadrons were up to strength." However, Colerne, following the departure of the Mosquitos, was very quiet from an operational point of view. This situation soon changed dramatically.

'Cat's Eyes' at Colerne

Just after noon on 5th June 1944 a tannoy announcement was broadcast throughout the Camp by the Station Adjutant. No one was to enter or leave the Station. Additionally, all GPO telephone kiosks on the Camp were sealed. The Station Diary records: "No explanation was available to account for these extreme measures of security and opinion and speculation were rife amongst all personnel as to the possibility of forthcoming events."

By the middle of the afternoon it became clear that some important operation was imminent, as no fewer than twenty-six Mosquito night fighters arrived at the Station. Twelve of these aircraft belonged to No 85 Squadron while the remaining fourteen were drawn from four other squadrons, Nos 29, 151, 410 and 604. The officer responsible for directing the operation, the Head of Night Operations at neighbouring No 11 Group, also flew in. This was none other than Group Captain John 'Cats Eyes' Cunningham DSO DFC, the most famous night fighter pilot of the war.

During the evening Cunningham and Wing Commander Constable-Maxwell of No 125 Squadron briefed the aircrews on their duties for the forthcoming night. These were to patrol, in four relays of six or seven aircraft each, the skies above Normandy. The first aircraft were airborne at 2300 hrs. The Station Diary takes up the story:

> During the period after midnight a continuous air armada passed over this Station – all comprised part of the Troop Carrier and Glider formations transporting airborne troops, both British and American, who were scheduled to invade Normandy. Additionally, that it had been the task of the aircraft from this Unit to carry out patrols south of the Cherbourg Peninsula and with the specific object of preventing any interference from the Luftwaffe during the various landings of the airborne forces, preceding the landings by sea.

By 0545 hrs on the morning of 6th, D Day, all the aircraft had returned safely to Colerne after their patrols, which were described as "completely uneventful." This is not to say, however, that the patrols were unimportant. During D Day the Allies employed 2435 aircraft and 867 assault gliders to carry almost 17 000 airborne troops into action. If even a few German fighters had got among the slow moving and unarmed transports and gliders they could have endangered the airborne, and hence the whole, invasion plan. By 0945 hrs all the Mosquitos had left for their respective bases.

This was not to be the last Colerne was to see of 2nd Tactical Air Force aircraft. In the period following the D Day invasion the Station became a base for several Mosquito squadrons. No 604 Squadron's Mosquito FN XIIIs provided night defence over Normandy invasion beaches, first operating from Hurn, in Hampshire and then, in July, from Colerne. In the first few weeks following the invasion the squadron destroyed fifteen enemy aircraft and in July No 604 celebrated their hundredth victory of the war. Before the month was out the squadron moved to Zeals, where No 488 Squadron, the other squadron in the wing was based.

On 28th July No 149 Wing of 2nd TAF arrived at Colerne. The wing comprised No 488 (RNZAF) and No 410 (Royal Canadian Air Force) Squadrons, plus a detachment of No 604 Squadron, all flying the Mosquito FN XIII. With the arrival of No 149 Wing at Colerne, No 286 Squadron departed to Zeals. While aircraft of No 149 Wing roamed the night skies over France with almost daily successes, No 410 Squadron began the slow process of conversion to the Mosquito

FN 30. During the night of 19th/20th August the squadron achieved its first success with the new type when one of its aircraft shot down two Ju 88s. Without doubt the highlight of the wing's stay occurred during a patrol between Caen and Lisieux, on the night of 29th/30th July. Flight Lieutenant George Jameson DFC of No 488 Squadron, together with his navigator, Flying Officer Crookes, shot down four German aircraft, three Ju 88s and a Do 217, in the space of twenty minutes. Jameson gained a total of eight enemy aircraft destroyed in the post-invasion nights. His award of a DSO was announced when he was almost back in New Zealand by ship!

No 604 Squadron had moved to France by early August, while No 410 left Colerne in September and No 488 in October. An arrival in September was No 406 (RCAF) Squadron which moved in from Winkeigh in Devon. Before the squadron departed at the end of November some of its members had the chance to vote, at Colerne, in the Saskatchewan General Election. No 406's replacement was No 264 Squadron from Predannack, but they too left just before Christmas 1944.

No 29 Squadron arrived at Colerne in February 1945 working up with its new Mosquito NF 30s. As late in the war as March this squadron had to keep two crews at 'available' in view of renewed German night raids on Britain. In April the squadron moved to Manston from where on 24th of that month Warrant Officer Dallinson shot down a Messerschmitt Me 262 jet and damaged another, the squadron's last action of the war.

The Station Diary's entry for April recorded an important change for the station:

> The successes of the Allied forces in Europe since D Day has slowly affected the policy of this night fighter Station and during this eventful month we have said goodbye to our last night fighter operational Squadron who have been on constant operations from here since November 1941. Also we have witnessed the closing down of the Operations Room, the departure of Squadron Leader C A Redgrove, Senior Controller, and of his Operations Staff and handing over of the duties of Sector Station to Exeter.

The following month saw the end of the war in Europe and another change for Colerne. The Station now came under No 11 Group.

As it turned out No 29 Squadron was not only Colerne's last night-fighter unit, it was also the very last piston-engined fighter squadron to be based there. However, for several months a new sound had been heard in the skies above Colerne.

The jet age

Colerne has the distinction of being the RAF's first permanent jet-fighter base. No 616 (South Yorkshire) Squadron arrived in January 1945 with their nineteen new Gloster Meteor IIIs, under the command of Wing Commander Andrew McDowall DFC, a former Battle of Britain Sergeant-Pilot. No 616 was the first jet fighter squadron in the RAF and the only one to become operational during the Second World War. The squadron had received its first Meteor Is in July 1944, while based at Manston in Kent. Early the following month it began anti-V1 (flying bomb) patrols, achieving thirteen confirmed victories before the V1 menace ended in September. No 616 had also acted as 'enemy' to USAAF bomber formations, allowing the Americans to work out tactics to counter attacks from German jets. In December the squadron began conversion to the Meteor IIIs, the first version of the aircraft to be manufactured in quantity. In the new year the move to Colerne took place and the squadron soon got down to training. One flight, however, was sent to join 2nd TAF on the Continent. No 616's stay at Colerne was a short one for in February 1945 the squadron moved to Andrew's Field in Essex. From there they joined their colleagues on the Continent where, having failed to find German jet opposition, they were employed principally on ground attack work.

No 616 Squadron's replacement was No 1335 Conversion Unit, formed at Colerne on 8th March, whose task it was to train new Meteor squadrons. They themselves were equipped with Airspeed Oxfords as well as early Meteors. This unit's first job was to work with No 504 Squadron, which arrived in March 1945 from Hawkinge in Kent and received its first Meteors on 10th April. In May the war in Europe ended and in that month No 74 Squadron returned from the

Fig 95 A Meteor F3. The Meteor was the RAF's first jet fighter (IWM CL 2930)

Continent with their Spitfire IXs to re-equip with Meteors. They, together with No 504, formed, at Colerne, the RAF's first jet fighter wing. Although too late to see action No 504's Meteors did go to Germany when, in July, the squadron's aircraft were detached to Lubeck, while the HQ remained at Colerne. The same month, with its work done, No 1335 CU left for Molesworth in Cambridgeshire. On 10th August No 504 Squadron was disbanded. On the same day a new squadron, No 245, was reformed at Colerne, from No 504's aircraft and most of their personnel.

Colerne's jets were of course a source of great interest. The Air Officer Commanding No 11 Group visited Colerne in May 1945, the month his Group gained responsibility for the station, and flew a Meteor. The following month 120 Naval and Army officers visited the Station to see its jets. In August the Meteors were shown off to visiting members of the national press and the Station Commander gave a flying display. The press came again in October when there was an opportunity for air-to-air photography and filming, with eighteen aircraft airborne. In April 1946 a five-man Swiss mission visited to see a jet-fighter base in action and was given various demonstrations. On 26th August 1945 eight aircraft of Nos 74 and 245 Squadrons escorted the liner Queen Elizabeth, on her departure to America, carrying returning US troops. The following month Colerne aircraft took part in the Battle of Britain Fly-Past in London. On 8th June 1946, after several days' practice at Bentwaters, Colerne's Meteors flew in London's great Victory Fly-Past. The next month, in yet another fly-past, they flew over the United States Embassy.

While all this ceremonial was going on the serious business of training continued. Many exercises were carried out with Meteors defending Bristol against mock attacks and engaging in dogfights against North American Mustangs. The safety record of these early jets does not appear to have been good. In addition to belly-landings, some nine Colerne aircraft crashed, including ones at Black Cross Wood in Colerne, at Weston-super-Mare, at Frome, near Lacock and on the airfield itself. The first death occurred when the Commanding Officer of No 1335 CU crashed his Meteor at Farnborough while giving a demonstration of low-level aerobatics. The writer of the medical section of the Station Diary could perhaps have chosen better words when recording the incident, "The aircraft struck the ground at over 300 mph so no medical problems arose."

No 74 Squadron and No 245 Squadron served at Colerne until August 1946 when they moved to Horsham St Faith in Norfolk which was to be the latter's peacetime base for almost nine years.

The final entry in the Station Diary for this period reads, "As from 23.59 hours on the 31st October 1946 RAF Station Colerne ceases to be under Fighter Command. From 00.01 hours on the 1st November 1946 Headquarters Maintenance Command assumes command." And so one era ended and another began for Colerne and its station.

The bombing

On 10th April 1941 a lone German bomber crossed the aerodrome. Tom Kent recalls the incident. He and Bert Jenkins were coming down off the runway when they saw the aircraft, "He's letting something out – leaflets?" It was in fact a stick of bombs. A single bomb struck the NAAFI canteen situated near the present car park between the Northwood and Southwood housing estates.

Cyril Rogers was one of the few people in the canteen when the bomb struck.

> When the bomb hit the roof I didn't see it. The concrete came down and I blacked out because I was only five feet from it. I was on a form at the side of the window writing a letter saying what a good time I was having! I came round in about five minutes I suppose. Not a soul about, only the other two lying on the floor and one was badly knocked about – his back was blown away – and I went round the counter and there was Flossie Sheppard, she was there and I consoled her. I stayed with her for a while. The other chappie got out of the place – he ran out. I stayed there till someone else came in, till the all clear went. How I got away with it I don't know.

Remarkably Mr Rogers received only minor injuries, a shrapnel wound to the shoulder and a small fragment in the eye, for which he had treatment at the Royal United Hospital in Bath. A concert was to have started in the canteen at seven o'clock and two musicians had been rehearsing. One of these was killed and a second airman, Sammy the pianist, lost an eye. Minutes before the attack the canteen had been full with diners. A little later the hall would again have been packed, this time for the concert. It was only by remarkable good fortune that the number of casualties was not much higher.

A report of the raid, suitably uplifting if not entirely accurate, appeared in the press. Very much in the 'somewhere in England' style of the time, it was entitled "Two Brave Women."

> Here is a story indicative of the spirit of England; the spirit Hitler cannot break but which will break him. A correspondent writes to tell me that when a canteen in the South-West was struck by a bomb a few days ago two women attendants had a narrow escape from death. The canteen was crowded at the time, and three persons were killed, among them the pianist and the singer he was accompanying and a number of others were injured. The two attendants were knocked over by the force of the explosion and received minor injuries. One of them, who comes from a military family, lost her husband in the last war.

Fig 96 Two of Colerne's squadron commanders. S/L J R Pennington-Leigh DFC (left), W/C A D McNeill Boyd DSO DFC (right) (IWM CH 10301/2802)

> Next morning, however, they were back at their post, cleaning up the wreckage and making the canteen presentable again. They simply said that the needs of the other men must be attended to, and there was no one else who knew where the canteen goods were stored. This simple devotion to duty is yet another of the countless examples to be found all over the land of the courage of ordinary men and women which is going to win us the war.

The two women were Mrs Flossie Sheppard of Tutton Hill, mentioned in Mr Rogers' account, and a Miss Aggie Ham.

In his account Cyril Rogers states that the bombing occurred at 5.45pm. A number of other witnesses, however, place the incident at approximately four o'clock. Strangely, the entry in the Station Diary for that day reads, "0230 [hours] 3×50 kilogram bombs dropped on the Aerodrome between the Main and temporary Landing Grounds, no damage." It is odd to say the least that this document, which records events in such detail, should, on this matter, be at variance with so many people's recollections. There are only two other references in the Station Diary Record Book to bombs falling at Colerne. Firstly, on 3rd May 1941, "A number of incendiary bombs were dropped on western side of the Aerodrome by enemy aircraft, no damage. Also 2×250 kilogram bombs fell about 200 yards from the south west corner of the Aerodrome, both unexploded;" secondly, when bombs fell close to the Station during the bombing of Bath in April 1942.

Luckily Colerne and its airfield were not normally the main target of enemy bombers. However, being on the direct route of aircraft attacking Bristol and the other Bristol Channel towns, it did, for a period, see and hear a good deal of the enemy. Jack Scrivin remembers on occasions, "The sky black with bombers and their fighter escorts – Scary." "It used to be Bedlam", Cyril Rogers recalls, "you didn't know where the bombs were dropping. We used to refrain from opening up with the twin Lewis guns even if they came down because we'd be giving the position of the camp away." He does remember an occasion when a German aircraft was fired on from the ground. A young airman opened fire with his swivel mounted Lewis gun from the back of an armadillo [a lorry converted into an armoured car for airfield defence] positioned outside the Officers' Mess. The aircraft finally came down at Marshfield, but as the victim of a pursuing Hurricane!

Fairhead employee Frank Champion remembers the advice he and his fellow workers were given,

> We all had instructions about what you had to do in an air raid. We all collected up there. A chap came along and talked to us. He said, "Don't forget lads, if you hear the siren going and you're in the open, you get up and you run like hell till you get to Lucknam Woods over there." So we had to run all the way over there. [That could be] about two miles away from the other side of the airfield all up to Lucknam. If one had dropped in there it would have wiped out the lot of us. So there was heck of a run – everyone scurrying about like rabbits and that used to happen sometimes two or three times a week when enemy aircraft were passing.

Waifs and strays

A striking feature of the war years is the number of aircraft, of every description, making unscheduled landings at Colerne. This, at times almost daily occurrence, was the result of damage sustained on operations, of engine trouble, lack of fuel, diversions caused by bad weather or simply the pilot having become lost. In these circumstances Colerne became a welcoming haven. The Station Diary gives a picture of the impressive work done by the staff of Colerne's Air Traffic Control, or Flying Control as it was then known, who were constantly on the watch for aircraft in distress.

Most often distressed aircraft arrived singly. In June 1942, a Hampden bomber from Waddington in Lincolnshire was guided to Colerne by radio and made a safe night landing. The aircraft was low on fuel after its return from an operation. Two nights later a Wellington bomber, lost while on a training flight, was guided to Colerne by a Beaufighter and landed with the aid of pyrotechnics (flares) owing to poor visibility. In an incident the following month a Hurricane of No 87 Squadron was homed into Colerne by radio following an engine failure. Although the cockpit was full of fumes owing to glycol coolant leak, the pilot landed safely. In November

1942 an Armstrong Whitworth Whitley bomber was homed in safely at night using 'Darkie'. This was a system by which an aircraft could call for a homing using the call-sign 'Darkie', so allowing operators on permanent Darkie watch to obtain the aircraft's position. The next night an Avro Anson from Bobbinton, Staffordshire, was landed with the aid of searchlights and pyrotechnics. There were three searchlight batteries situated around Colerne and one of their responsibilities was to form a cone of light over the Station to assist distressed aircraft to locate the position of the airfield.

On other occasions, especially later in the war, these unexpected visitors could arrive in numbers. The period following D Day was particularly busy. On 7th June 1944 fourteen Avro Lancasters and a Handley Page Halifax arrived for re-fuelling and because of bad weather. On 9th June nineteen Dakotas landed because of the weather conditions. Two days later another nine Halifax bombers re-fuelled when returning from operations. In all Colerne played host to almost 70 aircraft in that June alone. Among the other mass landings was that of 29 B-17 Flying Fortress aircraft of the USAAF on their return from a raid over the Continent on 16th November 1944. "This diversion was quite unexpected", states the Station Diary, "and accommodation and rations were provided for a total of 116 aircrew in the Officers' Mess and 135 in the Sergeants' Mess." All the Fortresses left two days later, except two which were flak damaged and another which ran into a parked aircraft while taxying. The greatest unplanned mass landing of all, however, occurred on 19th December 1944 when no fewer than 46 Fortress aircraft were diverted to Colerne owing to the weather conditions.

Night-fighters, such as the Beaufighters and Mosquitos based at Colerne, do not feature among the 'lost'. The reason is that the A I radar these aircraft carried had a secondary purpose quite different from the prime one of locating their quarry. At the turn of a switch the radar transmitter in the fighter would trigger a beacon at the aircraft's base enabling the navigator to read off his bearing and distance from the airfield. Each ground beacon responded with its own Morse letter code so the navigator could identify his own base.

The Yanks

As we have already seen, Americans, both civilian and military personnel, were working at Colerne airfield long before their country officially joined the hostilities in December 1941. The early visitors were involved in the assembly, testing and maintenance of US aircraft supplied to Britain, but later Colerne was also to see many Americans from combat units.

The first of these combat units to arrive was 27th Fighter Squadron, 1st Fighter Group, XIIth Air Force, USAAF in their 23 Lockheed P-38F Lightnings. The large and powerful twin-engined, twin-boomed aircraft must have made quite an impression on their arrival at Colerne on 15th September 1942. While they were at the station, the 27th spent most of their time training. However, on 9th October they took part in an 'offensive operation' with other US aircraft of the Fighter Group from Ibsley, Hampshire. On 6th November the Lightnings left for Chivenor, North Devon, en route to North Africa.

On 26th October 1943 a flight of nine Republic P-47 Thunderbolts of 357th Squadron, 335th Fighter Group, VIIIth Air Force arrived from their base at Steeple Morden, Cambridgeshire, for 'defensive training.' The flight consisted of ten officers and 24 enlisted men. These departed on 10th October, to be replaced four days later by a second flight of eight aircraft from the same squadron. Four more flights were to arrive at Colerne for training before the last group of four aircraft left early in February 1944.

On 3rd December 1944 two American officers arrived at the station seeking a suitable site for a tented camp to accommodate some 2000 US Army personnel. Two days later, and to the surprise of the Station authorities, an advance party of approximately 100 Americans arrived without tents or equipment. The RAF provided these men with food and accommodation for the night and next day made arrangements for them to use the Northwood Farm aircraft dispersal site for their tented camp. An old Airmen's Dining Room, which had not been used for several months, but which the Station Works Department said they could get fully serviceable within five days, was put at the Americans' disposal.

During the afternoon of 11th December some 2300 troops from

units of the US 17th Airborne Division arrived, to be joined the following day by their commander Brigadier General Whitehead. Also arriving on the 12th were no fewer than 97 Douglas C-47 Skytrains, or Dakotas as they were known to the British. The USAAF personnel arriving with these aircraft, numbering about 750, were accommodated in huts at Ashwicke Park and Barrack Block G provided further offices and accommodation. With nearly 100 American aircraft on the airfield in addition to Colerne's own fighter squadron, the aircraft passing through the MUs, No 10 Group Communications Flight and an odd unexpected visitor, the camp must have been bursting at the seams. Next day, as the Station Diary records, the airfield was "the scene of intense activity during the morning, with long columns of American Airborne personnel – heavily armed and equipped – proceeding to the airfield to embark in the awaiting Dakota Troop Carrier aircraft." However, news arrived that the 'Exercise'[18] in which the troops were to take part had been postponed owing to bad weather. Following a further postponement the next day, the operation was finally cancelled on the third day of bad weather. This would have come as no surprise to those involved with airborne operations as cancellation was, for one reason or another, the fate of many. Over the next few days the Dakotas left to return to their base in France, although one group of six aircraft was forced to turn back to Colerne by the continuing poor weather conditions. The six finally got away on 21st December. It was 28th January before the last of the American troops left Colerne. Wing Commander Wooliams, for one, was not sorry to see them go, "they were a bit of a nuisance rushing round the woods and shooting at the pheasants."

The main camp site

Colerne was one of the last Expansion Scheme aerodromes to be completed. The start of the war and the changed role of the airfield caused many planned buildings not to be completed while others were constructed to meet the new circumstances.

[18] The quotation marks are in the original document indicating the 'Exercise' may have been more than that word would otherwise indicate.

The area of the aerodrome, as originally planned, and to which it would revert after the war, was mainly within the triangle spoken of earlier and this constituted what was called Site No 1 Airfield.

The Station's main administrative and domestic buildings were completed broadly on the pre-war Expansion Scheme pattern, laid out on a neat network of roadways. These included the Station Headquarters, Guard Room, Officers' Mess, Sergeants' Mess and Airmen's Mess and Institute, and the six H-block barrack buildings. Other 'permanent' buildings included those housing the Motor Transport Section and Fire Section as well as services such as power plant. The change in the airfield's role added a requirement for an Operations Block. All these buildings lay in the 'Fighter' area of the site. Slightly to the north 'Maintenance' had their Headquarters.

With the expansion of the station many additional buildings were required to accommodate the men, women and equipment operating there. Temporary hutted accommodation and storage buildings of all sorts were erected on the airfield, as well as on the dispersal sites to be discussed later. Buildings such as the dance hall and the cinema were added for the entertainment of the men and women of the camp. The Station church was formally dedicated by the Bishop of Bristol on 12th October 1941. One or two buildings remained from the time before the airfield's construction. Mr Pope's house was put to various uses and was only demolished long after the war.

The three tarmac-surfaced runways, laid out in the standard 'A' pattern, and surrounded by the perimeter track, occupied the southern part of the aerodrome. These were of course an addition to the original plans.

Runway	Length	Direction
No 1	1200 yards (1100 metres)	N–S
No 2	1950 yards (1780 metres)	NE–SW
No 3	1150 yards (1050 metres)	SE–NW

All the runways were 50 yards (46 metres) wide.

Around the edges of the airfield were four sub-sites used by the Maintenance Units. To the south of the former Back Road and nearest to the village lay Aircraft Storage Unit (ASU) Site No 1 and ASU Site No 2. These housed, respectively, three and two L Type storage hangars. ASU Site No 3 consisted of the two hangars, to the north of the airfield, alongside the Fosse Way. At the Doncombe end of the airfield, to the far north, ASU Site No 4 had three more hangars.

On three of these ASU sites Air Ministry Warden's cottages were built. These cottage were in fact substantial semi-detached houses. A pair were sited alongside Totts Lane on Site No 1, two more on Site No 3 and the final pair beside Doncombe Lane on Site No 4. Jack Scrivin recalls "After our dad had done the marking out [on the airfield] he went on as a warden. I don't know what they did as a warden, I'm sure." he also states that the cottages were not used by wardens. It is certainly the case that soon a pair of these cottages were used as the WAAF Officers' Mess, while the others served as married-quarters for warrant officers and their families.

Dispersal sites

RAF Colerne not only occupied the main sites described above but during the war years, and a few years subsequently, it spilled over into the neighbouring land and beyond. The Station Diary records that on 31st October 1940 a detachment of the Staffordshire Regiment, which was involved in the defence of the airfield, was quartered in Ashwicke Park. The Fosse Way and Doncombe Lane were closed to the public on 31st May 1941. Ashwicke House itself was requisitioned in July 1941 to be used as an accommodation and rest area for officers involved in night flying operations. Major Pope, the owner of Ashwicke, thus became another of the dispossessed. Surprisingly, Wing Commander Richard Johnson, Colerne's very last Station Commander, commented that the RAF was still paying the water rates for Ashwicke House in 1970, although by then it had not been in Air Force hands for more than twenty years. There were RAF buildings on either side of Ashwicke Lodge. There were Nissen huts and a strange, totally enclosed building, the purpose of which is obscure, although it may have been an anti-aircraft training dome. North of the lodge on the Ashwicke estate the wooded area bounding the Fosse Way was used as a dispersal area for aircraft. A stretch of the Fosse

Way was widened so aircraft could be wheeled along it to gain access to the woods. Wing Commander Wooliams of No 39 MU remembers he had great difficulty in obtaining permission to carry out this widening. Aircraft were also concealed under trees in the field in front of Hunters Hall, on Northwood Farm land and on a strip of land south of Sewell which stretched up to the Lucknam Park drive.

In the woods down the hill from the present Pinewood estate there was an emergency water supply for the camp which consisted of several large water tanks let into the hill one above another and a small asbestos building that housed the diesel-powered water pumps. To the north of the camp in North Wood astride Doncombe Brook was a small-arms firing range. This range was also used by the Colerne Home Guard.

The RAF made much use of Northwood Farm land. Norman Alford recalls:

> There was a hangar about 500 metres down a wide track from the farm house. It was camouflaged with dark green and black matt paint. About 50 metres away under the trees there was a wooden tower structure that looked something like a windmill without the sails. This building was a radio beacon transmitter/receiver installation operated by WAAF personnel who also had a small brick building for resting and eating [Site 12]. Close by in another brick building was a small diesel-powered generator, used for standby purposes (as a young lad of sixteen I can remember attending this generator weekly with the fitter, Mr Lionel Williams of Charter Square, known to us as Bill Williams, to service and run up this machine). Further down the same track there were two wooden radio masts installed, this was at a later date of course. A brick building housed the receivers which were operated from the old control tower on the airfield. The transmitters were located at the top of Bannerdown Hill, now the property of British Gas, also with two masts of wooden construction.

A track ran from ASU Site No 1, by Totts Lane, to two hangars near the former post-war married quarters at Thickwood. Along this, small aircraft were taken for repair. The point where this track crossed Doncombe Lane is still marked by the original, and now rather dilapidated, wheeled gates. When the fields to the south of the now closed Lucknam Road are newly ploughed, a line of cinders in the soil still marks the route of this track. The hangars, of iron and asbestos construction, were well disguised under the trees, having imitation chimneys made of wood and hessian and sprayed to look like houses, complete with doors, windows and shadows! Mary Guy recalls that the fields around this area were littered with boxed aircraft awaiting construction.

Searchlight and anti-aircraft batteries as well as pill boxes also appeared around the village. There were pill boxes situated at the corner of the airfield near Hunters Hall, at the bottom of Doncombe Hill and in the field opposite the main entrance to Lucknam Park. Parts of the Recreation Ground and Mr Payne's adjoining field were requisitioned in the spring of 1941 and a Bofors anti-aircraft gun was located along the hedge that separated the two fields. A defensive blockhouse building and Nissen hut were constructed at the top of the Recreation Ground (the hut on the Rec became the property of the Colerne Parish Council in February 1946 and until the 1990s was used as changing rooms for football teams). Trenches were also dug on the Rec and an entry in the parish records on 15th October 1941 expressed concern that these trenches might present a danger to children at play as they were not fenced off. They were inspected by the Chairman of the Parish Council who decided no action was necessary. There were also gun emplacements opposite to the entrance to Green Lane in Bath Road. One of the searchlight batteries was located between Colerne village and Thickwood beside that stretch of Thickwood Lane later destroyed but the current main road. For many years after, the two Nissen huts on this site were used to store hay. Their bases can still be seen.

In and around Thickwood and along the road to Ford, hutted living accommodation was built.[19] At the centre of these sites, where the married quarters were later built, was Site No 2, the Communal Site, for use by both male and female personnel. This had a cookhouse and other facilities including a dance hall complete with stage and floodlights. There were nine of these Living Sites (Nos 3 to 11), six of

[19] When the foundations for the Thickwood huts were being excavated another Romano-British find was discovered. On 25th April 1941 a John Williams unearthed a small red pot containing a hoard of Roman siliqua coins *c* AD 407. The coins, which probably originally numbered over 200, were declared Treasure Trove.

which were for airmen. Four of these (Nos 3 to 6) were alongside the Thickwood to Ford road. The most distant was at Down Plantation, another around Raffinwood House and two more, one each side of the road, around Lucknam's Chippenham Lodge. Site No 7 was just to the north of Thickwood Farm and No 8 was near Fox-Corner Farm, on what later became a caravan park. Sites Nos 9 to 11 were used by the women and slightly confusingly known as WAAF Sites Nos 1 to 3. WAAF Site No 1 was near Hall Farm, No 2 Site was located where later Berwyn Engineering had their works and No 3 Site was at the end of Thickwood Lane alongside the hamlet. Joan Long, a WAAF Corporal Cook, remembers that the Nissen huts had eight beds down each side and there was a solid fuel stove in the centre of each hut. On each site there was a picket post inside the gate and generally six felt clad huts. They also had latrines (on the male sites separate ones for officers, NCOs and airmen), ablutions and cycle stores. This last was very important on these dispersed sites, although personnel at Colerne were quite lucky. On some highly dispersed stations, with sleeping, eating and working sites far apart, it was necessary to travel up to 30 miles a day.

Colerne did, however, have some outposts a little further afield. The Sick Quarters were at Middle Hill House in Box, some two and a half miles south of the airfield. Colerne also had an Emergency Operations Room located at Ditteridge, just to the north of Box, for use if the Ops Room on the airfield was out of action. An exercise to test a move to Ditteridge was held in August 1942, and the Ops Room was in action within an hour. Women soldiers of the Auxiliary Territorial Service (ATS) were also billeted at Ditteridge, in Cheney Court.

As a major station and sector HQ, Colerne also had wider responsibilities. For instance, Charmy Down, some five miles to the west, was Colerne's fighter satellite for much of the war and that station's Commandant reported to Colerne's Station Commander. In September 1944 Colerne absorbed Fairwood Common sector. As we have seen, No 39 MU also had its satellite airfields. Colerne sector also had its GCI radar stations. In July 1942 one moved from Huntspill near Highbridge in Somerset, to Long Road, near Somerton in the same county. Two months later Cricklade GCI station, north of Swindon, was transferred from Middle Wallop sector to Colerne.

Pains and pleasures

Life must have been difficult for the service personnel on the camp in the early days, living and working on what was literally a building site. Although the Station Diary was able to report that "Steady progress was made throughout the month of October [1940] on the construction of Station buildings and runways of the new landing area", Colerne weather again intervened. "The first week of November was marked by almost incessant rain both by day and night. As a result Colerne camp and Aerodrome became a morass which greatly interfered with the progress of the construction." As well as preventing the Station from becoming fully operational and causing general inconvenience the state of the camp was a source of real danger. On 22nd October an airman "was found dead in the early morning at the bottom of an un-railed and unlit stairway in Barrack Block B, having apparently fallen down accidentally in the black-out whilst carrying out his duties as Station Orderly Corporal."

Cyril Rogers remembers his arrival at Colerne on 15th August 1940. "We found it in a very rough state. It was in the building. They were erecting hangars and part of the runway. I was in the first batch of 40 airmen on the camp. Before long we saw things taking shape and there were more airmen coming in and things began to get better for us."

By October the number of personnel on the camp was increasing with a station strength now at twelve officers, two warrant officers, 53 non-commissioned officers and 401 men. Accommodation was said to consist of "barrack blocks, huts and billets in surrounding parishes." October also saw the opening and first meeting of the Sergeants' Mess. The Officers' Mess first met on 1st November, though at this stage its members had to share accommodation in the Sergeants' Mess. Officers also had use of two small houses near the camp. The cost of messing for officers was set at two shillings a day, although this was later reduced to 1s 9d. It was not until 23rd July the following year that the Officers' Mess building, with its ante-room, dining room and kitchen, was opened. On 20th September 1941 a dance was held in the Officers' Mess to celebrate its opening. Numerous guests attended including senior officers of the Group and Sector and other station commanders in the Group. Army guests and 'local friends' also attended. The music was provided by the dance band of RAF Ibsley, near Ringwood in Hampshire, although it seems Colerne's own Station Band had arrived two days before the dance and they also attended. Also celebrating no doubt were the sergeants who now had the Sergeants' Mess building to themselves. The WAAF Officers' Mess also opened that year. This happened on 12th September 1941 when the two Wardens' cottages on ASU Site No 4, near Doncombe, were taken over for the purpose.

Parties and dances became a regular feature of life on the Camp. A small informal party was held in the Officers' Mess on 1st August 1941 for the officers of No 316 (Polish) Squadron on the eve of their departure. Other units were given a similar send off. On 3rd September 1941 the Sergeants' Mess held a dance that was also attended by a number of officers including the Station Commander, Group Captain Harvey, accompanied by his wife. The hospitality was returned the following December when the Officers' Mess entertained the members of the Sergeants' Messes of both Colerne and Charmy Down. On 21st November an Airmen's Dance was held at the Pavilion in Bath with Colerne's Station Dance Band playing to a large audience. On Christmas Day 1941 the airmen were given a full Christmas meal together with beer, minerals and cigarettes. In the evening a dinner was held in the Officers' Mess which was thrown open to lady guests. The Stations of Rudloe and Colerne jointly held a subscription dance in Ashwicke Hall to see the New Year in. Some 200 guests attended. Only the writer of the Station Diary seems to have been lacking the festive mood. "The month, December 1941, has been exceptionally quiet and there is little of real interest to report. The slow, and what must be regarded as normal progress in the completion of the Station and provision of work and services has continued, but apart from the change in routine occasioned by Christmas festivities, generally speaking one day has been much like another."

Colerne personnel also attended dances at other bases. On one such occasion, in June 1944, service women from Colerne went to an American organised dance at Warminster. However, at about 11.45 pm, while on their way back, the American truck in which they were travelling was in an accident with a second truck, on the road

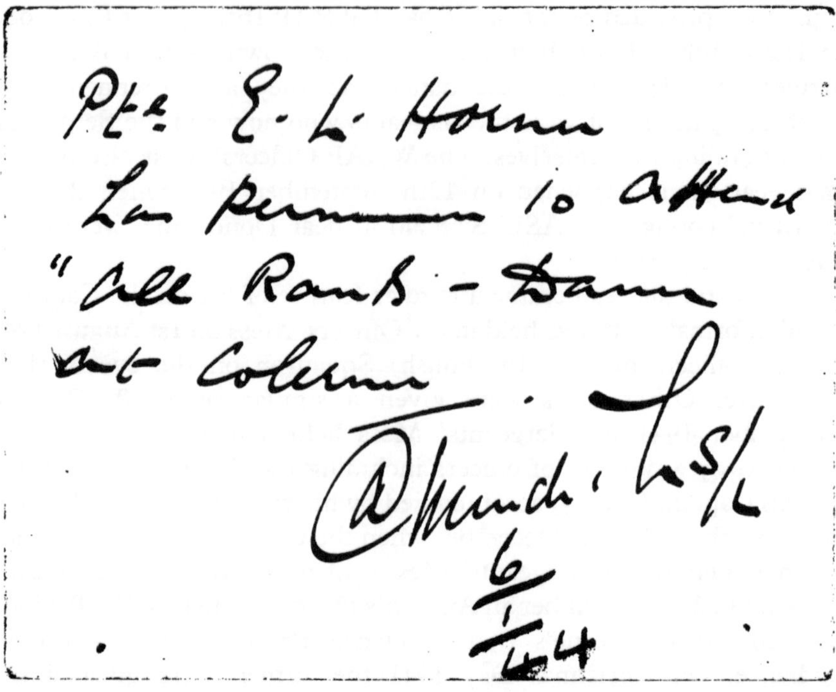

Pte. E. L. Horner
has permission to attend
"All Ranks" - Dance
at Colerne
[illegible] S/L
6/1/44

Fig 97 Pass allowing Pte Horner (ATS) to attend dance at RAF Colerne (E L Hitch)

between Warminster and Bath. Thirteen ATS and four WAAF were taken to Box sick quarters. Six were detained but 'severe shock' was luckily the worst effect of this incident.

Wing Commander Wooliams of No 39 MU remembers that for this unit at least having time for recreation was not always easy. "They used to play football and that sort of thing when they had time. We sometimes had a cocktail party, but rarely, we were so terribly busy. We were working day and night to get the aircraft out as quickly as we possibly could."

Service weddings were always a highlight of the Station's social scene. On 12th January 1942 Flight Lieutenant Roscoe of No 87 Squadron married Section Officer Brock, Senior Cypher Officer, at Colerne Parish Church. They were married by the Station Padre, Squadron Leader A Raley. The bride was given away by her father,

Air Commodore Brock DSO, and the best man was the CO of No 87 Squadron, Squadron Leader Smallwood. The reception was held at Ashwicke Hall and was attended by a large number of officers. But, as so often happens in war, pleasure can quickly turn to sorrow. In February, while on exercise, Flight Lieutenant Roscoe flew into power lines and was killed. The Station Diary records crashes both of Colerne-based aircraft and of others that came down in the sector area. Sadly such crashes were not uncommon.

RAF Colerne was a community in which there was birth as well as death. On 3rd March 1942 Mrs Harvey, the wife of the outgoing Station Commander, gave birth to a son. Five days later Mrs Donaldson, the wife of the Acting Station Commander, Wing Commander A H Donaldson DFC AFC, had a daughter. A week later on the 18th Mrs Fieldsend, wife of Squadron Leader Fieldsend, the Senior Controller, gave birth to a son.

Another off-duty distraction on the camp was the ENSA concert parties, which Wing Commander Wooliams recalls, "used to come fairly frequently." One such was *Cafe Colette*, performed on 3rd July 1941. Plays were also staged by the Colerne Amateur Dramatic Society. Their offerings in 1945, in the Station Cinema, included three one-act plays by Noel Coward and a performance of *The Ghost Train*. By 1945 entertainment was provided on a large scale. On the afternoon of 20th April an All Ranks Dance was held in the newly re-floored and re-decorated Dance Hall. This was followed by a cabaret show provided by five London artistes, with no fewer than 1200 personnel of all ranks attending. Afterwards Mrs E M Donaldson, the Station Commander's wife, presented prizes.

Sport was, of course, an integral part of service life. Among the more unusual sporting competitions held was one in March 1942 when a men's team with an average age of 46, and none under 40, took on a WAAF team at hockey and won 4-nil. In a return match a week later the over-40s again won, this time 7-nil.

In 1945, with the end of the war in sight, much attention was given to the future. Lectures were given on Release and Resettlement. By October, 80 'Educational and Vocational Training' classes were being run, with over 1000 students enrolled. A staff of 22 full-time and part-time instructors were employed. By 1945 'current affairs' too had a

Fig 98 Pilots of 501 Squadron formed their own model aircraft club (IWM CH 2818)

more pressing and political feel with a General Election expected. On 12th April 1945 Group Captain Viscount Stansgate PC DSO DFC "visited the Station and talked to all officers and a large number of airmen and airwomen about the many aspects of home and international affairs, including the Dumbarton Oaks and San Francisco Conferences".[20]

Guests and gardens

By the spring of 1941 RAF Colerne was judged to be in a fit state for a royal visit. This occurred on 24th August when Queen Mary (mother of the then king, George VI) arrived, accompanied by the Duchess of Beaufort, Lady Cynthia Colville and a Major Coke. This was not

[20] Stansgate had been a minister in Ramsay MacDonald's Labour government and was to be appointed the first Secretary of State for Air in Clement Attlee's government. Tony Benn MP is his son. The Dumbarton Oaks and San Francisco Conferences were concerned with the creation of the United Nations.

Fig 99 HM Queen Mary visiting Colerne (17 April 1943) accompanied by G/C M B Hamilton and W/C W G Wooliams (W G Wooliams)

Queen Mary's only visit to the station. It seems she passed through occasionally when visiting Badminton and she made a second official visit on 17th April 1943. On this occasion she was accompanied by her Lady in Waiting, Lady Airlie, and Equerry, Captain Lord Claud Hamilton. Wing Commander Wooliams remembers the occasion. "They looked around the aircraft and we gave them tea in the Mess."

There were other royal visitors to Colerne during these years. The king's brother Group Captain the Duke of Kent toured the Station on 16th July 1942 and took an interest in both the domestic and operational aspects of the camp, especially in the Mosquito aircraft.[21] Their sister Princess Mary, the Princess Royal, visited on 27th November 1943. The princess was accompanied by the Director of the

[21] The following month, on 25th August 1942, the Duke of Kent was killed in an aircraft crash in Scotland while *on active service*.

ATS and their tour included an inspection of the ATS detachment on the camp. On 18th July 1942 Prince Bernhard of the Netherlands landed and was met by AOC No 10 Group, Air Vice Marshal Orlebar, and by the Station Commander.

The Secretary of State for Air, Sir Archibald Sinclair, visited the Station on 8th May 1943 to carry out a short inspection but his itinerary was disrupted by the now notorious Colerne weather and the planned programme had to be cut short. Some less august visitors came in strength. On 9th August 1941 the Station entertained some 700 members of the Royal Observer Corps. They were shown various types of aircraft before being entertained by an aerobatic display by a Spitfire piloted by none other than Group Captain Stainforth. Later they were provided with tea and selected groups visited the Operations Room, to which they provided vital information, and had flights in a de Havilland Dominie aircraft.

Colerne was the base for No 10 Group Communications Flight. This provided an air taxi service for the Air Officer Commanding and his officers and ensured a regular stream of visitors passing through Colerne on their way to and from Group HQ.

Visits by senior serving officers, Army as well as Air Force, were frequent but one officer, although 'retired', ranks as a VIP visitor. This was the 'Father of the RAF', Marshal of the Royal Air Force Viscount Trenchard GCB GCVO DSO DCL LLD. Although not officially active in the Air Force since 1929, Trenchard remained the most senior member of the RAF until his death in 1956 and was, during the war, still a figure of great authority in his medal-bedecked uniform. On 22nd July 1944 he arrived by air from St Davids, then lunched in the Officers' Mess before continuing his journey to Hendon. More than two years earlier, on 29th March 1942, Lord Trenchard had made his first visit to the Station. On this occasion, before lunching, he addressed the officers and aircrew who were attending a talk given by Flight Lieutenant Shaw on his escape from a German prison camp.

On 12th March 1944 two members of No 157 Squadron visited Colerne to give a talk on their experience "after ditching in the Bay of Biscay." Talks on work-related topics were of course common but so too were those classed as 'current affairs'. Among these was one given in June 1942 by M Paul Bartel on "The Secret Army in France."

Certainly amongst the more unusual talks must have been one given on 6th June 1941 when "Captain Knight, the well-known owner of eagles, attended the Station and delivered a lecture."

A lecture which, it seems, had more effect on the Station than most, was given on 16th April 1942, when Flight Lieutenant Rawnsey talked about Fighter Command's agricultural policy! The following month the Station Diary recorded, "A widespread interest is now being taken in the cultivation of land on the Station. At the moment there are over 5 acres of gardens under production. Frequent talks are heard over the tannoy on aspects of gardening and its national importance, and the scheme is meeting with an enthusiastic response." In July the Station was informed that it had been adjudged to have the best garden in No 10 Group's Unit Garden Competition. On 14th April 1944 Mr R A Guyatt, the Air Ministry's Horticultural Adviser, visited Colerne. By this date over 20 acres of the airfield were under cultivation and some 70 pigs were being reared. At a major (100 per cent) Station Parade, held on 20th July 1945, Colerne was presented with the Fighter Command Unit Gardens Challenge Trophy for the best gardens in the Command in 1944. A quoted figure of 50 tons of vegetable foodstuff was produced that year. It is a little ironic that the nation's Dig for Victory campaign should have caused some of the land, so recently taken from agricultural use, to be returned to cultivation.

Food, friction and friends

Food was of course a matter of great importance. Joan Mortley, a 23-year-old Cardiff girl, joined up in September 1940. After a short time at the WAAF Initial Training Depot at West Drayton, in Middlesex, she travelled to Melksham for Trade Training as a Cook. On completion of about two months training she found herself one of twelve women posted to Colerne. At that time, at the end of 1940, the camp had no WAAF accommodation at all, so she and the others found billets in the village and walked to the camp daily. But within a year the hutment sites at Thickwood had been built and Joan moved to WAAF Site No 3. She then remembers cycling to work on the camp. Food was prepared in the big hangars as well as in the main cook house. "We catered for several hundred per sitting." The cooks worked in shifts. Providing food on a night-fighter base was a 24-hour-a-day task. Not only the aircrew but ground crew, controllers and many others had to be fed at all hours, but Joan says "It was fun." And it seems the airmen and women did not have cause for complaint, "There was no rationing on the camp, we had plenty of food." On 8th August 1942 Joan married Joe Long, a member of thc ground crew of No 264 Squadron, at Colerne Parish Church. She bought her wedding dress in Bath. Friends donated clothing coupons and she had some extra from the RAF. She remembers too that she had a cake, "But only a small one – one tier." They moved into married quarters in Bath, but when Joe was posted to Cornwall, Joan moved back to the camp. Of her five years' work at the camp she says, "They were good days. . . . We had a wonderful time at Colerne."

Another source of food for personnel on the camp was provided by a W V S mobile canteen from Vale Court, residence of Captain James Bowes-Lyon, a cousin of the queen. The van travelled around the camp twice a day providing drinks and extra food for the troops. Alan Coward, then an airman on the camp, remembers the visits when Captain Bowes-Lyon's wife was serving:

> She used to come around to the aerodrome during the war in the W V S van – they used to lift the top. You used to have a cup of tea and two wads [buns]. And then if you were lucky sometimes we used to get chocolate. You used to get four ounce and the little two ounce bars. The aircrew used to line up in one queue and we, the ground crew, in another. There was a little cockney fellow queuing in front of me. She was giving all the big bars to the aircrew and we were getting all the little bars. So when this chap got up to the front he said to her, "Can I have a block of that democracy chocolate." She said, "What do you mean?" He said, "Well all the big ones are going that side and all the little ones are coming this side." She said, "Do you know who I am? I'm the Honourable Lady Bowes-Lyon, related to the queen", or something like that. "I don't care about that", he said, "It's about time we had some of those big bars of chocolate coming our side." "What's your name?" He got put on a charge and confined to barracks.

Joan Mortley remembers an occasion that she too got into trouble. "We went out to Castle Combe on our bikes. I said, 'Don't get on your bikes till you get out of the village.' Of course we [did]. A policeman came out of the bushes. Caught us for cycling with our lights on in [the blackout]. They stopped us a month's privileges. We were going to go to Wales, the other girl was Welsh, from Newport. We were going to her twenty-first birthday but that was all cancelled, we had to sign-in every day."

Another Colerne WAAF, Violet Rymer, also remembers trips to the famous Wiltshire beauty spot. "Sometimes one or two of us hitch-hiked to Castle Combe and patronised the one and only shop. Here we bought pasties and cakes from 'Mrs Cooked Meats' as we called her." She recalls too her arrival at Colerne and a fortuitous meeting.

> I remember gathering at Gloucester after my calling-up papers for the WAAF had arrived. There seemed to be vast numbers of us doing tests of all kinds. We were measured and issued with uniforms. Then came a long train journey to Morecambe, an ideal place for 'square bashing' up and down the prom (which seemed never ending!) regardless of the storms and high seas. Five of us shared a billet – my friend and I were in the attic. We had to work out who was getting dressed first and what we should do to keep the skylight open or shut, accordingly must we suffocate or perish with cold? The day came when we were summoned to a very large hall to receive our postings and the officer who spoke rather quickly seemed to say to me "Coloque" – it was of course Colerne. I don't think many of us had much idea where that was! We went by train to Bath and then Box. From here our transport lorry rumbled up the country road through the village of Colerne and up to the Camp. And so to the Nissen huts – on the iron bedsteads we had 'biscuits' [square mattresses] and rough army blankets, but you can get used to anything really. The wash rooms were across the road and before the cold weather set in we sent for warm boots.
>
> One morning I attended a service held in one of the big hangars. We had been told a new RAF chaplain had just come to the Camp and that he was splendid. The hangar was packed and the service had a profound effect on me. Suddenly I heard a voice saying "And I said to myself, I Derick Greeves . . . " My thoughts raced ahead – of course this was where my school friend would be, who married an RAF chaplain. I decided to lose no more time, found the officers' quarters and the door marked "Padre." I had barely had time to wonder whether to salute, give my number or . . . ? The door opened and a voice said, "You must be Vi. Have you a bike? If not we'll borrow one. We have a cottage in the village and you will find Nan there with Roger crawling around on the floor."

Fig 100 Wedding of WAAF cook Joan Mortley and airman Joe Long, 8 August 1942 (J Long)

Fig 101 Cooks at Colerne (J Long)

The role of the WAAF was in fact a very important one. By the end of the war they worked in 89 trades, including those of flight mechanic, fitter, electrician, radar mechanic and wireless mechanic. Across RAF bases in Britain as a whole they made up something like 22 per cent of personnel, a figure borne out by the manning at Colerne on 1st December 1944:

	Officers	Senior NCOs	Other ranks	Total
RAF	82	250	2739	3071
WAAF	15	22	907	944
				4015

Victory

On Tuesday 8th May 1945, VE Day, the war in Europe officially ended. At 1100 hrs the Station Commander announced over the Station's tannoy system that the Prime Minister would broadcast to the nation at 1500 hrs. He also announced the arrangements he and the Senior Administrative Officer, Squadron Leader F R Offord, had made to allow the Station's personnel to celebrate. These included two special performances of the film *Rebecca* in the Station Cinema and a VE Day All Ranks Dance in the Station Dance Hall. On the 9th the cinema was open all day, with three performances given, and an athletics meeting was held in the afternoon. In the evening some 1500 personnel attended an All Ranks Dance with free beer and refreshments. On Saturday 12th, a VE Dance was held at Ashwicke Hall and was attended by some 250 officers and guests. "It is worthy of record" the Station Diary states "to say that during this memorable month with the celebrations which immediately followed the announcement of VE Day, airmen and airwomen of all ranks had a most joyous time at this Station and behaved themselves in an exemplary manner worthy of the highest traditions of the Royal Air Force. During VE Day and the four succeeding days not a single case of bad behaviour was witnessed or reported at Colerne." The Station Sick Quarters reported "Casualties were very small consisting of one airman with concussion and abrasions of face, having come off his bicycle into a wall [while] under the influence and one airman with minor lacerations of the thumb from a broken bottle."

Sunday 13th was Victory Sunday. In the morning an officer and 50 other ranks took part in a parade in the village, followed at 1100 hrs, by a service in the parish church. Squadron Leader Offord took the salute at the march past which consisted of contingents of Home Guard and defence organisations as well as the Air Force personnel. In the afternoon Colerne provided a contingent of an RAF officer and 50 other ranks and a WAAF officer and 50 WAAF other ranks for a service at Bath Abbey. After the service there was a march past. At the saluting base were the Mayor of Bath and senior naval, army and air force officers including Colerne's Commanding Officer.

There were other occasions to celebrate in 1945. On 6th June a half day holiday was given to commemorate the anniversary of D Day. The Japanese surrender was announced by the Prime Minister, Mr Attlee, at midnight on 14th August. Thanksgiving services were held on the Station the following day, as was another All Ranks Victory Dance. The 15th, together with the next day, was declared a VJ holiday.

In May 1945, with the end of the European war, peace time schedules of working hours were introduced on the Station. This allowed more time for recreational activities. Sport came even more to the fore. In 1946 the Station Diary records that swimming and water polo took place every Wednesday and that mixed swimming was organised on Fridays at the pool in Bath. Netball, badminton, squash and tennis were played with the Station courts in great demand. The Station cricket team did not have a successful season that year although the football team seemed to hold their own. RAF Colerne also fielded hockey and rugby teams. Some units at Colerne also had their own teams. On 15th June the football teams of No 39 MU and Colerne village met and drew one-all.

Impact on the village

How did the construction of the airfield affect the village? The physical changes, the change in the pattern of employment and the relative prosperity it brought has already been mentioned. Businesses in the village also had a boost to their trade. For example the blind newsagent Johnny Savine, who lived in Ogbourne, extended his business to include the Camp. Pete Sheppard recalls that the bus which brought construction workers up from Bath used to drop the papers off at the top of Silver Street, "I used to pick them up and put them on a little trolley and take them to Johnny Savine." Pete Sheppard delivered newspapers to Sunley workers along Doncombe Lane. Norman Alford also had a paper round delivering to Thickwood and Lucknam. After delivering to the regular customers he quickly sold the remaining papers to the troops, "Needless to say the Daily Mirror was always the favourite because of the ongoing antics of 'Jane', a cartoon which appeared daily." His round was quite lucrative; he recalls that at one time a field at Thickwood was completely occupied by Canadian troops under canvas. "These men were always good for American chewing gum and the occasional packet of twenty Canadian cigarettes, which were discreetly smoked, although I was under age at the time."

The village Post Office was run by Vernon and Sarah Notton and the service men and their wives had to use it to draw their allowances and savings.[22] Mrs Dowding, then Patricia Wale, remembers the wives queuing up for the Post Office to open, "Colerne Post Office was then upgraded. It had to provide more services. Mr Notton's salary was increased by the Post Office. There were different grades of sub-post master." This was often a first point of call for newly arrived personnel. Cyril Rogers remembers his arrival at Colerne in 1940.

> We came to Box railway station. There was no transport on the camp seemingly and we had to walk all the way up Tutton Hill with all our kit. Our first visit was to the Post Office to let my parents know what part of the country I was in. Of course I got talking to Mrs Notton, she was Welsh, I'm Welsh and we had a good old chin wag. Before I left there she gave me a big piece of Dundee cake. We were friends always after that!

Gaisford's nursery provided flowers for weddings of service personnel. Joan Mortley, the WAAF Corporal Cook who married Joe Long of the RAF, obtained her bouquet from Gaisford's.

[22] There was no Post Office on the camp until one was opened in 1964. Mr Notton became postmaster of this too.

The two village pubs, The Fox and Hounds and the Six Bells were popular haunts. The Six Bells, affectionately referred to as 'The Clangers', was run by a Mr Kelly. Joan Long remembers the Six Bells as "our pub" and Wing Commander Wooliams recalls his 'troops' also frequented 'The Clangers.' Beer, like so much else, was in short supply; it came in on Wednesday and was sold out on Friday.

Voluntary groups extended hospitality to the service personnel. As we have seen, a mobile canteen from Vale Court travelled around the camp twice a day providing extras for the troops. The Evangelical chapel also helped sustain the men and women of the armed forces. They initially opened a canteen in Chapel Path but later the pastor, Mr Matthews, was offered the use of one of the huts on Living Site No 4, by the Station CO. Nancy Fletcher worked there, "It became known as 'Holy Joe's Place.' I used to cut up about twelve huge loaves every day making Oxo sandwiches and the airmen would come in at night. We made no charge, they could put a donation in the box if they wanted to."

Probably one of the most momentous changes was the great influx of people. Everyone who had a spare room had to take in construction workers, service personnel or evacuees. WAAF were billeted in the village before their living accommodation at Thickwood was built. Tutton Hill House was requisitioned for this purpose on 13th August 1941. There were no married quarters so married couples lived in the village. Mr and Mrs Kent, for example, rented out their house in Ogbourne to the cinema manager, Mr Grainger, and his family; steelmen, who erected the hangars, were billeted with Mr and Mrs Guy; Tim Palmer, who worked for the Cement Gun Company, lodged with Stan Gay in Tutton Hill. Several families in Box View housed men who drove the 'Queen Mary' articulated transporter lorries that brought crates of partly constructed aircraft from Box Station to the camp. These must have been quite a spectacle driving through the village! A Polish pilot lived with Mr and Mrs Jefferies of 11 High Street . . . the list is endless.

Almost everyone it seems did 'their bit.' Meals were frequently on offer, Cyril Rogers: "The people in the village were always very kind to us. We used to go out to lunch almost every Sunday. The Camp

Fig 102 Members of 256 Squadron outside the Six Bells, March 1941 (Postcard sent to F Webb from New Zealand)

Fig 103 Group of WAAFs outside Six Bells (J Long)

showed their kindness in return." Joan Champion remembers her mother, Mrs Tanner who lived in the High Street, having service men in for meals. Anne Kent often had "a houseful after the pubs shut."

Village dances took place in the village school, now the Church Hall, on Friday evenings with Ted Johnson on the piano and brother Jack on drums. Service people would be invited to these 'hops'. There was a reciprocal arrangement with the camp. Patricia Dowding remembers "You could go to dances on the camp and to the cinema if someone met you at the gate." Pete Sheppard also recalls walking to Thickwood for dances in the Nissen huts. Mrs Merry of Lucknam Park gave occasional dances for service personnel as well as civilians.The coming of the camp provided endless interest for the young lads of Colerne, spending many hours at the airfield getting to know the aircraft. Men from the RAF became involved with the life of the school, helping with sport and plays and even teaching classes.

The Colerne platoon of the Home Guard used the camp's firing range in North Wood. They also received extra training, two or three times a week, from the Suffolk Regiment, when that unit was based at Ashwicke.

Not all the influence the camp exerted on the village was positive. The bus service for instance proved to be very frustrating. Villagers recall having to queue at the crash barrier at the entrance to Lucknam on a Saturday at least an hour before the bus was due, to be sure of getting on. At a Parish Council meeting on 11th February 1942 the Clerk was asked to write to Bath Tramways about the unsatisfactory bus service. Villagers were being left behind in both Colerne and Bath. The RAF were also to be approached on the question of providing their own transport for their men. Bath Tramways did respond by providing two extra buses but an inadequate and over-subscribed bus service was a recurrent theme throughout these years.

Initially the construction work and then the constant activity of aircraft, both night and day, shattered the peace of the village, but as Pat Dowding recalls "We didn't notice after a while." The air raids, however, were quite a different matter. Mrs Rogers, then Mary Foster, found them very frightening:

When the sirens went we always had a bag or a small case packed. If it got

> too noisy and if we could hear too many bombs in the distance I used to get up, my mum didn't nor did my sister but I did. I used to meet my friend down the road, Mrs Seale. She had a baby. We used to go down Widdenham Lane and get underneath the hedges. We did this several times when it got too bad and the sky used to be absolutely alight with flares. I just used to panic. We used to stay underneath the hedge, wrapped in blankets until the all clear went. We weren't the only ones. There used to be sometimes about twenty or thirty down there.

Mary Guy, who was living at Rockfield at the time, remembers one night the sky was so lit up that you could stand outside and read the newspaper. An enemy plane had dropped a series of flares in advance of a bombing raid, which on this occasion did not materialise.

The bodies of two German airmen were found amongst the crops in one of George Gifford's fields (in which the landing lights were later placed). These men were buried in the village churchyard, but later exhumed and returned to the Continent.

There were a few incidents of deviant behaviour by airmen which were recorded in the minutes of the Parish Council. At a meeting on 9th October 1940 one councillor reported holes had been dug in the Recreation Ground and he believed that they had been used, presumably as latrines, by men in the RAF hut close by. On 25th September 1941 a complaint was made that members of the forces used the street and some private yards as urinals especially after dances and after public houses closed.

The Station Diary entry for 29th August 1943 notes that a small boy in the village was burnt with a smoke bomb during "a Para and Invasion" exercise.

The building of the airfield and the arrival of a new community appears to have had little effect on the members of the Parish Council. Despite the enormity of the events happening to their village, their concerns continued to be parochial in the extreme. Incredibly, there is no mention in the Parish records of the construction of the aerodrome until 16th October 1939 when the council resolved to write to the Rural District Council complaining that the Air Ministry had not given them due notice of the closure of the footpaths across the aerodrome site! It was obviously difficult to dissuade the inhabitants of Colerne from using their former rights of way because even in June

1940 there were complaints made, to the Council, that people were still trying to use them!

A good thing

At the beginning of the twentieth century Colerne's population was in decline. It had fallen from 1060 in 1901 to 844 by 1931. Agriculture and stoneworks at Box and Corsham were the only sources of male employment. Colerne was a run down village. Mr Billett, then a regular visitor, remembers that there were many empty properties in Colerne when he was a boy. The arrival of the camp changed all that. By 1951, the population had risen to 2035 and it continued to grow. As well as the transient population many airmen and WAAF married villagers and made their homes here.

What of the dispossessed? The evictions, at the time, were undoubtedly very traumatic, and for the older Henry Knight the final blow, but most of the families went on to rebuild their lives. Henry and Linda Knight first rented, then went on to buy, a farm at Wellow. Mr Pope and Harold Marsh moved to Church Marsh Farm near Calne. Tom Pullen eventually gained the tenancy of a farm at Ford. His daughter recalls, "Afterwards my father wished he'd moved years ago. It was a much superior house, a much nicer sort of place altogether."

Mrs Mortimer described Colerne before the war as a very narrow-minded community and, perhaps because it was geographically isolated, its concerns were certainly very parochial. The arrival of the airfield, the war and the immense influx of people challenged the long-established way of life. Some village men employed on airfield construction moved with their firms to other parts of the country. Men and women from many different parts of the world including America, Australia, Canada, Poland and the West Indies, came to this small out-of-the-way village. The village itself became more accessible. Air Force snow ploughs would clear the roads quickly in a bad winter, as the RAF required good communications. The bus service, although a constant source of complaint, would improve. The RAF did quite literally put Colerne on the map.

The aerodrome brought prosperity to the village. Airfield workers were relatively well paid. Businesses thrived and lodgers put money in villagers' pockets.

Lifelong friendships were made. Pete Sheppard remembers the wartime years with affection, "I know there was a war on, but the number of people that were here, it was friendly, closer together somehow. I don't know why." Anne Kent says "We got to know so many people." People who were stationed here still return. Nancy Fletcher recalls that when the Evangelical Church celebrated its 150th Anniversary in 1974 "no end of airmen came back." Many people still remember their time at Colerne with affection. Former WAAF Violet Rymer rekindled fond memories on a visit in 1993. "I stayed with my cousin in Bath, and her friend drove us to Colerne. It was like old times to see the perimeter, stop at the Guard Room and joke with them. We went on our way to Castle Combe, sleepy and attractive as ever. We sat in the sun on the bridge enjoying our ice creams – what a day of memories for me."

One can only speculate about what Colerne would have become without the Camp. Perhaps it would have virtually disappeared apart from a few farms and country retreats for the wealthy. Instead it survived and thrived. A larger school was needed to accommodate the airforce as well as village children. It provided continuing employment for Colerne people . . . and with pensions! The present sewage treatment plant, built by the Air Ministry, was sold to the Rural District Council. The presence of the airfield led to the construction of the 'New Road' by-pass to Colerne. The Parish Council were looking at proposals for a new road to replace the 'Back Road' as early as 1946, although it did not become a reality until the early 1960s. Colerne also has the RAF to thank for affordable housing; the former married quarters now relinquished by the Ministry of Defence.

Cordial relations between village and RAF continued right up to 1976 when the station closed. The RAF supported village activities and the pensioners enjoyed their splendid Christmas meals.

Villagers interviewed about the camp unanimously declared it "a good thing."

Appendix 1

Equivalent Officer Ranks

Royal Air Force	WAAF	Royal Navy	Army
Marshal of the Royal Air Force		Admiral of the Fleet	Field Marshal
Air Chief Marshal		Admiral	General
Air Marshal		Vice Admiral	Lieutenant General
Air Vice Marshal		Rear Admiral	Major General
Air Commodore	Air Commandant	Commodore	Brigadier
Group Captain	Group Officer	Captain	Colonel
Wing Commander	Wing Officer	Commander	Lieutenant Colonel
Squadron Leader	Squadron Officer	Lieutenant Commander	Major
Flight Lieutenant	Flight Officer	Lieutenant	Captain
Flying Officer	Section Officer	Sub Lieutenant	Lieutenant
Pilot Officer	Assistant Section Officer		Second Lieutenant

Appendix 2

Principal Contractors Working on Colerne Airfield 28th November 1940

Allen Fairhead Ltd – Main contractor
B Sunley and Co – Concrete work, runways, etc.
Richardsons Ltd – Platelayers, plasterers
Newman and Sons Ltd – Plumbers, glaziers
Haden and Co – Hot water engineers
Constable Hart Ltd – Sub-contractors to Fairheads
J. Long and Sons – Builders
Duncan Watson Ltd – Electrical Engineers (cable laying)
Moor and Rowley Ltd – Builders
D A P S Ltd – Decorators
Downing Rudman & Bent – Builders
Cement Gun Company – Concreters
Braithwaite and Co – Structural Engineers

Appendix 3

RAF Colerne Commanding Officers

Early Camp Commanders	
Squadron Leader Chalmers	May 1940
Wing Commander R B Harrison	July 1940

Station Commanders of the Fighter Command Era	
Wing Commander C E St J Beamish DFC	September 1940
Group Captain A V Harvey	April 1941
Group Captain H M Pearson	March 1942
Group Captain H Eeles	September 1942
Group Captain M B Hamilton	March 1943
Group Captain E M Donaldson DSO AFC	December 1944
Group Captain R W Stewart OBE AFC	September 1945
Group Captain G E Sampson OBE	February 1946

RAF Fighter Squadrons Based at Colerne 1940 - 1946

Sqd	Dates	Main Equipment	Commanding Officer
87	28-Nov-40 - 11-Dec-40	Hurricane I	S/Ldr R S Mills
256	06-Feb-41 - 26-Mar-41	Defiant I	S/Ldr G H Gatherall
307	26-Mar-41 - 26-Apr-41	Defiant I	S/Ldr Grodzicki
118	05-Apr-41 - 08-Apr-41	Spitfire II	S/Ldr F J Howell DFC
501	09-Apr-41 - 25-Jun-41	Spitfire I/IIa	S/Ldr E Holden DFC
			S/Ldr Boyd DFC (3/6/41)
600	27-Apr-41 - 17-Jun-41	Beaufighter IIF	W/Cdr G H Stainforth AFC
125	16-Jun-41 - 07-Aug-41	Defiant I	S/Ldr H M Mitchell DFC
316	18-Jun-41 - 02-Aug-41	Hurricane	S/Ldr C J Donovan
		I/IIa/IIb/c	S/Ldr J Frey
317	26-Jun-41 - 27-Jun-41	Hurricane I	S/Ldr A Brzezina
600	27-Jun-41 - 06-Oct-41	Beaufighter IIF	W/Cdr G H Stainforth AFC
			W/Cdr G H M Pearson (?/10/41)
87	07-Aug-41 - 27-Jan-42	Hurricane I/IIc	S/Ldr I R Gleed
			S/Ldr D G Smallwood (?/?/41)
89	25-Sep-41 - 24-Nov-41	Beaufighter 1F	W/Cdr G H Stainforth AFC
125	25-Jan-42 - 14-May-42	Defiant I/II	S/Ldr E G Barwell
		Beaufighter IIF	W/Cdr D V Ivins
417	26-Jan-42 - 23-Feb-42	Spitfire Vb	S/Ldr C E Malfroy
263	26-Jan-42 - 11-Feb-42	Whirlwind I	S/Ldr T P Pugh DFC
402	04-Mar-42 - 17-Mar-42	Spitfire Vb	S/Ldr R E Morrow DFC
264	01-May-42 - 30-Apr-43	Defiant I/II	S/Ldr C A Cook
		Mosquito II	W/Cdr H M Kerr DFC (14/5/42)
			W/Cdr W J Alington DFC AFC (?/3/43)
19	23-Jul-42 - 31-Jul-42	Spitfire Vb	S/Ldr P R G Davies
263	15-Aug-42 - 07-Sep-42	Whirlwind I	S/Ldr R S Woodward DFC
184	01-Dec-42 - 01-Mar-43	Hurricane IId	S/Ldr J Rose DFC
456 *	16-Mar-43 - 30-Mar-43	Mosquito II	W/Cdr M H Dwyer
183	25-Mar-43 - 08-Apr-43	Typhoon Ib	S/Ldr A V Gowers DFC
175	08-Apr-43 - 29-May-43	Typhoon Ib	S/Ldr J R Pennington-Legh DFC
124 *	28-Apr-43 - 13-May-43	Spitfire VI/HF VII	S/Ldr J C Nelson (US)
151	30-Apr-43 - 16-Aug-43	Mosquito II	W/Cdr D V Ivins
		Mosquito XII	W/Cdr S P Richards AFC (?/5/43)
183	29-May-43 - 05-Jun-43	Typhoon Ib	S/Ldr A V Gowers DFC
456	17-Aug-43 - 17-Nov-43	Mosquito II/VI	W/Cdr G Howden
151	17-Nov-43 - 24-Mar-44	Mosquito XIII	W/Cdr G H Goodman DSO DFC
137	02-Jan-44 - 04-Feb-44	Typhoon Ib	S/Ldr J R Dennehey DFC
131	10-Feb-44 - 31-Mar-44	Spitfire VII	S/Ldr J J O'Meara DFC Bar
165	10-Feb-44 - 04-Apr-44	Spitfire IX	S/Ldr M E Blackstone
219	26-Mar-44 - 01-Apr-44	Mosquito XVII	W/Cdr A D McNeill Boyd DSO DFC
488	05-May-44 - 11-May-44	Mosquito XIII	W/Cdr R C Haine DFC
604	13-Jul-44 - 25-Jul-44	Mosquito XIII	W/Cdr D F Hughed DFC 2 Bars
604	28-Jul-44 - 06-Aug-44	Mosquito XIII	W/Cdr D F Hughed DFC 2 Bars
410	28-Jul-44 - 10-Sep-44	Mosquito XII/NF30	W/Cdr G A Hiltz
488	28-Jul-44 - 09-Oct-44	Mosquito XIII	W/Cdr R C Haine DFC
406	17-Sep-44 - 27-Nov-44	Mosquito NF30	W/Cdr D J Williams DSO DFC
264	30-Nov-44 - 23-Dec-44	Mosquito XIII	W/Cdr E S Smith AFC
616	17-Jan-45 - 28-Feb-45	Meteor F3	W/Cdr A McDowall DFC Bar
29	22-Feb-45 - 12-Apr-45	Mosquito NF30	W/Cdr J W Allan DSO DFC
504	28-Mar-45 - 10-Aug-45	Meteor F3	S/Ldr M Kellett DFC
74	11-May-45 - 14-Aug-46	Spitfire IX	S/Ldr A J Reeves DFC
		Meteor F3	W/Cdr H C Kennard DFC (28/5/45)
245	10-Aug-45 - 16-Aug-46	Meteor F3	S/Ldr T D Williams

* Detachments only

Sources
Interviewees and Correspondents

Mr Harry Billet, Mr Frank Champion, Mrs Joan Champion, Mr Alan Coward, Mrs Patricia Dowding, Mrs Nancy Fletcher, Mr Horace Guy, Mrs Mary Guy, Mrs Violet Hall, Mrs Eva Hitch, Mr Jack Hoskins, Mr Frank Jenkins, Wing Commander Richard Johnson, Mr Tom Kent, Mrs Anne Kent, Mr William Knight, Mrs Linda Knight, Mrs Joan Long, Mrs Margaret Mortimer, Mr Cyril Rogers, Mrs Mary Rogers, Mrs Violet Rymer, Mr Jack Scrivin, Mr Peter Sheppard, Mr Alex Sleap, Mr Robert Struthers, Mr Frank Trumper, Mrs Kate Trumper, Wing Commander Walter G Wooliams.

Published Sources

Ashworth, Chris et al *Action Stations* - 10 Vols, especially Vol 5 (Patrick Stephens 1979-1987)
Bath & Wilts Chronicle & Herald (various 1939 additions)
Battle of Britain (*The Daily Telegraph* an editorial supplement 1990)
Bowyer, Chaz *Beaufighter* (William Kimber 1987)
Brandon, Sqd Ldr Lewis DSO DFC *Night Fighter* (Goodall 1992, originally 1961)
Butler, JRM (Editor) *History of the Second World War - Defence of the United Kingdom* (HMSO 1957)
Castleden, Rodney *British History - A Chronological Dictionary of Dates* (Parragon 1994)
Deighton, Len *Fighter* (Panther 1979)
Drew, P R A *Short History of Colerne Airfield 1940-1990* (Drew 1990)
Escott, Sqd Ldr Beryl E *Women in Air Force Blue* (Patrick Stephens 1989)
Gilbert, Martin *Second World War* (Fontana 1989)
Green, William *War Planes of the Second World War* - Vols Two & Four (Macdonald 1961)
Halley, James J *The Squadrons of the Royal Air Force & Commonwealth 1918-1988* (Air-Britain 1988)
A History of Colerne (Colerne Branch of the Women's Institute)
Hunt, Lesley *The RAF and the Westcountry* (an article in *Wiltshire Life* 1968)
James, John *The Paladins - The story of the RAF up to the outbreak of World War II* (Futura 1991)
Langley, Andrew & Utting, John (Editors) *The Village on the Hill* Vol 1 (Colerne History Group 1990)
Macdonald, Charles *By Air To Battle* (Macdonald 1970)
Parkinson, Roger *Encyclopaedia of Modern War* (Paladin Granada 1979)
Rawlings, John *Fighter Squadrons of the R.A.F. and Their Aircraft* (Crecy Books 1993)
Taylor, MJH *The Aerospace Chronology* (Tri-Service Press 1980)
Wainwright, Martin *The Bath Blitz* (1992)
Willis, Steve & Holliss, Barry *Military Airfields in the British Isles 1939-1945* (Enthusiasts Publications 1987)

Other Sources

Alford, Norman *Random Memories of Colerne Airfield 1939 & On*
Colerne Yesterday Today (an RAF booklet circa 1970)
Royal Air Force Rudloe Manor - 50 Years of Service 1940 -1990 (RAF commemorative booklet)
Description of Colerne Airfield (Ministry of Defence, Air Historical Branch (RAF))
Aerodrome Improvement Board Final Report (Air 2/3993 Public Record Office, Kew)
Opening up of RAF Station Colerne 1940 (Air 2/6118 Public Record Office, Kew)
Station Diary - Royal Air Force Operations Record Book (Air 28/166 Public Record Office, Kew)
Details of Roman remains (NMR ST 87 SW 7 & 9 National Monument Record, Swindon)

Acknowledgements

Crown Copyright material is reproduced with the permission of the Controller of Her Majesty's Stationery Office.

IWM photographs are reproduced with the permission of the Trustees of the Imperial War Museum, London.

The Junior Leaders Regiment at Colerne

A Personal Memoir

David Coates

The posting order to Colerne came as a pleasant surprise. After three years of Garrison life on the North German plain, the chance to work in the West of England, within easy reach of home came as a welcome change. The letter was quite specific: "Azimghur Barracks Colerne, as Chaplain to the Junior Leaders Regiment Royal Corps of Transport." A quick consultation with the road atlas confirmed that this hitherto unknown community was a very promising looking village on the extreme southern end of the Cotswolds within striking distance of Bath. The type of Regiment, Junior Leaders, promised two great advantages: first, it would absorb all my available energies and would thus be the only Army Unit I should be called upon to serve, and second, there would be plenty of regular block leave periods offering at long last the chance of more frequent visits to my much neglected cottage.

A few weeks later, in the early summer of 1979, I was flown home from Germany to attend a course, and managed to undertake my first reconnaissance of the village on the hill and the surrounding countryside which were to become so familiar to me over the next dozen or so years. The Barracks' former status as an active RAF Station was still much in evidence, right down to a set of derelict traffic lights which had until recently guarded against any conflict of interests between users of the mile long main runway and the lane from the village to the Camp gate. A month or two later, calling in to drop off some of my luggage at the Mess, I met the Commanding Officer who kindly gave up an afternoon of his leave to show me around. At once I was impressed by the sense of space and the spectacular views which unfolded on every side as we drove round the disused runways. Our final port of call was the Church of England church. (I was pleased to note that the Camp had two other places of worship!) This, my guide observed as we scanned the very long and narrow interior, would test my powers as a preacher to the full. Holding the attention and goodwill of the 350 teenage boys in such a building would not be easy.

Driving away through the lanes, it occurred to me that this beautiful corner of Wiltshire was not after all such an incongruous site for an army camp; two thousand years ago the Fosse Way, now a narrow lane, then a vital military road, must have been familiar ground to generations of Roman soldiers. Now the soldiers were back.

The closure of the Royal Air Force Station must have come as a bitter blow to the people of Colerne. The once busy airfield fell silent, jobs vital to the village economy vanished overnight, married quarters were suddenly unoccupied and long-standing friends moved on to new postings. Worst of all, with the departure of the aircraft and the workforce which had maintained them, the huge airfield complex which for well over thirty years had played so important a part in the life of the hilltop community, abruptly lost its reason for existence. Inevitably, the slow but steady process of decay began. It must have seemed as if even the village itself would soon begin to slip back into its pre-war isolation.

Happily for all concerned, a welcome reprieve was soon announced. The erstwhile airfield was to suffer the fate common to so many other redundant RAF stations and was to be handed over to the Army for use as a barracks. At least then, some form of life would continue. The first occupants of the Army's new acquisition were destined to be the Junior Leaders Regiment of the Royal Corps of Transport. They arrived in the autumn of 1978 to take over what had by now been given the rather exotic sounding name of 'Azimghur Barracks Colerne', recalling an act of heroism during the Indian Mutiny. The incoming Regiment had previously spent many years in a large wooden-hutted camp at Norton Fitzwarren near Taunton, now deemed inferior to Colerne with its brick-built accommodation blocks, vast aircraft hangars and seemingly endless sports fields. Another, perhaps surprising, factor in the decision to move to Colerne was its more central location, at least in relation to the rest of the Army in southern England.

The new Regiment was part of what was then known as the Junior Army, the purpose of which was to enlist school leavers and to give them a year's military training whilst at the same time continuing their general education. After three terms at Colerne, successful recruits would move on to a separate squadron at Driffield in North Humberside to complete the transition into the adult Army whilst learning to drive heavy vehicles at the nearby Army School of Mechanical Transport (itself occupying another ex-RAF station at Leconfield). In short, the Regiment could best be described as a kind of military boarding school. The permanent staff who were posted in from other parts of the Army in the normal way, included not only members of the Royal Corps of Transport, but others such as the Royal Army Educational Corps and the Army Physical Training Corps who manned the Military Studies Wing and the Gymnasium respectively. As a posting, Colerne was popular, chiefly because of its location and the regular and generous block leave periods. In addition to the military staff, the Regiment employed a number of civilian 'Burnham Lecturers' to help with the teaching in the Military Studies Wing, as well as many local people in various capacities.

Once the Regiment had become established in its new home, it quickly settled into a fairly relaxed routine. Long crocodiles of Junior Leaders learning to ride motorcycles became a familiar sight in the local area, as did cars from a well-known driving school, each with its complement of three uniformed occupants in the care of a civilian instructor. The camp itself was busy again; from time to time the peace of the countryside being disturbed by small-arms fire from the range and by go-carts on hobbies evenings, of which there were two each week. The sails of land-yachts were to be seen tacking to and fro on the runways which at other times saw light aircraft staggering into the air laden with novice parachutists. The 'new' control tower by the water towers eventually became the home of the Silver Stars parachute display team who would sometimes descend in free fall, only opening their canopies at the very last moment. Small groups of breathless soldiers in combat uniform undergoing endurance tests were often seen on local roads. From time to time there would be an opportunity

Fig 104 Junior Leaders – training (JLR RCT/RAOC)

Fig 105 Junior Leaders – recreation (JLR RCT/RAOC)

for the Army to make itself useful to the village community, as for example with their efforts at snow-clearance during the winter of 1986. Each year, just before Christmas, a party was held in the barracks for elderly people from the village who were brought in by coach and given tea and entertainment by Junior Leaders and members of the permanent staff.

The first major change came at the beginning of 1986 when a Company of Junior Leaders from the Royal Army Ordnance Corps arrived to form part of an augmented Regiment renamed 'The Junior Leaders Regiment RCT/RAOC.' The routine of life in the Regiment continued relatively undisturbed until the end of the 'Cold War' and the fall of the Berlin Wall dictated changes in the country's defence needs. A few members of the permanent staff went to the Gulf War, during which the Regiment had the sad task of organising the funeral of a former Junior Leader who had died as a result of an accident while serving with the British contingent.

The full force of the changes ahead became evident with the publication of the 'Options for Change' proposals for the slimming down of the armed forces in the new climate which followed the collapse of the Warsaw Pact. It soon became clear that the Junior Army could no longer be afforded and that recruitment and initial training were to be rationalised and reduced in scale. The first redundancy scheme was announced and many were faced with the prospect of leaving what they had always regarded as a secure career for an uncertain future in civilian life.

The first cuts in the Regiment's budget led to the end of one of the three RCT squadrons and such costly activities as driver training. This was followed by a process of gradual decline which led to the final disbandment parade in February 1992. Many happy memories of a rewarding job carried out in the delightful surroundings of the village on the hill were tinged with sadness as the Regimental band played for the last time and the diminutive pony Taku, the Regiment's mascot, led the final batch of Colerne Junior Leaders off parade.

I had been fortunate enough to enjoy two tours of duty in Colerne. I will never forget either the people or the place.

A Naval Connection

Barrie Austin

RAF? Obviously! And now the Army – but a Naval connection with Colerne sounds altogether improbable. We can wander down Watergates but it's a long way before the Bybrook finds its way into the big sea. Yet there hangs in the Parish Council office a framed certificate headed by the Admiralty seal to commemorate the 'adoption' by the village in March 1942, halfway through the Second World War, of *HMS Cyclops*, an ageing submarine depot ship.

The ship's particulars were:

Displacement	11 300 tons
Length overall	477 ft
Beam	55 ft
Draught	21 ft
Engines	Single screw triple expansion, 3500 shp
Speed	13 knots
Coal capacity	1600 tons
Armament	2×4-in guns (originally 6)
Complement	266 (had been as high as 314)

Cyclops had a varied career. Laid down in Sunderland in 1905 as the passenger/cargo liner *Indrabarah*, she was purchased while building and converted for Royal Navy use as a repair ship, also described as a "floating workshop and distilling ship" (not for whisky, alas – just making boiler feed and drinking water!).

She was deployed throughout the Great War in support of ships based at or visiting Scapa Flow. A notable achievement during this period was the innovative connection of a telegraph link with Kirkwall post office. She also earned a more sinister reputation for equipping 'Q' ships – innocent looking merchant vessels fitted with concealed guns, intended to lure U-boats to the surface and sink them.

Converted in Chatham in 1922 to a submarine depot ship, *Cyclops* subsequently enjoyed the peaceful role of HQ for the Malta submarine

Presented by the Lords
Commissioners of the Admiralty
to the Civil Parish of
Colerne
to commemorate the adoption of
H.M.S. CYCLOPS
during Warship Week March, 1942

Fig 106 The 'Adoption Certificate' (Colerne Parish Council)

squadron from 1926 to 1938. The outbreak of World War Two found her in Harwich, whence she was moved as hostilities hotted up to Rothesay (Bute) as "depot ship of a new 7th Submarine Flotilla under the command of Captain Longsden now in command of that ship".[1]

The primary function of this flotilla was for training submarine officers and ratings, including 'chariot' crews, and also in anti-submarine warfare. Alistair Mars in *British Submarine at War* says "Clustered around *Cyclops*, a veteran depôt ship from the First World War, were a few old crocks, part of the motley bunch of elderly submarines in which all training had to be carried out". Commander E P Young, in *One of Our Submarine*s, says that only the wartime shortage of shipping had saved old *Cyclops* (known as the 'Cycle-box') from the scrap heap. Once a year she was taken to sea on exercise, to disprove the rumour that she was aground on a self-made reef of empty tins.

In this role she served for the duration, being adopted the while by Colerne and neighbours. She returned home to be paid off in 1945 and was broken up in Newport in 1947.

Being a coal burner, everyone who served in or near the ship will have memories, of which the following are no doubt typical. "I still have memories of coaling ship on *Cyclops* from sunrise to sunset, continuously for 2–3 days up to the eyeballs in coal dust all day, and in the afternoon the issue of lime juice to wash the dust down, drinking this and, from the boat deck, watching Captain Conway doing his stint in the collier, too".[2]

Another recollection, albeit apocryphal, is of a Northumbrian Chief Engineer being promoted, but with the clothing store bereft of 'brass hats.' It is said that a young destroyer commander had cause to complain to *Cyclops*' captain about a casually dressed Geordie leaning on the taffrail as his ship's bridge drew level while coming alongside, demanding "where did you get that nice new hat?" One wonders how soothed he might have been to hear "It seems you have just met my Commander(E)!"

Research back home reveals that Colerne's certificate was not the only one, *Cyclops* having technically been adopted by several parishes

[1] Signal from Vice-Admiral Submarines to Admiralty, 23 June 1940
[2] Letter from Mr Bob Mundy to SM Museum Curator, 31 Oct 1986

Fig 107 *HMS Cyclops* (RN Submarine Museum)

in Chippenham and District during their allocated 'Warship Week.' *The Wiltshire Times* of Saturday March 14, 1942, prints a photograph with the caption "Chippenham's Warship Week was opened on Saturday in the Market Place by Rear Admiral G R S Watkins DSO, pictured taking the salute in the parade. With him are Mayors of other towns, and officials" [presumably including the Chairman of Colerne Parish Council].

A report two weeks later says "The total amount subscribed during the Chippenham and District Warship Week, which ended on March 14th, was £246 751 0s 7d. This sum, which was announced by Alderman G L Culverwell (Chairman of the Committee) in the Market Place on Saturday evening, exceeds by £16 751 0s 7d the objective of £230 000 for the 'adoption' of the submarine depôt ship *HMS Cyclops*." The report goes on to list fifteen prizewinners in a competition for estimating the total.

In fact the paper reports over several weeks the preparations and achievements by many towns, districts and individual villages who got together to adopt various ships. Amongst advertisements for Burton's Victory Suits (£3 15s 0d) and second-hand Austin Sevens (£60) the paper reports a cable received by Trowbridge/Bradford from the Commanding Officer of *HMS Avon Vale*, saying "Your kind efforts are very much appreciated by all on board." Bromham put the £40 profit from the week's entertainments to "a Carley float [liferaft] for a Destroyer;" Sutton Benger's budget aimed for "£5000 for two naval launches." Notwithstanding Colerne's evident participation, their only mention over the period is that the WI was busy knitting "pullovers, gloves and socks, large numbers of which [were] needed for urgent despatch to Russia."

We have also established that the Admiralty badge on 'our' certificate was used generally where a print of a ship's badge was not readily available. The real thing, as one might expect for a *Cyclops*, is formally described as:

Field:	Black
Badge:	A sixteen pointed star red, bordered gold, within which an eye proper
Motto:	With eye and hand

Fig 108 Submarines alongside *Cyclops* in Rothesay (Bob Mundy)

Fig 109 PO Bob Mundy (B Mundy)

Sadly we have not been able to unearth any record of communication between the village and the ship. One can only suppose that several socks and mufflers went that way – possibly not so many of the latter since it seems that in some quarters *Cyclops* was believed to be berthed in Colombo (that was *HMS Lucia*). It would be nice to think that something more romantic might be recorded, and we should be more than pleased to hear from any reader able to contribute any information for our archive, or possibly for inclusion in a reprint.

Footnote:

Having read the draft of this article, Mr (formerly Petty Officer Ordnance Mechanic) Bob Mundy wrote to say: "During my time on *Cyclops* I cannot recall any mention of Adoption by any town, etc – pity that, the winters outboard on sub casings were mighty cold I recall, and woolly socks and scarves would, indeed, have been very welcome." (He did, however, get a 4 ft scarf from his wife's workmates at Vickers Armstrongs, and is still using it!)

The RN has one repair ship in service today, the 10 000-tonne *RFA Diligence*, which also started life in the merchant service as the Swedish-registered oilfield support ship *Stena Inspector*. Coincidentally the author, who had previously served in the depot ships *Tyne* and *Forth*, was associated with her acquisition and subsequent conversion during the Falklands conflict.

Acknowledgements

The help of The Wiltshire Record Office, Colerne Parish Council and the Royal Navy Submarine Museum, Gosport, is gratefully acknowledged.

J. Mullins and Sons: Water Finders

Lesley Yeo and Joyce Utting

The following is an extract from the *Daily Mail* of 19th March 1920.

> Have you ever asked one of those people who scoff at spiritualism how they explain water-finding? They can't do it. Here your seance room is under the open sky and your paraphernalia a hazel twig. No cabinets! No curtains! No darkness!
>
> The water-finder – or dowser, as he is called – walks slowly across country clasping his twig by its forked end, the points towards the earth. Perhaps for an hour or even more he draws a blank; and then suddenly the twig begins to twitch and jerk like a leashed hound struggling for freedom. A subterranean stream has been discovered, you are told. And in nine cases out of ten, if you care to fall-to with a shovel then and there you can prove it.
>
> The genuine water-finder's failures are so few as to be negligible.

Mullins is an old Colerne name and as early as 1676 there is a record in the Colerne Marriage Register of a John Mullens marrying Anne Woodman. In the first published census return of 1841 we find recorded the family of William and Jane Mullins. William and Jane, both 30 years old, had at that time six children. John, with whom this chapter is mainly concerned, was their second son and aged 3 years. By the time of the 1861 census John aged 23 was married and living in 'the Street' [High Street]. Although his occupation is listed as 'Stone Sawyer', his powers as a water diviner had already quite by chance been discovered. In 1859 he was employed on the estate of Sir John Orred at Ashwick, which at that time was in the county of Gloucestershire, situated on the road between Colerne and Marshfield. Sir John had employed a diviner from Cornwall as he was wanting to sink a new well. The diviner successfully found a good supply of water, but, rather as an entertainment, a number of people

Fig 110 John Mullins and his sons Joseph and Henry (from *The Divining Rod*)

present also had a try with the hazel twig and it was discovered that Sir John's own daughter had the gift. Intrigued by this he decided to have all the workmen on the estate try to see if they had the gift. Immediately John Mullins had his turn the twig reacted so violently that it snapped. Gradually over the years his outstanding ability as a water finder led to his being employed all over the country.

The 1881 census lists John as having seven children, two of whom were stepsons. Two of his sons, Henry and Joseph, by his first wife Sarah, were also 'dowsers.' Despite this success as a water finder, he did not entirely give up his trade as a stone worker (he is eventually listed as a stonemason) until 1893 when he was 55 years old. Yet in various trade directories, the first entry being found in 1879, John Mullins is entered under Colerne as a well sinker and water finder. In 1895 a *Kelly's Directory* entry lists "John Mullins and Henry Mullins, water finders." This indicates that John had by then gone into partnership with his son Henry. In 1911 the entry lists "Joseph and Henry Mullins, water finders." By that time 'water' had become a family business. The proof of this is in a small book *The Divining Rod* published in 1905 to advertise their flourishing business. It contains lists of satisfied customers, from owners of mansions to owners of breweries, not only lists but glowing testimonials, some from newspapers and trade magazines. At the end it advertises Mullins Improved Steel Wind Engines specially designed for pumping water, and Mullins's Special Pumps "constructed to be worked by any power giving the best result with the minimum amount of labour."

The family's increase in fortune can be traced through the census returns. In 1861 the Mullins were living in a cottage in the High Street. By 1871 a move had been made to Watergates and they remained there until some time between 1881 and 1891. The 1891 census has them living at Berry Cottage, in Quarry Lane, where a live-in domestic servant was employed. Finally, by the end of the century they owned Elmsleigh, a house of some substance in the Market Place. There are no further entries in the trade directories after 1919. By 1920 the Mullins, Water Finders, had left.

The following undated cutting has come into our possession, but we cannot trace its origins.

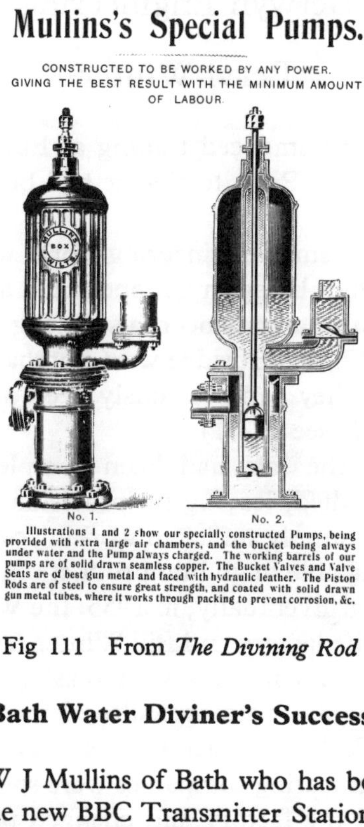

Mullins's Special Pumps.

CONSTRUCTED TO BE WORKED BY ANY POWER.
GIVING THE BEST RESULT WITH THE MINIMUM AMOUNT OF LABOUR.

No. 1. No. 2.

Illustrations 1 and 2 show our specially constructed Pumps, being provided with extra large air chambers, and the bucket being always under water and the Pump always charged. The working barrels of our pumps are of solid drawn seamless copper. The Bucket Valves and Valve Seats are of best gun metal and faced with hydraulic leather. The Piston Rods are of steel to ensure great strength, and coated with solid drawn gun metal tubes, where it works through packing to prevent corrosion, &c.

Fig 111 From *The Divining Rod*

Bath Water Diviner's Success

I learn that Mr W J Mullins of Bath who has been very successful in divining water at the new BBC Transmitter Station at Beaumaris, in the Isle of Anglesey, thereby saving the Company considerable trouble and expense, has been invited to broadcast about water divining. It is of interest to note that Mr Mullins located water at a depth of 54 feet.

Mr M T Tudsberry, M.Inst.C.E., the civil engineer, has expressed his satisfaction with the work, Mr Mullins's prognostication having been positively fulfilled, both as regards depth and supply. The Office of Works has taken advantage of Mr Mullins's experience at the anti-gas school which is conducted by this department.

Could this be a grandson?

Berwyn Engineering

Beryl Winter

Berwyn Engineering commenced trading at Euridge Works, Thickwood, on 1st July 1960. Prior to that it had been known as Jeffery Engineering.

In 1953 the idea of a small engineering works was conceived by Mr Jeffery, a tannery owner living in Chippenham, and Richard William Winter (known as 'Bill') an engineer, also living in Chippenham.

The land and buildings at Euridge were purchased from Mr George Gifford of Colerne. They had previously been used as a WAAF site during World War II (see p 221).

Ten months after the sale had been completed and machinery installed, Mr Jeffery died, leaving no provision for the factory. Bill Winter was unable to supply sufficient working capital to complete the factory, and not being able to go into production, was forced to seek a buyer to keep it going. Eventually, in 1955, the West of England Sack Contractors bought the factory and Bill Winter remained as Managing Director. They traded for five years, increasing the staff from ten to 30–35, and developed and sold agricultural machinery. In 1960 the West of England Sack Contractors were taken over by another company and the engineering companies were sold off. This was when Bill Winter acquired the factory and changed the name to 'Berwyn Engineering' – a combination of my names (*Ber*yl *Win*ter) and also a reference to the fact that the Berwyn Mountains in Wales were a favourite holiday haunt of the Winters.

Bill Winter as Managing Director of the Company and Beryl Winter as Company Secretary continued to trade for the next seventeen years.

The staff increased to about 35 on the shop floor and eight in the offices and stores. During that time the Hydrostatic Release was designed for the MOD. It was a mechanism attached to a life-raft to enable the raft to inflate automatically under certain depths of water pressure, and it was patented by Bill Winter. It was sent on trials in competition with other larger manufacturers and subsequently accepted as standard equipment for the Royal Navy, and then sold through them, to many other navies throughout the world.

This contact with the MOD led to other contracts for specialised design and development work. The company also designed and marketed agricultural products for British Petroleum and ICI. A great number were sold to Scandinavian markets and also to Canada.

Bill Winter was a dedicated engineer, always enthusiastic and a great innovator. He believed passionately in the skill of the craftsmen of today. His hobby was restoring and working steam engines. He first of all owned a steam roller but later sold it to acquire a Sentinel steam lorry. He also possessed a collection of model steam engines and hoped to create a model steam railway at Thickwood. Sadly, this was not to be; he died at the end of 1977. The business was sold in 1978 to Mr Buchanan and Mr M Reed.

On a personal note, being married to an inventive engineer does have some hazards – on returning home one day, I found my new plastic mackintosh had been sacrificed to make diaphragms for test on a prototype hydrostatic release. Quite often the Sunday joint was taken from the refrigerator so that the shelves could be filled with rows of mechanisms being tested for their reaction to cold temperatures!

Memories of the Vineyard Restaurant

Iris Fuller

My husband George and I married in Beckenham, Kent, in 1941 when air raids were at their height. We were both then working in the Admiralty, which had been evacuated to Bath, and we left a happy reception for a traumatic journey back to Bath, encountering snow storms and an air raid before finally catching the midnight train from London. We worked together, I dug for victory and George joined the Home Guard. But this quite comfortable routine was shattered when our flat was completely destroyed in the first air raid on Bath. With so much property destroyed it was hard to find new accommodation and after moving five times in two years we eventually found the Vineyard, on the Bath side of Colerne village.

The face of the old quarry on which the house is built still exists at the rear of the building. The stone from this quarry was used for road building. With the Fosse Way only a few hundred yards away, it is possible that some of its stones were trodden by the Roman Legions. From records we know that in the mid-nineteenth century the Vineyard was the main (possibly the Bailiff's) house of a small rectangular cluster of cottages which were occupied by farm labourers. Part of the house was rebuilt in 1857, but a fine cellar of late seventeenth century brick construction remained. This vault, comfortably restored and heated, later made an attractive restaurant.

Our adventures began when we moved to Colerne in a snow storm in the winter of 1943–4. We were greeted by a frozen well and no water, but a kind neighbour, Mr Hall of Ranch Farm, came to our rescue, allowing us to get water from an unfrozen stream on his land. However, in no time at all, pumping water from the well, cooking with an oil dutch oven and coping with oil lamps became part of everyday life.

After the end of the war in Europe in 1945, I found myself with unaccustomed time on my hands. Sitting in the garden one Sunday afternoon, we were aware of a number of people, cars and buses passing along the road. A chance remark, "What about opening a Tea Garden?" had unforeseen repercussions!

On 7th October 1945, after negotiations with the Ministry of Food, the local town planning authority and building surveyor, we had permission to open a catering establishment. A rough ply-wood sign went up announcing that 'The Vineyard is Open for Teas and Suppers'. That afternoon six customers turned up from the RAF camp; three weeks later we served sixty teas on one Sunday afternoon. Eventually we became so popular that the bus company put on an extra bus on Sunday afternoons, and we were baking 700 to 800 cakes each week for teas.

AFTERNOON TEA.

TABLE D'HOTE.

2s. 0d.

Bread and Butter
Jam
Home Made Cakes
Pot of Tea

2s. 3d.

Hot Buttered Toast
Jam
Home Made Cakes
Pot of Tea

2s. 6d.

Mixed Sandwiches
(Tomato, Egg, Ham, Tongue, Sandwich Spread, Cucumber, according to availability)
Home Made Cakes
Pot of Tea.

2s. 0d.

Bread and Butter
Jam
BOILED NEW LAID EGG
Home Made Cakes
Pot of Tea.

SUGGESTIONS FOR TEA TIME SNACKS.

Spaghetti on Toast	1s. 6d.
Tomatoes on Toast	1s. 6d.
Mushrooms on Toast	2s. 6d.
Sardines on Toast	1s. 6d.
Poached Egg on Toast	1s. 6d.
Fresh Fruit Salad and Ice Cream	2s. 0d.
Wall's Ice Cream (Vanilla, Strawberry, Chocolate or Coffee).	9d.

LEMON IS AVAILABLE FOR YOUR TEA
if you so desire.

Fig 112 An early menu (I Fuller)

Coping with inconveniences had its amusing side. At times when we were very busy and ran short of water for teas we would ask for volunteers from our customers – work the pump 365 times and get a free tea! It worked extremely well.

By 1948 modernisation had set in, and the old brick vaulted cellar had been comfortably restored and turned into a restaurant. We had gas cylinders for cooking and a donkey engine for our electricity. But one day disaster struck. By that time George's sister, Grace, was helping me, and while changing a gas cylinder we had an explosion. We immediately phoned the fire brigade, then rescued the dogs. Our attempts to douse the resulting fire with buckets of water were not too successful – we just made ourselves very wet. Fortunately the fire brigades from the RAF, Chippenham and Bath came extremely quickly and damage was confined to the kitchen.

We began to build up a reputation for good English cooking and our situation, not too far from the edge of town, brought us many new customers, though many of the best came from RAF Colerne. Early in the 1950s Fanny Craddock, who at that time was writing a column in the *Daily Telegraph*, visited the Vineyard and gave us an excellent write-up in the paper. This gave us a tremendous boost and really the nature of the restaurant changed. We obtained a 'full' licence instead of just a 'table' licence, our menu became more exotic and we had to take on more staff to cope with the immense increase in trade. We extended the premises to provide live-in accommodation for two members of the kitchen staff and we were able to employ a number of people from the village. Most importantly we had a thatched 'uniport' built in the garden. This was known as 'The Round House.' It was at first used for wedding receptions, cocktail parties and as an overflow for the main restaurant. Eventually we linked it to the main building making a splendid bar-lounge. George retired from the Admiralty and worked full time in the expanding business. He became an acknowledged connoisseur of wines, and to store these the old vault became a wine cellar instead of a restaurant.

It is no exaggeration to say that 'The Vineyard' is remembered by customers not only up and down this country but in other parts of the world. We had many American customers and have two very useful

Fig 113 The old cellar as a dining room (I Fuller)

Fig 114 After the fire (I Fuller)

Fig 115 The Round House (I Fuller)

Fig 116 The Elizabethan Revel (I Fuller)

A First Elizabethan Revel
for the
Six Good Trenchermen
and
Their Guest.

In the chair — W. George Fuller.

The Guest — Doctor Eric Forrest.

Elly Stuart-Lockwood

Spring Soup

First Remove:— Broiled Royal Sturgeon
Shrimp Sauce — Caper Sauce

Second Remove:— Boar's Head
Winter Salet
Salamagundy

Third Remove:— Roast Sucking Pig
Buttered Parsnips, Swedes and Carrots

Champ

Syllabub

Ices Nuts Fruit

Sherris Sack. Mead. Ale. Claret.

Fig 117

recipe books given to us as thankyou presents to remind us of happy visits.

After a time we extended our business into outside catering, a most interesting venture. We catered for banquets in the Guildhall, Bath, and one of our buffets at the Bath Octagon was for M. Andre Simon, the distinguished gastronome and wine expert. Most exciting of all, we catered for cocktail parties at Badminton House, often attended by members of the Royal Family including the Queen and Queen Mother.

Memories of those years of hard but rewarding work are myriad. Writing this memoir in 1995, fifty years after the end of the Second World War, I cast my mind back to our special party for friends and invited guests from the RAF. Great fun, ending with dancing in the road! Also our New Year's Eve celebrations, when the haggis was piped in, and the evening ended with the hokey-kokey which we danced all around the house, garden and restaurant.

Our expertise as fine cooks was tested when, in 1961 we provided an Elizabethan banquet for a group of six gourmets. The group was set up in 1957 and they had previously met six times a year to eat regional meals of traditional local dishes. But in 1961 they decided to go 'historical' and they held their feast at the Vineyard. Every effort was made to make all aspects of the occasion authentic. The walls were hung with medieval tapestries and the floor was covered with six inch deep straw. The tables were laid with wooden platters, daggers and posset cups. The menu will be seen in the illustration.

After twenty-one years we sadly decided that the time had arrived to sell the business. We sold it to Ben Warriss, the comedian, and his wife.

Now I have good and fond memories of a hard-working but happy life. We had lots of fun and made lasting friendships.

The Village Constable

Ron Read

In Anglo-Saxon times, the kings expected the people to keep good order and any crime was an 'Act Against the Peace'. More serious crimes were 'Against the King's Peace'. It was the duty of citizens themselves to see that the law was not broken and, if it was, to catch the offenders. All males in the community between the ages of 12 and 60 were responsible for this duty. Dwellings were grouped into a 'tything' (usually ten dwellings) and each person was held responsible for the good behaviour of the others. If one member committed a crime the others had to catch him and bring him before the Court (called the 'moot'). If they failed to do so, they were all fined. Very serious offences were tried at the 'Shire Court' which came under the control of the 'Shire Reeve', or 'Sheriff' as he came to be known.

The chase to catch a known criminal was called 'the hue and cry' and all men had to drop their tools and join the chase. A criminal who reached the precincts of a church could claim 'sanctuary' as long as he remained inside. The 'Tytheman' was the forerunner of the Constable.

In the Middle Ages the Normans continued the Anglo-Saxon laws and, as persons lived at peace and were more law-abiding, the role of Sheriff was taken on by the Lord of the Manor who annually appointed an ale-taster, a swine-ringer, a bread-weigher and a Constable. The Constable was not paid and had to combine his duties of keeping the King's Peace with his ordinary work as best he could.

The Statute of Winchester in 1285 was made to "abate the power of felons" and ruled that certain citizens had the power to act as 'watchmen' and hand over any suspicious stranger to the Constable who would in the morning, take the person before a court. The Constable would be provided with a 'lock-up' or 'Blind House' in which to imprison the suspect temporarily.

The Justice of the Peace Act of 1361, gave each county the right to appoint Justices to "restrain offenders and rioters and to arrest, take and chastise them." These men became known as 'Justices of the Peace' and today's Magistrates are still known by that title.

In Tudor and Stuart times the Justices assisted the Parish Council in local government. They appointed 'Parish Constables' who still had no pay or uniform but carried an official staff of office. Examples of the staff can be seen in local museums and some are similar to the truncheon carried by police officers today, except that they were adorned with pretty carvings and gilded coats of arms and the like. The Parish Constable could call on any citizen to help him and he sometimes kept criminals in his own house until they could be taken before a Justice of the Peace.

The Constable also had to carry out certain punishments. For example he had to whip vagrants "till their backs be bloody". He had to duck 'scolds' in the village pond and put some offenders in the stocks in the village market place. There was, of course, a village green at Colerne, in the area which is now occupied by the Walmesley memorial and a miscreant detained in the stocks would become ridiculed and abused by passers-by. Church records show that on 30th April, 1720, John Mullins was paid ten shillings for repairing the parish stocks. The stocks were still in evidence in Colerne Market Place at the turn of the nineteenth century.

When a well-to-do citizen was called upon to act as Constable for a year, he was permitted to pay another citizen to do his duty for him.

The Wiltshire Police Force

In 1829, Sir Robert Peel formed the Metropolitan Police Force in London and laid the foundation of what was to become the first fully-paid police force, which in the following ten years was copied in many towns and boroughs throughout England and Wales.

Following riots which took place throughout the country (including the Corn Riot at Devizes in 1839), Parliament passed the County Police Force Act of 1839 which permitted a county to appoint a Chief Constable. Against much opposition at Quarter Sessions meetings held at both Marlborough and Devizes, a Committee of Magistrates met at The Bear Hotel, Devizes, on 28th November 1839, and appointed Captain Meredith RN as the first Chief Constable of Wiltshire. Thus the very first county police force was formed.

The first records available show that in 1841 Pc Richard Sheppard was appointed to serve at Colearn [sic] with Luckenham as another principal place to visit on his beat. He is shown as serving under the 'Superintendence' of James Wright in the Chippenham Division, and appears to have served the village for six years. There is no record of a police station at Colerne and it seems likely that he rented a house locally. The first purpose-built police station was in Bath Road and was occupied from 1927 to 1965. This house still stands next to the old Colerne Bakery.

Pc Sheppard may well have had use of a 'lock-up' which stood at the entrance of the yard at Clyst House in High Street (No 27) and was listed in a report to the County until 1903, but not in later years, and may have been demolished at that time. A lock-up was usually a round, square or octagonal stone building with domed roof and a ball finial. It was erected to house petty offenders (mainly drunks). The purpose of these little buildings was summed up in an 1815 description: "A kind of prison for the nightly watch to secure persons in till they can be brought before the Magistrates." Sanitary provisions were non-existent, the building was airless and unheated. The upkeep was the responsibility of the parish.

An 1887 return of police stations and lock-ups shows that the police station at Corsham was used for prisoners conveyed from Colerne. The station consisted of one cell and one office, at an annual rent of £18.

From 1841 to 1975 some 38 Constables were posted to the village. A full list is given as an Appendix. Some Officers stayed for fairly long periods, whereas others were present for less than one year. One or two were dismissed from the Force for drunkenness – a charge which was not unusual in the nineteenth century!

Movement around the parish was by means of foot patrol and later by bicycle, although Officers were permitted to purchase and use their own motor cycles in the 1920s. The first motor vehicle officially provided was a small Triumph motor cycle in 1962. Communication was extremely difficult and information about active criminals had to

Fig 118 Two Colerne police houses: Box View (left) and Bath Road (Mrs Scrivin at gate) (I Alford and N Fletcher)

be passed by word of mouth when a Constable patrolled to the extent of his beat to meet his neighbouring Constable. A prisoner to be conveyed from Colerne to Corsham would be taken to Box and 'handed over' for delivery.

Pc Oatley served in the village from 1865 to 1873. This Officer was born in Bromham and had been a weaver by trade. He and his wife Anne had nine children and when he retired in 1891 he lived at Brinkworth until his death at the age of 92. (He clearly enjoyed more years on pension than he had served in the Constabulary which is every Officer's ambition.) A photograph taken with fellow Officers in 1880 showed that each of them had a full beard and, apparently, a Constable had to apply in writing to be permitted to parade for duty clean shaven!

Mr Oatley called a doctor to his home when at the age of 90 he had a tooth removed, this being the first tooth he had lost. He never smoked nor drank alcohol. He attended the last public hanging at Devizes Prison.

His great great grandson, Stuart Ponting, became a Superintendent who was at one time stationed at Police Headquarters, Devizes.

Pc Bertie Read was posted to Colerne from Sutton Benger on 22nd February 1922, and took up residence with his family at Box View. This house was owned by the Lucknam estate and when Pc Read retired on 26th September 1927, he purchased the house and continued to live in it with his family. His daughter still occupies the house. One of his grandsons is the present author, who has upheld a family tradition of policing in the Wiltshire Constabulary. He retired in 1995 as the Divisional Commander at Chippenham, with the rank of Chief Superintendent.

The Chief Constable of Wiltshire in 1927 was not greatly pleased that Pc Read had purchased the house but overcame the problem by purchasing land in Bath Road, where the first Police Station was built. The Police Station was later moved to Silver Street where in 1965 Pc Jack (Barry) Webster took up occupation. This station was finally given up in September 1975. Barry was well known locally and played in goal for the village football team. It is rumoured that he was the only Colerne player not to be 'sent off' in a local derby one fateful Saturday afternoon.

Fred Woodham was Colerne's Village Constable from 1927 to 1931. His widow Winifred (née Clarke) recalls that when they moved into the Police Station at Bath Road it was a fairly new house but had a toilet (bucket) at the bottom of the garden. Police Officers' wives were not permitted to hold separate employment and acted as unpaid stand-in whilst their husbands were on patrol. Fred was a motor cycle enthusiast and was paid a small allowance to use his own Norton motor cycle whilst on patrol, and Winifred remembers riding on the pillion for shopping trips to Bath.

Pc Woodham was succeeded in 1931 by Ernest Scrivin. Although he had not been long in the village when he retired in 1934, the people of Colerne made a collection for a retirement present. Because policemen were not supposed to accept gifts, special permission had to be

Fig 119 Pc Bertie Read with his wife, Elsie, and sons, Douglas and Ronald (I Alford)

obtained from the Chief Constable before he could be given a clock and a canteen of cutlery.

Villagers thought a great deal of their own Constables and often got round the ban on gifts by leaving vegetables or other produce on the front doorstep anonymously.

In 1934 (Arthur) John Barnbrook became Village Constable. Mr Barnbrook was a former Welsh Guardsman. His wife was a trained school teacher but was unable to accept employment. Pc Barnbrook patrolled mostly by cycle and was accompanied by his dog, a large Airedale terrier which had been donated by a member of the public. He recalls being summoned from his bed to search the area for an escaped convict from Parkhurst prison. Having searched all barns in the Fosseway and Bristol Road, he eventually located two men near a hedge at Ford who aroused the suspicion of his dog. He stalked them and later apprehended and searched them. Unhappy with their account, he 'marched' them towards Chippenham. Realising that they could easily escape en route, he flagged down a lorry and directed the driver to take them all to Chippenham Police Station which stood in New Road. He there announced to Superintendent Reggie Brevitt, "If they're right, then I'm wrong." They had in fact escaped from an institution in Bristol used to house sexual offenders and known as 'Hawthorn Colony.'

When the local Fox Hunt met in the village, it was traditional for the Master of the Hunt, Colonel Bartholemew to leave two pints of beer at the Six Bells for the Constable. On one such occasion a motor cyclist was held up in the mêlée and Pc Barnbrook suspected the rider of stealing it. He shouted in front of the crowd, "Get off, or I'll knock you off." With the help of villagers, the man was arrested and admitted stealing the motor cycle, as well as committing burglaries at Box and at Bath.

Pc Barnbrook also has fond memories of the village Fire Brigade who were volunteers led by their 'Captain', Jack Tanner. The pump was a box containing water and mounted on four wheels and was pulled by the volunteers. The pump was kept in a lean-to near the village church and was summoned by ringing of the high pitched tenor bell in the church tower. After one or two incidents in the village, the Parish Council decided that a secret test of the Fire Brigade's efficiency should take place one Sunday morning. Captain Merry of Lucknam Park agreed that a fire could be lit at Sewell and George Gifford, the Parish Clerk, would call out the Brigade by ringing the bell and then ride his motor cycle to Sewell and light the fire. He was to time the response. Over a few pints in the Six Bells, Jack Tanner was 'tipped off' by a member of the Parish Council. On the day in question George Gifford rang the bell and raced to Sewell. He had just lit the fire when the whole team of Firemen appeared from nearby woods pulling the pump. They quickly extinguished the fire and boasted for months about the speed of their call-out!

Pc Barnbrook could not afford a motor car but was determined to give his wife and young daughter a holiday each year. He remembers an 'arrangement' with Curtis the Scrap Dealer at Trowbridge whereby he would purchase an old car for £5 0s 0d, use it for two weeks and return it on receipt of £2 10s 0d. His posting to Colerne had an unhappy ending in 1939 when he was reported to the Chief Constable for spending one and half hours in the village pub on his day off. The Superintendent considered that such behaviour was unbecoming of an upholder of the law and posted him to Swindon as a punishment.

The Wiltshire Constabulary records indicate that either the Superintendent's Clerk could not spell or that village names have changed. The beats to be covered by the village Constable are variously shown as:

Colearn, Coleren, Colerne.

Luckenham, Luckingham, Lucknam.

North Wraxall, Donkham and Donkenham.

Since 1975 the village has been policed by rural Beat Officers who are stationed at Corsham and patrol the old village beats by motor vehicle. Closing village police stations was an unpopular decision made by the Chief Constable, but it was recognised that criminals were more mobile and were likely to 'visit' the area when it was known that the village Constable was off duty.

Villagers today expect a fairly quick response to calls for help and due to the advances of the telephone and radio services, are normally able to summon assistance fairly quickly. In a real emergency a controller can direct resources to the village and also send other Officers to 'check points' in an effort to apprehend an offender escaping by motor vehicle. The use of computers and the Force helicopter means that the Wiltshire Constabulary are at the forefront of the fight against crime and as the first County Force, are proud of their record. Hence their motto: 'Primus et Optimus' (First and Best).

In Saxon and Norman times, law and order was under a 'self-help' style and with the development of Neighbourhood Watch, householders are encouraged to be vigilant and keep an eye on their neighbours' property in vulnerable times. This is backed up by the Constabulary and the Special Constabulary and works quite well in small populated areas. It also builds on the 'neighbourly' feeling which has always been present and still exists in villages like Colerne.

Appendix

Village Constables 1841–1975

Year appointed to Colerne	Pc no	
1841	106	Richard Sheppard
1847	66	George Oram
1855	42	Thomas Proctor
1862	29	Edward Fry
1862	164	George Pead
1863	130	William Savage
1864	152	Edward Harris
1865	123	John Oatley
1873	91	Thomas Tanner
1876	152	William Davis
1877	92	John Barnes
1878	179	William King
1879	93	Frank Blake
1881	83	John Maloney
1884	89	Samuel Macey
1896	63	George Chandler
1898	28	John Fishlock
1902	63	George Chandler
1903	113	James Newman
1907	52	Frederick Hunt
1913	140	George Coles
1920	242	Seward Cross
1922	35	Bertie Read
1927	228	Fred Woodham
1931	31	Ernest J. Scrivin
1934	111	Arthur Barnbrook
1939	26	Sidney Pearce
1946	102	W J Webb
1946	250	R A Winchcombe
1946	222	J J Morley
1950	157	Thomas G Goff
1952	132	Gerard Flenk
1956	330	Ernest Walton
1962	465	Walter Lloyd
1964	83	Jack (Barry) Webster
1968	163	John Fletcher
1971	417	Paul Coombe
1974	785	Nigel Walker

Medical Care in Colerne

Introduction

Colerne has had a long association with Box doctors. We know from records of the Overseers of the Poor that doctors in Box were sometimes paid for the care of village paupers as long ago as 1726 and that later the Overseers paid a retainer to Box doctors for the care of paupers (*V on H* pp 105–8).

At that time, of course, 'midwifery' attention was in the hands of village women.

There are also records of payments being made in the nineteenth century to Bath hospitals, again for paupers. After 1834 when the care of the poor ceased to be a parish matter they became the responsibility of the Chippenham Union (together with a cluster of villages). Doctors were appointed by the Guardians of the Union to care for paupers, whether they lived in or out of the workhouse, but this meant that one doctor could be responsible for the care of the sick poor in a number of villages. In the 1840s these same doctors were responsible for the first vaccinations against smallpox.

We have been unable to find any record of the medical care available to the slightly better off members of the village community until the early part of the present century when, in 1911, a system of National Insurance was set up for the 'working classes.' An account of this legislation, which improved the medical care of the whole nation, is set out after this introduction. We have found no record of professional medical care in Colerne until Dr Martin arrived on the scene. He came to Box during the 1880s and did not retire until 1931. There are many memories of this colourful character who came up to Colerne from Box on his horse (see *Life on the Hill* pp 35–7). The association with the Box doctors has continued up to the present time.

The link with the medical practice based in Marshfield seems to have started in the late 1930s and this has also continued since then.

We print below accounts of both practices within the village. First a personal record by Dr D G Taylor of his experiences while working in Colerne from 1958 until his retirement in 1986, and second an account of the involvement of the Marshfield practice in the village.

Finally we add short notes about the Colerne Nursing Association and the establishment of surgery facilities in the Parish Council offices in 1961 for the use of both medical practices. Today there are two modern surgeries in the village. Dr J Morgan, who has links with the Marshfield practice, has one at the eastern end of the High Street, and the Box practice has another in the Firs estate at the western end of the village.

Fig 120 Dr Martin

National Health Insurance 1911–48

Joyce Utting

It might be useful to have a short note about the health care available to most ordinary people before 1948 and the advent of the National Health Service.

In 1911 a system of National Insurance against sickness was set up for the 'working classes.' This meant that the wage earner (usually the man) was able to obtain medical attention from a local doctor by being put on the list (panel) of a practice. It also provided some compensation for loss of earnings if he had to be off work.

In parallel with government provision some, not all, Trade Unions paid out a small amount of sickness benefit to their members.

The huge scale of the First World War (1914–18) forced the government to take control of large areas of the economy and infrastructure of the nation. New ministries were set up, such as the Ministry of Food to control rationing, and responsibility was vested in the government for railways (for troop movements etc) and coal mines (for fuel to power armaments factories etc). This involved an increase in taxes so that by 1918, when the war ended, the state had both more power and more resources. Also in that year the franchise was extended to all men over 21 and all women over 30. As a result there were demands for better welfare provision and, as the coalition government (Conservative/Liberal) led by Lloyd George now had the means, some improvements were made.

In 1919 all workers earning up to £5 a week (a respectable middle class wage then) were brought into the National Insurance scheme. But these schemes were not available to the wives and children of the wage earner, and the depression which hit the country from the mid-twenties to the end of the thirties caused immense poverty and deprivation particularly among the unskilled members of the community. Families were ill-fed and ill-housed and women and children in particular suffered. The doctor was called only at times of direst need and at times of childbirth women mostly relied on family and neighbours with the help of a local midwife who was not always trained.

There were, however, some improvements towards the end of the thirties. Under the 1936 Midwives Act, local authorities were required to provide trained personnel and by 1938 there were 1795 ante-natal clinics in England and Wales. In some areas these welfare centres were providing free or cheap milk to expectant mothers. Also during this period a number of public hospitals were established to supplement the care provided by the private and charitable hospitals, many of which had existed for centuries, and the state provided hospital care and fumigation services when scarlet fever or diphtheria struck.

The Second World War (1939–1945) brought into being the well planned rationing scheme which fulfilled its object of improving the nation's health. Essential vitamins were added to certain foods and extra items like cod liver oil and orange juice were available at a low cost for all mothers and children.

A need for more hospital beds was created not only by war wounded but also by civilian casualties from air raids, and treatment was of necessity provided by the state without charge. Therefore, by 1945 hospitals had many more beds available, and the war had accelerated better forms of treatment both medical and surgical. Also, during the war, a free immunisation programme against diphtheria became available, which resulted in a dramatic fall in the incidence of this disease.

As so often, the right person appeared on the scene at the right time. In 1942 Sir William Beveridge produced his famous report on social security for the wartime coalition government. This reasoned document put forward a balanced scheme for the population's welfare and was a major influence on the establishment of a national health service through the National Health Service Act, which was passed by Parliament in 1946 and implemented in 1948.

Memories of the Box Practice

Donald Taylor

(Interviewed by Joyce Utting)

When talking about my years in general practice in Box and Colerne, it has to be clear at the outset that there is no way that individual cases or people's medical history can be mentioned, so I can only talk in a general way about my own experiences during the years in which I worked in the area.

I came to the Box practice in 1958 when the National Health Service was ten years old. I do not have any accurate memories of medical provision before that time. For most people it was probably pretty basic and sparse. This would partly be due to cost. I seem to remember a sum of 7s 6d for a visit and 5s 0d for a surgery consultation – a considerable sum of money for people in those days, particularly if they had families. There was, of course, the old 'panel' system, but I am not absolutely sure how that operated. I think it only benefited people in work and able to pay Health Insurance contributions, so it would seem to leave wives, families and unemployed people without free or subsidised health care.

The succession of doctors in Box and Colerne during this century starts with Dr Martin, probably the best remembered by people in the village, often for his horse and eccentricities rather than his medical skill. Then came Dr Thomas, Dr Devine, Dr Muir, and me and Dr Davy from Box, with whom I worked for many years.

Before coming to Box, an area which I knew not at all, I had been working as an assistant GP in a Salisbury practice. I had been there for about two-and-a-half years, was married with children, and seemed to be working very hard for small pay. I saw the Box practice advertised in a medical journal. "Small single-handed practice" it said, and that is exactly what it was. I applied at a time when I was feeling somewhat disenchanted with my current post and was quite surprised to find myself appointed from about twenty applicants. The committee who conducted the interviews and finally decided to offer me the post were all local worthies. I well remember Mr Gifford, the farmer, who was a member. I was asked "Do you play cricket?" I said "Yes." "Oh that's fine" they said "you can bat for Box!" I don't remember much mention of my medical abilities, but that is how I came to this area.

When I arrived in Box there was no available surgery so I went to see my potential rival, Dr Jim Davy, who was also working single-handed and things then followed on in a logical manner. We liked each other although very different from one another – a good thing – and we eventually joined up as a practice of two instead of two single-handed practices. It worked very well. Although our house was over-run with builder's men and we had three small children, I hired a person to answer the front door, and we managed to run the surgery from this house, at Middlehill. The practice increased in size but we managed perfectly well.

But I must turn my attention to the Colerne practice. As you can see, I really had to work my way into the area. In fact, I visited Colerne on the very day that I took over the practice. My wife, Molly, had taken two calls for visits in the village. I set off in the car (had to ask where Colerne was) and I eventually found myself in Silver Street where there were two ladies chatting. I asked them where the surgery was, and one of them, Mrs Bass, said "I'll take you along and show you where it is." So we said goodbye to Mrs Jenkins (the other lady) and off we went. I was taken to Mr Bull's house in the High Street, where Dr Muir had held his surgery in the front parlour. Mr Bull was very deaf, so in a fortissimo conversation I made an agreement with him to rent his front room. It was very neat and tidy but old fashioned in its furnishings, with a table covered with a green baize tablecloth. For this I paid 7s 6d a week which I settled in cash at the end of each week before I returned to Box. There was no waiting room, patients either sat on the stairs or waited outside, and I am afraid they just got wet if it was raining. I had a surgery twice a week on Mondays and Fridays at 12.30pm. The practice simply snowballed. This was partly, of course, because the NHS made my services available to people, but also, I am sure, that if you fill a need in a caring and polite way, then the patient will come back to you and trust you. Of course, providing a good medical service, such as the NHS, for the community will lay it open to a small amount of abuse but, importantly, those people with real need will be helped.

The administrative side of the practice was managed by our two wives – just our two wives – who combined making appointments, taking phone calls, arranging visits and all the secretarial work with bringing up their children. We had three children and Dr and Mrs Davy three. We also had the services of a District Nurse. The present practice has a staff of something like twenty to deal with all the administration and nursing care that goes with present-day procedures. It is a business now, and I do not think it would have suited me very well.

My predecessor had done his own dispensing but I said I certainly would not take that on as I could not stick labels on straight! In all seriousness, however, new drugs had become available in tablet form, such as penicillin and tetracyclin, so that when I was confronted with bronchial or urinary infections I could effect a cure often within a week, where slow-acting potions had been prescribed hitherto.

Prescriptions did pose a problem, particularly when I started in the practice, when very few people had cars. If, as was the case with most patients, they wanted to collect their prescriptions in Colerne, I would take all the prescriptions to Box at the end of surgery. The chemist made them up and then delivered them to the house of a kindly volunteer in Colerne. Patients then collected them from that house. Eventually, Mrs June Notton provided this service at the Post Office, and then Mrs Sheila Knight took it over at the Spar shop. It worked very well. The chemist was most obliging also, and in an emergency would deliver a prescription himself. The system still operates except that the chemist now delivers the prescriptions to the new Colerne surgery in the Firs. I am sure that patients do appreciate this service.

When I started, there were no ante-natal clinics. On the whole, I thought it worked better to see mothers-to-be during general surgery rather than at a special clinic. The Midwife and District Nurse for the Colerne area was Nurse Twyman. Another nurse covered the Box area. Most deliveries took place at home, although it was also made clear to mothers that if there was any possibility of complications they should go to hospital. At one time hospitals preferred not to take normal deliveries. There were three available hospitals. One, the Royal United in Bath which had an up-to-date obstetrics department and two where the GPs were responsible for their own patients, Greenways, in Chippenham, and Bradford-on-Avon. Mothers had a choice and, naturally, after their first confinement, if they had felt happy in that hospital they liked to return to it; if not, they had the opportunity to try one of the others. But I cannot remember ever having any problem with obtaining maternity help when I needed it; one had the assurance that extra expertise was easily available.

I used to enjoy home deliveries. Nurse Twyman was quite a character, but extremely practical. She always wore a woolly hat! I can remember wading through snow on some extremely cold nights in Colerne. She could be abrupt and aggressive at times, and so obviously she was loved by some and feared by others. But she was an experienced nurse and passed some of her wisdom on to me. I can picture her now, sitting in a corner knitting away – she always brought her knitting if a long labour was likely – her legs crossed and old-fashioned underwear in view. She certainly knew her trade and did not always ask me to be in attendance if she felt confident that things would be uncomplicated. She would say to a mother "When you go into labour don't come running to me straight away, call me when the contractions are down to two or three minutes" – detailed instructions that she was not to be called a minute before it was necessary! She was all right if you gave as good as you got.

The Box nurse, a single lady, was quiet, subdued and reticent – just completely different and absolutely right for some mothers. Getting to know patients and their temperaments well is so important in medicine.

If a patient had to be taken into hospital, I had complete confidence in the efficiency and sense of responsibility of the ambulance service. It was superb.

As far as I can remember, there was a Nursing Association in Colerne. I think it worked in conjunction with the Red Cross and was able to supply medical aids, crutches, wheel chairs, bed pans etc., to members who might have need of them. I am fairly sure that it did not, in fact, provide any nursing care [but see below].

General Practice has gradually changed over the past forty years. It is much busier and, as I have said, involves a great deal more administration. People are living longer, and that involves the holding care of patients waiting for such things as hip replacements. We started with two doctors, two wives and five or six thousand patients. I cannot remember any major catastrophes. The work of the practice has increased, with many more clinics. There is more minor surgery, taking of blood samples etc, carried out at the surgeries.

The great improvement in my time was the immunisation programmes which got under way under the NHS. This meant the virtual end of epidemics and if children got measles or whooping cough etc, they made a good recovery. Most dramatically, inoculation against tuberculosis virtually ended the scourge.

The Marshfield Practice

Jocelyn Berry

I am grateful to Dr Eastes of Marshfield for much of the information in this brief account of the work of the practice in Colerne, to Mrs Monica Clarke for her memories of health care in the village from the Marshfield practice, and to Mrs Anne Kent for her account of the Colerne Nursing Association.

Dr Sam Mawson took over the Marshfield Surgery in 1930 and a few months before he died in 1939, he opened a branch surgery in Colerne where he saw patients in the 'front room' of Mrs Tanner's house in the High Street on two afternoons a week. Dr Henry Eastes continued with this arrangement for some years, during which time Dr Thomas of the Box practice asked him to take over those of his patients who suffered from gastric or duodenal ulcers.

Eventually the doctors had to move from Mrs Tanner's house and then held their surgeries in the lounge of the shop next to the Rectory, and later, when the shop changed hands, Mr and Mrs Preedy accommodated them for some years until Commander Cheetham, as Clerk to the Parish Council, organised the purchase and equipment of the Council Offices opposite, where the Marshfield and Box doctors had much better accommodation. When Dr Eastes retired in 1982, Dr John Morgan came to Colerne and held his surgery in his house at Elmsleigh in the Market Square and then, with the sale of Trimnells for building, he seized the opportunity to purchase a plot for Colerne's first purpose-built surgery.

When the doctors moved into the Council Offices, Dr Eastes started an antenatal clinic with a midwife on one morning a week plus surgeries on four afternoons a week. In addition some Colerne patients went to Marshfield for morning or evening surgeries.

Dr Eastes ran his own 'club' and for a few pence each week, wives and children could join and he undertook to attend them and provide medicines etc, as only wage earners were covered by the National Health Insurance scheme. In 1948 the National Health Service came into force and so this 'club' was no longer required.

As there was no pharmacy in Marshfield or Colerne, the doctors were obliged to dispense medicines themselves (which Dr Morgan still does) and this made it simple to carry urgent or emergency supplies with them so that patients often received their medication immediately. This was very convenient for those who lived in isolated locations and had no means of transport. A selection of commonly used medicines, pills and ointments etc, were locked up on the surgery premises and less commonly used items were delivered to Colerne the following day. Some time in the 1960s a dispensing chemist opened a shop in the High Street for a few years, in spite of being advised that it needed a population far greater than Colerne plus the Camp in order to survive.

Dr Henry Eastes was one of the first General Practitioners in England to take medical students for a short exposure to the real thing. This scheme started in the 1950s and one of those students stayed for four years as an assistant and acted as locum. She is Dr Jane Richards who is now working in a large practice in Exeter. In 1965 Dr Edna Dunn was introduced to general practice. She also acted as locum and is still remembered in Colerne with great affection.

The Colerne Nursing Association

This was a voluntary organisation supported by public subscription and was started by the Hon Mrs Merry of Lucknam Park during the winter of 1926–7 when there was an influenza epidemic and funds were needed urgently to provide help and comfort for the needy in Colerne. She organised a fête initially. Miss Molly Frowde of Elmsleigh was the secretary and Miss Burton, a teacher at the school, helped to collect subscriptions monthly from families. As a result it became possible to engage a nurse/midwife for Colerne.

When the Association was wound up in 1985, Drs Bullen and Morgan were appointed trustees of the fund, which is available for them to authorise the purchase of equipment which will assist in the care of their patients in Colerne.

Provision of Surgery Facilities by Colerne Parish Council

Extracted from a letter from the Clerk to Colerne Parish Council to the Hon Secretary of Wiltshire Association of Parish Councils dated 7th November, 1970.

During the period 1950–60 there were many complaints about the shortcomings of the service provided by the doctors from Box and Marshfield, mostly because of waiting room and consulting room arrangements in private houses.

In 1959 an old scheduled building used as two separate dwellings, was purchased by the Rural District Council to ensure its preservation as part of the village scene. One of the dwellings was uninhabited and Colerne Parish Council decided that this could be made suitable for a dual purpose – as a Parish Council office and as surgery and clinic accommodation for the visiting doctors.

The Rural District Council agreed to sell this empty section of the building to Colerne Parish Council. This enabled the Parish Council to go ahead with their plan, which they did with great success. All the necessary official approvals for the adaptations, including repairs to the structure, were obtained, as was the necessary loan sanction of eventually £2000 to be repaid at £160 per annum over a period of 20 years at 6¼% interest. The total cost of £2795 was met by this loan, an Improvement Grant of £400, and £395 from the Parish Council's own funds.

The visiting doctors agreed to the new provision being offered to them, and in September 1961 they were able to move into the newly adapted premises, which, by the clever use of dividing doors provided a surgery and waiting room. They paid an annual rent of £80 for the use of the premises.

Colerne Parish Council

Chris Phillips

Although borough councils had been established for a number of urban areas in England by the Municipal Reform Act of 1835, local government in rural areas remained the province of the 'Vestry' (see *V on H* p 99) and the Justices of the Peace for more than another fifty years.

County Councils were established by the Local Government Act of 1888 and the essentially ecclesiastical Vestry was replaced by Parish Meetings and Parish Councils under the Local Government Act of 1894. The proposal to create these new 'civil' Parish Councils had caused such an uproar that the Bill took a year to pass, and Gladstone's government had to deal with over 800 amendments.

Colerne's first Parish Council

The procedures to be employed for the election of the Parish Council were laid down in the Act. New Year's Eve 1894 was designated as the date of the first meeting of all the newly-formed Councils and 15th April 1896 as the date of expiry of their terms of office.

In Colerne a Parish Meeting to receive nominations was convened on Tuesday 4th December 1894 by Mr R Field, on behalf of the Overseers, with Mr Samuel Dowding, the Vestry Clerk, in the chair. He checked the validity of the 23 nominations received, and, as required by the Act, read out the names of the candidates in alphabetical order together with the names of their proposers and seconders. The public was given time to put questions to all the candidates. A vote by a show of hands was taken and the Chairman announced the names of the eleven candidates who had achieved the highest number of votes and were deemed to be elected.

Under the Act the public had a right to demand a poll if they so wished and ten minutes had to be set aside for this right to be exercised. Thomas Sprules demanded a poll on this occasion and an election was duly held on Saturday 15th December 1894.

The *Wiltshire Times* of 22nd December reported that 23 candidates fought a vigorous contest for the eleven seats and the first Parish Council consisted of:

Henry Baker	
Charles Bence	Blacksmith
George Alexander Gifford	Farmer
John Isaac	
Thomas Kent	Saddler
Gideon May	Shoemaker and Sub-Postmaster
George Maynard	Shoemaker
George Thomas Mitchell	Farmer
John May Osborne	
John Tiley	
Frederick Woodward	Baker

There was a significant difference between the votes of those attending the public nomination meeting and the subsequent election by secret ballot. George Gifford, Henry Baker and John Tiley had failed to be elected at the nomination meeting, yet were elected at the secret ballot, George Gifford having polled the highest number of votes. Thomas Kent nearly doubled his vote, but Henry Mullins, James Tiley and Charles Hulbert failed to be elected, despite being successful at the nomination meeting.

The first meeting of the newly-elected Parish Council was duly held on 31st December 1894 with Samuel Dowding in the chair until the councillors had signed their declarations of acceptance of office and could then elect their own officers.

Gideon May was elected Chairman, George Mitchell Vice-Chairman and Jasper Lane, the Manager of the Wilts and Dorset Bank in Chippenham, as Treasurer (this was probably because he represented Colerne on the Rural District Council and the Board of Guardians).

This first meeting dealt with just one item of business. The Council unanimously agreed that its meetings would not be open to the public. However, at a meeting on the following 13th May this decision was rescinded.

The Parish Council met sixteen times in 1895, its first full year of existence. Meetings were held in the school buildings in Vicarage Lane and the school managers were paid 2s 0d for heating and lighting.

Assistant Overseer and Parish Clerk

After the Poor Law Amendment Act of 1834 the duties of the Overseers of the Poor had been limited to the levying of the poor rate. The Parish Council continued to appoint two Overseers, but these were honorary posts and the work was done by an Assistant Overseer, a paid officer of the Council.

Initially, this post was combined with that of Parish Clerk and James May was appointed to both. He was paid £19 10s 0d per annum and this was raised to £22 in 1897. The salary was raised again, following an auditor's report, in 1903 with a statement in the following terms:

£27 10s 0d basic salary
£2 10s 0d for collecting special rates
£1 10s 0d for banking the money in Box
£1 10s 0d for attending assessment committees
a total of £32 10s 0d

Following legislation introduced in April 1927, the duties of the Overseers were transferred to the Rural District Council. This made the role of Assistant Overseer redundant within the Parish and the Clerk's duties and salary were significantly reduced. He now received £10 per annum.

Early days

The early days of the Council inevitably saw a number of disagreements of a personal nature, some of which centred around the appointment of James May as Assistant Overseer. It was eventually decided in May 1895 to retain his services, but by only one vote and after he had provided a bond of £300 against his good character.

However, things gradually settled down and in subsequent years the minute books record the routine of dealing with the public concerns for which the Council was responsible. These included the appointment of committees, complaints about the roads and rights of way, the submission of charity accounts, the administration of allotments and the maintenance of open spaces and watering places.The Rights-of-Way Committee and the Allotments Committee were both set up in the Council's very first year.

The celebration of Queen Victoria's Diamond Jubilee was raised at a meeting in March 1897. An attempt to obtain a plot of land for a recreation ground failed, and the official celebration did not take place until January 1898, when a red blooming chestnut tree was planted in the Market Place in place of an elm that had died.

Allotments were of vital importance at this time when many families had to be much more self-sufficient than today. When, in 1899, Mr F Sheppard defaulted on his allotment rent the Clerk took him to Bath County Court to recover the amount due. While his case was being heard, he was forbidden by the Council to enter his allotment and, upon defying this order, the Clerk wrote and warned him that if he did it again he would be prosecuted for trespass. The court imposed a fine and his counter-claim of £1 6s 0d to cover the cost of lost potatoes and vegetables was disallowed. The Council magnanimously agreed at its next meeting to allow him back on his allotment to collect his potatoes!

The Walmesley memorial in the Market Place had been erected by public subscription but was being maintained by his widow. By June 1901 the Council thought that this was an unfair imposition upon her and it was agreed that the maintenance be undertaken by the Council. The memorial and its enclosure continues to be maintained at the expense of the Council to this day.

Following the 1902 Education Act, the Council became responsible for providing the names of three "gentlemen" for the County Council to select one to act as a school manager. It also became entitled to nominate its own school manager, and this role lives on in the 'minor authority' governor of the local primary school.

A meeting in September 1908 was asked by the Postmaster at Chippenham if it had any objections to him giving the local Postmaster a half-holiday on Wednesdays. On being informed that his absence would interfere with the postal and telegraphic services of the parish, the Council decided to oppose the proposition and informed the Postmaster accordingly. A later request from the Postmaster to close the Post Office at noon on Bank Holidays was also given short shrift by the Parish Council.

After the First World War the Council was instrumental in calling a public meeting to consider the site for a memorial to record the names of village people who had given their lives in the war. The first site suggested was that of the Cross Tree in the Market Place, but this failed to attract any support from the meeting. Indeed, the meeting was greatly in favour of the Cross Tree being preserved and its base being repaired. The site chosen in the end was that of the 'open green' where it now stands. Mr J Walmesley's kind offer to pay for the enclosure of the memorial was gratefully received. The war memorial was eventually taken on as parish property at a meeting in November 1921.

The recreation ground first appears in September 1920 when the title deeds were presented to the Council for signature. Following this, the first decision about the ground was to permit goalposts to be erected. The use of the recreation ground for football still continues.

Not everybody was pleased to see the creation of the recreation ground, and following a complaint from Mr Beswick about the noise of children playing on the swings, the Council agreed to move them to the top of the field. This decision was helped, no doubt, by Mr Beswick's offer of £2 towards the moving expenses. It was also decided to fasten up the swings between Saturday evening and Monday morning.

In 1934 the Council was approached by the village constable, Pc Midgeley, about the need for a public telephone box in the village. This was because he was unhappy about the considerable inconvenience of having members of the public requesting the use of the telephone installed at the Police Station. Following representations from the Council, the Post Office agreed to install the first public phone box in the village, outside the Post Office.

An attempt was made to procure the services of a District Nurse in the village in 1927, but the costs were considered to be prohibitive and the Council decided to let the matter drop for the time being.

More problems in connection with the Cross Tree were raised in July 1928 when boys had been seen climbing the tree and getting stuck in the dangerous cleft at its apex. In fact, one or two boys had become jammed and had to be rescued. The Council decided to coat the tree with a zinc covering as a preventive measure.

Some problems seem to recur continually. In September 1935 a complaint was received about the noise made by children in the Market Place. The Clerk was asked to write to the village constable, Pc Barnbrook, drawing his attention to the matter.

Problems with the village pond at Watergates were discussed at a meeting held in July 1937, when the District Surveyor reported that water from the pond was leaking across the road. This was referred to the Rural District Council for action. Evidently the problem was serious because a letter from the RDC on this subject was read out at a meeting held in March 1938. The RDC stated that the cost of filling in the pond and erecting a trough with an overflow would be £18 6s 0d, of which £10 16s 10d was the cost of the trough and its fitting.

The Parish Council agreed to pay for the trough themselves and replied with a plan to install two galvanised troughs instead. This was unacceptable to the RDC and it was finally agreed to accept their offer to install one trough. The work was completed by March 1939 when the Clerk was instructed to write and thank the RDC and to ask for a chain to be fitted to prevent cattle crowding over the trough and onto the land behind.

As stated in the contribution on RAF Colerne, the construction of the airfield and its operations seem to have had little direct impact on the Parish Council. Nevertheless, they had to deal with a number of more parochial matters during the Second World War. For example, a meeting held in October 1939 agreed to paint white rings around certain lamp posts in the village, as they were dangerous in the blackout, and in July 1940 the RDC was asked for an air raid shelter at the school, as it was within one mile of the aerodrome.

Following the resignation of the Parish Clerk, Miss A L Wood, in August 1941, advertisements were published seeking a replacement. There was only one application, from Mr H Denis Tidmarsh, and an attempt was made to hold the post open to see if any other applications were forthcoming, but the Council decided to appoint Mr Tidmarsh anyway. At the meeting in September, notice was given by Mr J G May that at the next meeting he intended to "make an objection to the new Clerk on the grounds that he objects to sitting under a conscientious objector." A meeting held on 15th October considered the criticisms raised by Mr May and Mr F Bedford about this appointment and, after a full discussion, decided to take no further action.

This was not acceptable to Mr May who, at a meeting held on 29th October, sent in a letter "criticising certain rulings of the Chairman at recent meetings." These criticisms referred to the refusal of the Chairman to allow the names of councillors to be recorded during the vote about the appointment of the Clerk. The Council decided to support the Chairman and rejected the criticisms, but this was obviously the final straw for the Clerk and, at the same meeting, he tendered his resignation as from 30th November.

No applications for the position of Clerk had been received by the meeting in November, so Mr F Bedford volunteered to carry out the Clerk's functions for the time being.

A complaint was made at the meeting in May 1942 about the conspicuousness of the water tower on the Camp at night, and a letter was sent to the RDC asking for it to be camouflaged. A letter was also sent to Mr Gaisford asking him to camouflage his water tower at the nurseries.

The end of the war, and the first fifty years of the Parish Council, were marked by a proposal from Councillor Sheppard to make preparations for a 'Welcome Home' celebration for all the troops returning to the village.

We turn now to three subjects which were of continuing and frequent concern to the Parish Council in the past, although they are no longer its repsonsibility. These are street lighting, the parish bier and the village fire brigade.

Street lighting

Although the Lighting and Watching Act of 1833 gave rural parishes the power to raise money from the rates to provide lamps for lighting the streets, Colerne did not take action until 1895 when Councillor

John Isaac gave notice at the meeting of 8th August that he intended to submit a motion for the lighting of the village [by oil lamps]. A Parish Meeting was held in January 1896 to consider the issue.

This meeting was informed that the costs would be recovered by means of a rate made and collected in the same manner as the poor rate, but house property would cover three-quarters and land property one-quarter of the costs of erecting and maintaining the lamps. This apportionment was laid down in the Act and reflected the relative worth of lighting to house owners. A letter from Marshfield Parish Council was read about the costs it had incurred in providing and running its lamps and, following a discussion about the possible placement of the lamps within Colerne, the meeting agreed to light the village.

A committee of six councillors inspected the village and reported that twelve lamps would be required and should be sited at the bottom of Vicarage Lane, near the entrance to Trimnells Farm, near the old tree in the Market Place, near the Six Bells public house, near Victoria Place on Tutton Hill, near the Post Office, opposite Ogbourne Lane, near the middle of Totts Lane, near Mr Kent's carriage house, near Catley House, near Elisha Aust's house and on the top of Watergates Hill. It was also agreed that lamp posts would be used to keep lamps clear of private property.

A Lighting Committee was formed at the meeting held on 15th June with instructions to visit Marshfield to see what the situation was with their use of lamps. They reported back on 27th July when the Clerk was instructed to write to Messrs Crawford and Son inquiring about the prices of various sizes and weights of lamp pillars, to be delivered to Box station. The next meeting, on 31st August, agreed to buy pillars at a cost of £1 each. It was recognized that the lamps would need frames in which to sit, and tenders were invited for their provision. It was also agreed to employ someone to haul the lamp posts from Bristol at a cost not to exceed £1 5s 0d. The lamps themselves were bought from Mr Garland of Marshfield.

The office of lamplighter was contested by open tender, the first lamplighter being requested to service the lamps only until 31st December, a period of three months. Three tenders were received ranging from 6s 0d to 9s 0d per week. The lowest, John Sumsion's, was accepted and he became Colerne's first lamplighter. The contract for constructing the lamp frames was given to the village blacksmith, Messrs Bence and Sons.

In December 1896 the Council considered tenders for supplying oil and lighting the lamps from 1st January to 31st March 1897. Four tenders had been received and John Sumsion's of £6 2s 6d was again the lowest. It was accepted and he continued in post for the rest of the lighting season.

The additional work incurred by the Clerk, as a result of lighting the village, was recognised by a pay rise of £2 10s 0d.

Gas lighting reached the village in 1905 after the Council had made a comparison between the costs of lighting with gas and by oil. It was decided that the Bath Gas Company should light the village. Three oil lamps were to be stored, for eventual disposal by the Clerk.

In 1936, automation finally reached Colerne when the Council accepted the offer of the Bath Gas Co. to supply gas to fifteen village lamps, clean their lanterns, light and extinguish the lamps by clock controller, supply mantles and keep the lanterns in good order during the forthcoming lighting season for £1 15s 0d per lamp with another 2s 0d per lamp to fit the automatic controllers. The lamps were set to ignite half an hour after sunset and to extinguish at 10.30pm.

This automation marked the demise of the village lamplighter who had previously had to light each of the fifteen lamps with a torch every night and extinguish them later the same evening.

In the years just before the Second World War, several attempts were made by electricity supply companies to interest the Council in electric street lamps, but they were not introduced until 1954. The story of lighting within the village continues until the late 1980s when the Council handed over responsibility for maintaining the lights and paying for the electricity to Wiltshire County Council.

The lights on the Thickwood Estate were also taken over by Wiltshire County Council a few years later.

The bier

A meeting of the Parish Council in November 1907 approved Councillor Frederick Woodward's proposal that a hand hearse, or bier, be provided for use within the parish. It was also agreed to ask Messrs Moore and Son to construct the bier at a cost of £14 14s 0d. By the time of the Council meeting in July 1908 the bier had been built, and after a successful trial through the church, a small committee drew up rules and conditions for use. The charges were set at 1s 6d for parishioners and 5s 0d for 'outsiders.' A caretaker was appointed and paid 9d per use to keep it clean.

In 1911 the condition of the bier caused some concern. In fact entries in the Parish Council minute books relating to the bier were invariably complaints about its cleanliness. Its poor state could be attributed to infrequent use and poor storage. In 1911 John Savine was asked to undertake the cleaning of the bier. In 1927 the charge for its use was increased to 2s 0d, the hirer to be responsible for its return in a clean condition.

Mr W Hicks, the village undertaker and carpenter, collected the money for use of the bier and the meeting of October 1939 recorded the receipt by the Clerk of £2 10s 0d from Mr Hicks for hire of the bier. At the same meeting Mr Hicks was asked to provide an estimate for its renovation.

After a history of infrequent use and small returns from hire charges the bier went out of use in about 1955, although it was stored in Colerne until 1963. After this it was for many years in the care of the Clerk and finally taken away by a Devon vicar in the 1980s.

The saga of the storage of the bier is bound up with that of the fire engine and is told later on in the chapter.

The Colerne Fire Brigade

The history of the Fire Brigade, under the Parish Council, is a story of continual maintenance of the engine and its apparatus, interspersed with the occasional industrial dispute. Its first mention in the Parish Council minutes occurs on 8th August 1895 when Thomas Kent gave notice of a motion to repair the Fire Engine, which was then kept in a building owned by Mrs C Randall, the landlady of the Six Bells, for which she was paid 10s 0d per year rent.

At this time the brigade consisted of eight men: J Osborne, T Osborne, E Tiley, G Tiley, F Aust, F Whale, W Holder and T Dixon.

It was felt that the fire service was not all that it should have been and, in January 1896, John Isaac, Vice Chairman of the Parish Council, proposed reinforcing the brigade from eight to twelve men with a Captain in charge. Four more men were taken on: H Reid Jr, F Sheppard, H Baker and J May. It was also agreed to pay the Fire Brigade £3 per annum and to hold six practices each year.

The engine was inspected and found to be "perfectly useless" and in March 1896 the Council agreed to ask Mr Lewis, a plumber of Batheaston, to examine it and to give a quote for its repair. The estimate of £8 6s 0d was evidently outside the Council's price range. They put it to a forthcoming Parish Meeting, who referred it back to the Council, and eventually the village blacksmith, Charles Bence, repaired and painted the engine at a cost of £7.

Further repairs were carried out by the Gaisford brothers in 1897, but then the brigade does not feature much in the minutes until 18th December 1901 when, following an application by the Captain, the Council agreed to raise the salary of the Fire Brigade to £4 per year.

In September 1902 the Fire Brigade was called to account for its non-attendance at a rick fire on Mr Sprules' land at Made for Ever. At the subsequent inquiry held by the Parish Council, Mr Sprules admitted that he did not send for the Fire Engine and Brigade but "took it for granted" that the Captain would hear of the fire and come anyway. He also admitted that, even if they had come, their service would have been of little use. The Fire Brigade Captain, W Holder, stated that he had heard "casually" of the rick fire at Made for Ever but immediately realised he could do no good by trying to take an engine to a fire at such a place. This account satisfied Mr Sprules, although he did point out that in future the Fire Brigade should attempt to fight all fires wherever they occur, in order to show intent and purpose.

The initial enthusiasm for the relaunched Fire Brigade waned between 1902 and 1907 when it was agreed to reconstitute it with eight new members and to take out insurance on all its members against loss of earnings if injured while attending a fire.

More repairs were carried out in 1908 when a quotation of £8 18s 6d from William Tanner was accepted. These included repairs to the lead-lined water container, and the Clerk was instructed to sell the old lead. The Fire Brigade Committee reported back in January 1909 that the repairs were very satisfactory and it was agreed to pay Mr Tanner's account.

In September 1909 the Council agreed that the Fire Brigade Captain be paid 10s per annum "for keeping the enginc in order the leather hose well oiled and the new canvas hose in such position to keep dry during intervals of usage." At the same meeting the Clerk was instructed to have the fastening on the engine house made good and to procure a strong lock for the door.

The question of insurance arose again in July 1910 when the Clerk was asked to cost up premiums for insurance and to determine the remuneration that would be paid by the insurance company if a fireman was disabled while working with the Fire Brigade.

At the end of the same year two vacancies in the fire brigade were published and Mr A Gaisford and Mr H Tanner were duly appointed.

The brigade was called to a fire at Euridge Farm on Saturday 19th August 1911, where three wheat ricks owned by Mr A Webb were destroyed. The *Wiltshire Times* of 26th August reported that the Colerne Fire Engine arrived on the scene as soon as possible but with the fire being out in a field and with a shortage of water caused by being some distance from a supply there was little they could do.

Following the fire, the customary report was sent to the Parish Council. After some consideration, it was agreed that refreshments for the men were to be paid for by the Council.

The same meeting approved the following scales of payment for the brigade while attending a fire:

Brigade Captain – 5s 1d for the first hour & 1s 7d for each subsequent hour or part hour

Lieutenant – 3s 4d for the first hour & 1s 4d for each subsequent hour or part hour

10 men – 1s 2d each for the first hour & 1s $2\frac{1}{2}$d each for each subsequent hour or part hour

The Clerk was instructed to write to Mr Tidmarsh, John Jefferies and F Perren requesting an explanation for their failure to attend the fire at Euridge Farm. John Jefferies was the only one to respond to the letter but his explanation was deemed to be unsatisfactory and, at the next meeting of the Council, all three were dismissed as from the date of the fire that they had failed to attend. The meeting of 26th October approved the appointment of Mr F Fletcher, Mr F Tiley and Mr L Baker to replace the sacked firemen. Following a practice and inspection in 1913, it was reported that repairs were required to the piping and that the iron plates on the side of the engine needed fixing. This time the repairs were left to the Brigade Captain to organise.

Competition to join the brigade increased and, in March 1915, three men applied for one vacancy in the brigade, Mr M Hulbert being the successful candidate.

On Saturday 2nd June 1917, the Fire Brigade faced a major incident when the parish church was struck by lightning and caught fire. Mr Tucker, the schoolmaster, was on his way to his usual weekly organ practice when he witnessed a vivid flash of lightning just before he reached the church. He hurried on and, upon entering the vestry door, noticed fire and smoke coming from the roof of the nave at the west end. He then rushed over to the Rectory and told the Rector, the Revd H Stephens, and summoned the Parish Clerk, Mr W M Holder, who rang the fire alarm bell from the church tower.

In less than ten minutes the village Fire Brigade and its manual engine were on the spot under the command of its Captain, Hubert Bence. The engine was taken into the church where all twelve brigade members worked hard fighting back the flames. A plentiful water supply was available from a large tank outside the church and, as fast as it was emptied, the heavy rainfall filled it again. Practically all available men, women and children turned out to help with buckets of water from numerous sources – and even George Gifford sent down barrels of water by cart.

After half an hour inside the church the Fire Brigade regained control and they turned their attention to the outside. They climbed onto the roof and removed tiles to get at the smoking wood and felting.

By 4pm the fire was out and the women set to work to clear up the mess. The floor of the church was one foot deep in water and dirt but they got it ready for service next day. The local newspaper was happy to report that "valuable assistance was rendered by inhabitants generally (churchgoers and non-conformists alike)."

The Council accepted £10 from the Ecclesiastical Insurance

Company in settlement of their account for attending the fire and instructed the Clerk to distribute the money among the Fire Brigade, Mr Ings and Mr G Gifford. Mr Gifford, however, refused to accept the 10s 0d allowed by the insurance company for the two 'Kyl Fires' that he had used in the fire so the Clerk purchased two replacements and presented them to him instead. The Kyl Fire was a glass sphere containing a fire extinguishing liquid that would put out a fire when thrown into it.

In 1919, while the Fire Brigade Committee was inspecting the sheds where the fire engine and parish bier were kept, Thomas Gray, landlord of the Six Bells, from whom they were rented, said that he could do with them back. The Clerk reported this to the next Council meeting on 23rd December and said that he knew of a suitable building that the Council could purchase for storage of the engine and bier instead of the one they rented.

The committee agreed to meet at 11.00 on Christmas Eve to inspect the building, and it was agreed that they be empowered to offer up to £25 for it. Following payment of a deposit of £2 against the £25 cost, a meeting in March 1920 agreed to give Mr Gray six months' notice of the intention of the Council to quit the parish store house. An inspection of the new premises by the Fire Brigade Committee found that alterations were needed, and tenders were invited to carry out the work. Mr Tyley was awarded the contract, but by the time the Council had completed its deliberations in September, the six months' notice had expired and temporary storage for the engine and bier was urgently required.

A letter from Mr Gray was read to the Council on 29th September in which he delivered an ultimatum to the Council to remove the engine and bier by twelve noon on the following day or double rent would be charged for any continuing storage. Luckily, the brigade Captain, Hubert Bence, offered to store the two items for three months for 10s 0d at his premises in the Market Place and the Council gratefully accepted his offer.

The new storehouse was inspected in December of the same year and was deemed to be "good enough." It was then agreed that Mr Tyley's account for alterations and repairs at a cost of £28 17s 6d be paid.

The cost of running a local Fire Brigade became an issue in 1926 and at the Parish Meeting of 21st October, the Clerk was asked to obtain information about the terms required by the Chippenham Fire Brigade to attend fires in rural districts.

The list of charges was duly received from Chippenham Fire Brigade and, at the next Parish Meeting in April 1927, it was agreed that the Fire Brigade be allowed to carry on as at present. The same meeting also asked for the question of insuring members of the brigade to be fully investigated. On 16th May the Clerk reported that the Fire Brigade members would be covered for ordinary daily earnings and not for loss of Fire Brigade earnings. This apparently met with Council approval, for the premium of £3 less 4s 9d rebate was duly authorised for payment.

At the same meeting, a request for an increase in salary and decrease in the number of practices was received from the Fire Brigade in the following terms:

> To Clerk of Parsh Counsil
>
> Sir All members of Fire Brigade wish for their wages rose
> Caption £1 Luietinernt 15s all others 10s year and 24 hour notice for a practic four practic a year
> Hubert Bence
> Captain

The meeting of 16th June considered this request and agreed to reduce the number of practices from six to four per annum, but to retain the pay as at present. The Clerk was also to receive 24 hours' notice of a practice to enable him to arrange for the Lighting and Watching Committee to attend and report on the condition of appliances and the number of firemen present. The Fire Brigade were, however, dissatisfied with this response and the Captain sent a letter to the next Council meeting in which he stated that the entire brigade wished to resign as the Council would not raise their salaries. The Council deferred this issue to the next meeting when the resignations were accepted and it was agreed to advertise the twelve vacancies with the same rates of pay.

Nine applications had been received by the closing date and the meeting appointed S Woodward, F Perren, B Read, E Pocock, E Reith Jr, J Tanner, H Guy and R Hood. They were instructed to select their

Captain and Lieutenant and were to be paid at the following rates: Captain 15s 0d, Lieutenant 10s 0d and firemen 6s 8d each. The meeting of 18th October learnt that J Tanner had been elected Captain and B Read was to be Lieutenant. Four more applications had been received and, without interview, the Council appointed A Tiley, D Beer and H Gaisford.

Absenteeism again presented a problem when the Clerk made his report on 4th April 1928. Of the two practices of the fire brigade in the previous six months three men were absent from the first and two from the second. The rules stated that absentees from Fire Brigade practices be fined and they were duly fined 1s each, a not inconsiderable sum in those days.

In 1932 the Parish Council decided that the fire engine should be discarded as being obsolete and arrangements made to link up with a District Fire Brigade. The Clerk was instructed to write to Bath and Chippenham brigades asking them for their terms. Chippenham Fire Brigade responded with a letter stating that they would be unwilling to enter into an arrangement with one particular parish but would attend any fires, subject to its usual charges.

The Council proposed holding a surprise practice to ascertain the time that it would take the brigade to turn out in case of a fire and would also test its efficiency. It was decided to hold the practice at Sewell on Thursday 22nd April 1932 at 6.30pm. Councillor Grainger undertook to arrange for a fire to be started and Councillor Spirell agreed to ring the fire bell. The practice proved to be a success because the Council subsequently received a letter from Mr D S Grainger, on behalf of E J H Merry, expressing his satisfaction with the very creditable display the Colerne Fire Brigade gave at the surprise practice at Sewell and enclosing £1 10s for the turnout (but see also p 279). The Council passed a vote of thanks to him for his kindly interest and decided to split the money among the members of the brigade who turned out: Captain 4s 6d, Lieutenant 3s 6d and eight men at 2s 9d each.

A letter from Chippenham Town Fire Brigade was tabled in which it detailed its charges for attending fires outside the borough. The charges of £2 10s for turning out, mileage at 7s 6d per mile, motor pumping at £2 2s per hour, appliances at £1 1s per hour, chief officer at £1 5s for five hours or less, second officer at 12s 6d for five hours or less and firemen at 5s for the first two hours or less and 2s per hour thereafter were thought to be prohibitive and the matter was dropped.

In 1936 the brigade was called out on Sunday 12th January to Mr L B May's premises and a bill for £3 10s was submitted to the insurance company for payment. The insurance company wrote back in early March with a cheque for £2 to cover the cost of the fire and declined to pay more. The Clerk was told to reply that the Council considered the claim to be very reasonable and fair and unless full settlement was forthcoming the Council would remove its business which hitherto had been transacted with the company. The insurance company responded by stating that if the scale of payments to the brigade were revised they might be induced to settle the claim in full. The proposed rates were:

Captain, 3 hours at 5s 0d per hour	15s 0d
Lieutenant, 2 hours at 3s 6d per hour	7s 0d
7 firemen, 2 hours each at 2s 6d per hour	£1 15s 0d
3 helpers, 2 hours each at 2s 0d per hour	12s 0d
person for ringing the bell	1s 0d
Total	£3 10s 0d

The revised scale of payments was accepted and the insurance company paid out in full in April.

At the Council's meeting in January 1936 the Clerk was again instructed to ascertain the charges of the Chippenham Fire Brigade for fire attendance and the retaining fee, if any. The scale of fees remained the same but the Council decided to request a demonstration to be organised on Sunday 6th June, and the Clerk was asked to write and ask the water works manager to arrange for the reservoir to be full of water so that maximum pressure could be obtained.

After the demonstration by Chippenham Fire Brigade their chief officer advised that hydrant equipment for the Colerne brigade be bought at a cost of £20 and provided a list. It was provisionally agreed to purchase the suggested equipment at a meeting held in July.

In 1938 problems with the water supply became apparent when the brigade Captain complained that at a practice held on 5th March, no pressure had been obtained from the hydrants, the water was very dirty and the stand pipe could not be fixed on the hydrant at the top of Vicarage Lane. The Clerk referred the matter to the Rural District Council for attention. The RDC replied that pressure from the hydrant had been satisfactory and that the waterworks manager had been instructed to raise the hydrant at Vicarage Lane and flush out Eastrip Lane.

Following a fire at the premises of Mrs H Jones at Victoria Place, Tutton Hill, a discussion on the Captain's report questioned the efficiency of the brigade and the Clerk was instructed to obtain an amended report giving the names of the brigade members who were in attendance at the fire. An amended report was received and a claim sent off to the insurance company after the meeting of 19th September 1938.

However, a letter from the Alliance Insurance Company informed the Council that, under the Fire Brigade Act of 1938, fire brigade services throughout the country were now a public service free to all members of the community, and the insurance company had therefore decided that it would not pay the claim. The Council replied expressing surprise at the content of the letter and the lack of notification received and requested reconsideration of the decision.

In November 1938, it was agreed unanimously to give notice to the Fire Brigade to dispense with their services as from 31st December. They were also informed that the Council would, in the meantime, accept no responsibility in the case of fire and that after 31st December any services they rendered would be entirely voluntary.

A letter to the insurance company inquiring about a rebate from the policy now that the services of the brigade had been dispensed with prompted the reply that they would not consider contributing to the costs of the fire at Victoria Place and that no rebate on the insurance policy was possible because the premium of £3 was a minimum figure.

The Council agreed to pay the Fire Brigade themselves for attendance at Victoria Place at the following rates: Captain 5s 0d, Lieutenant 3s 6d, 5 firemen at 2s 6d each and S Sheppard for ringing the bell 1s 0d. They also wrote a letter of protest about their treatment to the Alliance Insurance Company.

With the advent of war fast approaching, a letter from the Rural District Council was received in March asking for particulars of the village precautions for air raids. The Clerk was told to ask the Chief Warden, D S Grainger, for details of the number of auxiliary firemen enrolled.

In February 1940 the RDC wrote again requesting details of fire fighting equipment held by the parish, the date it was purchased, the price paid and the estimated value of it as at 31st January 1939. The Council replied that modern equipment had been acquired in September 1936 at a cost of £19 2s 6d and that its estimated value was now £20. On 3rd June the Council was asked to consider an offer of £16 from the RDC for the standpipe, hydrant key, a branch pipe, two nozzles and five lengths of hose. No offer was made for the old fire engine. This offer was accepted with the proviso that the equipment remain in the parish for the duration of the war. It was also decided that a voluntary Fire Brigade would be formed under the discipline of the Corsham Fire Brigade and that the Clerk was to issue notices inviting volunteers aged between 30 and 45.

The fire engine house was to be retained for storing the old lamps and the bier. The RDC's offer of £50 for the building was refused and the Council made repairs to it.

The meeting of 15th July 1940 was informed that no response had been forthcoming to the invitation to form a fire party. The Council decided that they would meet themselves and try out a stirrup pump, a two-man manual pump and other fire equipment which had recently been provided for parish use. The members of the party were Mesdames W James and G Wood, Miss Ruddle and Messrs R Hood, H James, H Maynard, J Sheppard and W Tiley.

The small size of this fire fighting party was giving cause for concern to the Chief Warden and the Clerk was instructed to exhibit a notice to this effect. Messrs D May, H Bence and J May volunteered to join the fire party. It was also reported that ladders were kept on the premises of T Guy, H Bence and S Gaisford, where there was easy access to them at all times.

In April 1941, the Council received a request from the RDC to use the bier and fire engine house as an emergency mortuary. As it would be necessary to remove the old manual fire engine, it was suggested that it be sold for scrap. The Clerk was instructed to write to scrap dealers and accept the highest written offer. A broken lamp standard was also to be included in the sale.

Two offers were received for the old fire engine: Mr Derrick offered £1 5s 0d and Mr Pike offered £2 10s 0d. Mr Pike's offer was accepted; he paid the money over and removed the engine.

The RDC wrote and said that, of the equipment taken over by them, two hose lengths had burst under a small pressure, so their offer had been reduced from £16 to £14; this was accepted.

In August 1941 the Clerk reported that the fire party was now up to strength and that a small portable power pump had been promised for Colerne. In the meantime, three agricultural stirrup pumps were available. Little else is recorded of the activities of the fire party in Colerne during the war.

In May 1945 a letter was received from the District Council soliciting views on a proposal to retain the manual fire pumps now that the National Fire Service was to be wound up.

It was agreed to reply asking them to remove the pump and return to the pre-war state "when the Chippenham Fire Brigade was sent for, if necessary", but the responsibility for the fire service in the parish was still unclear in 1946 and the RDC was contacted to supply information and notices to clarify the position.

The notices were received and posted in January 1947, thus removing any lingering doubts that the responsibility for controlling fire within the parish was no longer that of the Parish Council. This marks the true end of the Colerne Fire Service.

The old bier and fire engine house at 5 Watergates was sold at auction for £260 in the Six Bells on 20th May 1963. The council netted £210 13s 6d. The money raised by the sale of the storehouse was used to provide toilets on the recreation ground.

Bibliography

The Overseer's Handbook by W Mackenzie KC, 8th edition, 1915
Local Government Administration by Charles Arnold-Baker, 2nd edition, 1981
A Handy Book of Parish Law by W A Holdsworth, 3rd edition, 1872
The Minute Books of Colerne Parish Council